THE
TORCH
PRINCIPLE

Light up your mind

Javier ideami

Sound of Touch

Contents

About the Author

Javier Ideami is a multidisciplinary creative director, engineer, artist and entrepreneur. Javier is the founder of Ideami Studios and many other ventures all around the world, from Silicon Valley to the jungles of Bali. He has spoken at prestigious institutions, from Stanford University and UC Berkeley in California, to the United Nations FAO Headquarters, the financial center of London, the faculty of architecture of the University of Rome, the International Cultural Diplomacy Conference in Berlin and many others. He has received awards in areas as diverse as software engineering, music, filmmaking, photography, technology installations, etc. His central web is at:

[Web] **ideami.com**

Preface

Let's expand

Are you facing personal or professional challenges that require original and innovative solutions? Are you tired of the typical solutions that don't produce lasting results? Would you like to find a better balance between your creative and your analytical muscles in order to empower your career, health and well-being?

The happiest moments of my life, both professionally and personally, often had something in common. They are moments in which my analytical processes and ego were not the dominating part in my mind. Through different experiences and projects, I have witnessed how creative divergence can transcend the limits of analytical thinking, for the purpose of accelerating the generation of innovative solutions to our professional and personal challenges. Through a mixture of understanding and exercises, the torch principle will help you discover that beyond the analytical shore there is a vast ocean of possibilities that can enrich your professional and personal life in extraordinary ways. We set our limits, and it is time to take those limits much further. How does that sound?

Perspective and context

Context is everything. Let's reflect on how this book relates to the global innovation context. In the torch principle we review the complete innovation process, from establishing a challenge till the generation and evaluation of its solution. However, the book focuses particularly on the phases where creative divergence is the protagonist. And it is important to explain why. In our society there is a great emphasis on those processes that are analytical, systematic and logical. Most adults are well trained in them. An excess of these kinds of processes can be harmful both professionally and personally.

Because of that, we focus on helping you regain the balance between your analytical and your creative muscles. And as there is no lack of information or training regarding the analytical side of things, we focus on the part that is most often neglected in our society: the creative divergence. We have two objectives: Firstly, to give you strategies and exercises that you can use to strengthen your creative muscles and improve the balance between them and the analytical ones. And second, to provide you with tools that help you overcome complexity and competition through creative divergence, using all of your potential.

How to Read this Book

*"Once we rid ourselves of traditional thinking
we can get on with creating the future."*

— James Bertrand

More than a book

With the Torch Principle you obtain not just a book, but also an online platform where you can access infographics, videos and tools related to brainstorming processes and creative innovation.

First of all

Open a web browser and visit this page:
[Web] **torchprinciple.com/join**

On that page you can join the platform. You will have to enter in the form the place where you bought the book as well as the transaction code related to the purchase. Soon you will receive your login and password by email and you will be able to access all the content associated with the book.

In the different chapters of the book I will occasionally include web addresses that you can use to access infographics, videos or tools connected to that part of the book.

The first time, do the exercises and watch the videos in sequence.

In the [Web] **torchprinciple.com**, you will be able to access short videos that show examples of each of the exercises. To limit the duration of the videos, the content of each of these examples incorporates the ideas generated by the previous modules. Therefore we recommend that the first time you read the book, you practice the modules and watch the videos in sequence. After a first round, you can practice them again in any order or create your own variations.

Music playlist

In some of the exercises of this book you have to play music in the background. You can use tools such as Spotify to find the music you need:
[Web] **spotify.com**

Alternatively, in the following addresses you can access musical tracks that you can use in the exercises. Due to legal constraints the tracks cannot be downloaded, only streamed from the web.
[Web] **torchprinciple.com/soundmap**
[Web] **torchprinciple.com/music**

We share a mission

In this mission we are together. That's why I invite you to contact me directly whenever you like to share any doubt, question or thought connected to the book. It is possible that I won't have the time to answer all the emails, but I promise to try my best. You can contact me on ideami@ideami.com.

Dedication

To my family and my loved ones, and to all of those that have the courage to exercise their creative divergence, to go beyond the repetitive and the conventional, to generate progress and joy in their personal and professional lives and in those of others.

CHAPTER 1:

Operation Free Your Mind

"Great is the human who has not lost his childlike heart."

— Mencius (Meng-Tse), 4th century BCE

How many times does the word "problem" appear in this book? 71. What about the word challenge? 504 times. You might ask, what is the difference between these two perspectives? Whether you look at something as a problem or as a challenge is the key to making your life more innovative, fresh, original and joyful.

A quick summary of what this book is about

If you live on planet Earth, there are many challenges you face, both personal and professional. Some of them are too complex to deal with by just using logic and analysis. In addition to this, typical conventional solutions are not practical because competitors are already implementing them or because the value they provide doesn't last long enough.

In order to succeed, you need to raise your game and produce innovative, different and unique solutions to your personal and professional challenges. You cannot run a marathon without first training your body muscles regularly, similarly, you cannot become a master at innovating original solutions without first learning to exercise your creative muscles as well.

In this book I will show you how to make the transition from a personal or professional challenge to an innovative solution and how to exercise your creative muscles to become a master at this process.

We will also explore how creative thinking can benefit both your health and well-being.

Structure of the book

This first chapter is an introduction. The second chapter, "The electric mind", introduces the theater of operations, our brain. The third chapter, "Two powerful friends", covers the two key strategies our mind uses to process information: analytical and creative thinking. The fourth chapter, "Race for survival", connects these two strategies with our biology and our transition from children to adults. The fifth chapter, "The torch principle", guides you through the stages that occur in most successful innovation processes. The sixth chapter, "Exercising your creative muscles", provides you with specific ways to train these muscles. Finally, chapter seven explores how creative strategies can benefit your health and well-being. The second part of the book includes 10 small chapters covering extra and complementary information that expands on some of the topics covered in the previous chapters. They delve deeper into storytelling, education, marketing, business, etc.

Welcome to the journey

Welcome to a fascinating journey. I acknowledge your courage and bravery in accepting this challenge, for the mission we are about to embark on is not for the faint-hearted. It has the potential to transform your career, health and well-being in dramatic ways.

Together, we will accomplish a fundamental change in the core and base of how you think and function.

The objectives of this book are clear. First, to make you a more balanced, complete and successful human being. Second, to help you raise yourself above the complexity and/or competition around you and find innovative solutions for the challenges you face both professionally and personally. We will focus on giving you practical exercises, strategies, tools and tips that you can apply during and after the reading.

Nowadays, complexity and competition are constant companions in our professional and personal lives. It is not enough to create a product or service that works. It is also not enough to use logic to manage professional and personal relationships. Their complexity requires a deeper approach.

Today, we need innovative solutions to our professional and personal challenges. To thrive and succeed in a given environment, to continue to stay on top of any situation, we need to first diverge in intelligent ways before we converge onto extraordinary solutions.

Getting there requires some effort. Nobody runs a marathon without training. We all understand the need to exercise our body muscles to be healthy. Likewise, we also need to exercise our creative mental muscles in order to be fit and ready to find innovative solutions to our challenges. In this book there are specific exercises and tools you can use to keep those creative muscles strong and supple.

Along the way I will have a companion with me. I believe in dialogue and interaction rather than long speeches. That's why I will be interacting with my own mind (metaphorically speaking) as I go through the book.

Introducing dialogues is also a way to remind us that there is always a new perspective and angle on any topic, a new twist waiting for us around the corner. Keep an open mind and enjoy the journey. Every time our companion says something, it will be surrounded by double quotes.

"That's me!"

That's correct, thank you mind. Feel free to give us your perspective at any time please.

"Will do, this is fun!"

Thank you mind, I look forward to a great interaction!

A genderless mind

The mind will express itself in the book sometimes with a male voice and at other times with a female one. It is a way to celebrate the flexibility of our best tool.

Professional and personal

Let's begin by emphasizing something very important.

Many people think of innovation and creativity in relation to their jobs and careers only. But the benefits of what we will be covering here apply equally to your professional and your personal life. If you follow this journey, you will become a more balanced and complete human being and as a consequence you will become a more creative and successful professional as well.

The resistance effect

Empowering your creative muscles is not easy. You will feel resistance in your mind. You will get defensive. You will think it's not worth it or it's too difficult.

Let's understand why this happens.

There is a mixture of reasons, but we think it's important to focus on the cultural ones.

Our societies have traditionally overemphasized the importance of efficiency, quick results and analytical thinking. In the past, competition and complexity were not as important as other basic priorities.

"Most people wanted to get things done in the fastest and easiest way possible."

This creates unbalanced adults that tend to live most of their time in their analytical mental space. This reinforces the resistance effect. Analytical thinking craves immediate security and certainty. Any other option smells fishy.

"How do we overcome this?"

You need to fight this resistance effect in positive ways. It is the only way to recover your balance. The rewards are big. It ultimately means becoming a more balanced and complete human being and a more successful professional.

"Can I really do this…?"

It takes some courage and determination to change any habit. Imagine that you spend a full month eating cakes every day. After 30 days, you feel bloated and terrible. You cannot continue like this. You need to balance the way you eat. But there is a problem. You have created a habit. Your body craves sugar every day. You need to fight that craving and adjust your thinking, helping your body get used to a more balanced diet.

"That's after 30 days…"

Yes. If that happens after 30 days, imagine what happens after x number of years overemphasizing the analytical side of your mind!

A word of caution. As we will see later, fighting a habit does not necessarily mean fighting it straight on, which often fails. Instead it often means opening new routes, new paths and strategies that little by little and organically generate a new and healthier balance.

I don't need that. I am ok as I am.

It is very tempting to say this. The problem is that the consequences of our habits take some time to become fully visible. If you eat cakes every day, you may feel ok, even great for a while. It will be after a few weeks that you start feeling the effects of this insane diet and a few more months before your body starts to react negatively. Our bodies and minds are resilient, up to a point.

If you don't exercise your creative muscles, you will be constraining your horizons both personally and professionally. This will eventually produce symptoms that are just as strong and dangerous as the physical ones. You will feel anxious, stressed, empty, unsatisfied, constrained, restricted, small, limited, purposeless, etc.

"Not good…"

It is a matter of choice.

"Is it really?"

Is it your choice to be a couch potato or to exercise and move around?

"Definitely yes."

Well, then it is also your choice that you spend your mental currency in the constrained and repetitive analytical kingdom you've built for yourself, or exercise your creative muscles to expand your horizons and widen your mind.

The first choice produces unsatisfied, stressed, anxious and repetitive individuals. The second choice produces balanced, fresh, complete, satisfied and creative people.

"Take me there!"

Let's begin with some terms.

Establishing the terms

Before we start this fascinating journey, let's clarify some terms that we will be using regularly throughout the book.

- **AT:** Analytical thinking. We love to analyze, don't we? Adults are great at living on this tip of the iceberg of our potential. AT thrives in our conscious mind and around language. Logic and analysis are its friends and it is typically systematic and sequential in its behavior. AT is convergent; it tries to get to answers and solutions as fast as possible. It loves the past because it is faster to use past information than to spend time exploring what is always new, the present moment.

- **CT:** Creative thinking is the cornerstone of innovation. It thrives on subconscious processes that are wide and organic. It is visually tasty and capable of simultaneous processing. CT is divergent; it widens your horizon and opens new paths in your mind.

- **AT/CT, the AT and the CT:** The abbreviations AT and CT will be used with or without article. "The CT is a way of thinking" or "CT is a way of thinking. Each is equivalent to the other.

- **Subconscious:** When we use the word subconscious in this book, we are referring to processes which clearly are not consciously being controlled.

- **Cliffs of closure:** They are mental patterns that have been repeated so often as to render them very easy to reactivate, thereby keeping us away from other more innovative possibilities. They close down and narrow our horizons.

- **Diverge before you converge:** One of the key mantras of this book. Divergence keeps us away from the cliffs of closure and allows us to explore new possibilities before we converge onto specific answers and solutions.

- **DITS:** Divergence done correctly requires Depth, Ingredients, Time and Space, DITS.

- **Paths of least resistance:** Our thoughts tend to follow mental patterns/paths we have used before.

- **Subconscious pot:** A metaphor to describe our subconscious as a cooking pot where we gather quality ingredients for our creative processes.
  [Web] **torchprinciple.com/subconsciouspot**

- **Depth elevators:** We can engage with a challenge at different levels of abstraction and depth. The lower we descend on the depth elevators, the closer we get to the roots and foundations of our challenge and to its raw complexity.
  [Web] **torchprinciple.com/depthelevator**

- **Texture elevators:** We can engage with visual textures at different levels of abstraction. The lower we descend, the

more we diverge and are able to connect with unexpected insights.
[Web] **torchprinciple.com/textureelevator**

- **Soundmap/Soundscape:** Audio track that reproduces a specific acoustic context. Examples: sounds of a jungle, of a pub, of rain, of birds singing, etc.
[Web] **torchprinciple.com/soundmap**

- **Soundstorming/Lightstorming/Emotionstorming/ Contextstorming/Gesturestorming/Linestorming/ Patternstorming/Wordstorming:** Brainstorming techniques that work with sounds, visual textures, emotions, changes of context, movement, body gestures, improvisation, drawing, visual patterns, words, etc.
- **Challenge vs problems:** Think of challenges (positive), not problems (negative). In the words of Thomas Edison on his unsuccessful attempts at inventing the light bulb, "I have not failed. I've just found 10,000 ways that won't work." Those attempts are seen as failures if we think in terms of problems. Also from the perspective of a challenge, such attempts are simply useful steps on our path towards finding the best possible solution.

"Can you give me examples of what you mean by challenges?"

A challenge is any complex situation for which you need to find a solution. Not just any solution, but an innovative and original solution. This will put you ahead of the competition and help you adapt to the changing nature of any complex situation.

Here are some examples of the infinite number of professional and/or personal challenges that require innovative solutions.

- At my company we are working on an app that encourages people to practice sport. We need ideas to make the app useful but also entertaining.

- Our human resources department has problems identifying the best candidates for key positions in our company. How can we improve the process of identifying these candidates?

- I want to market a cleaning product by using storytelling, creating an original story around the product. I need ideas for that story.

- My partner and I are looking for original ideas for activities to do during our holidays or weekends.

- Our company wants to organize team-building events that improve our teamwork. We are looking for ideas to do this.

- Our company is researching ways to interfere with the blood flow that powers tumor cells. We are looking for new creative insights based on our current knowledge.

- I want to write a fiction book about a bank robbery. I would like to develop the base of the story.

- We are an events company specialized in organizing events for seniors. We are looking to find new original and creative ideas to surprise our customers.

- We are a company designing wearable tech, making clothing more interactive. We are competing against many others. We are looking for original ideas to make clothing more interactive in useful ways.

- I am creating a jingle to advertise a product. I need inspiration for the lyrics of the song.

- I am working on the script for a short film that will advertise our company. I need to generate the story.

- My partner and I argue because of our different views on tidiness. We are looking for unique ways to organize ourselves around this issue.

- Any other. There is no limit to what challenge you can work on. Anything is possible. The best idea is to pick challenges you care about, either professionally or personally.

And for each of those challenges you can choose to reuse old solutions, if they exist, or to find a new solution.

"Is a new solution always necessary?"

There are no absolutes and it is not always necessary. But Innovation has personal and professional benefits whose effects are deep and long lasting.

Let's travel with our imagination for a minute. It is a quiet winter day. As you open your eyes, in front of you is a wide and beautiful fresh fallen, snowy field. The field extends in all directions, full of so many possibilities. It is a great challenge, but you want and need to cross it. The snow is deep and you fear that a wrong step could get you injured. You hesitate and yet you need to cross it, you need to move.

"I need courage…"

Then you notice something. Footprints created by somebody else. Footprints that seem to cross the field in a safe and predictable way. And you wonder: should I follow those footprints, which will guide me safely and predictably through the field? Or should I take a risk and open a new path across the snow, a path that can take me somewhere different, somewhere new where others haven't gone before?

"What about combining both options?"

Should I even combine strategies, begin my path following the safe footprints of others, but deviate from the route at different times to explore new possibilities?

It is your choice if you want to follow the apparently safe path or open a new one, but keep in mind what often happens with that path that looks so safe…

"There is no free lunch…"

So many other people have followed that path that it has become really deep. So deep that as you walk over it you may get stuck in a deep trench. Becoming stuck, bored, and empty, that's how we feel sometimes when we decide to follow the easy and predictable paths in life.

"What begins easy doesn't always end easy…"

These paths typically begin safe and easy, but boredom and repetitiveness are often what we find when they come to an end or whenever we get stuck along the way.

Opening new paths requires courage and determination, but the rewards are many including more excitement and a younger and more dynamic professional and personal life.

"I say that's worth it!"

Find your kind of joy

Everybody wants to feel satisfied and whole. Which kind of satisfaction are you after? The one that gives you a powerful and quick rush of excitement and fades away just as fast? Or the one that provides a steady stream of excitement and satisfaction that keeps going strong over the years?

"The answer is clear to me!"

If what you are after is the second kind, you are in good company. This book is about creating the kind of lifestyle that engages with the world in ways that keep your health, mind, and career fresh and exciting.

It is easy to eventually fall into boredom and routine. By the end of this book, you will have understood and discovered many ways to keep the most important part of you fresh and revitalized. You will be looking at the world around you in a completely different way.

Introducing myself

After the initial concepts, it is time to introduce myself.

I am Javier Ideami, in charge of this vessel whose mission is to guide you on your way to balance your thinking, freeing your mind to regain your true potential as an innovator and a creative human being.

During my career I have earned recognition across multiple creative fields: media, technology, business and engineering. This is a story that began when I was a child, filled with an intense yearning for exploration and proactive problem-solving.

After many years working as a multidisciplinary creative director, artist, entrepreneur and engineer, I am bringing it all together, sharing with you a mixture of understanding and unique tools designed to help you transform the way you think and exercise your creative muscles.

During this mission you will explore how innovation and creativity affect your career, health and relationships. These are pillars that hold up the edifice of our lives and the way we process information, the way we think, shapes them moment by moment.

This deep understanding is just half of the process. The other half is putting that new understanding in practice in order to strengthen your creative muscles and balance your analytical and creative thinking skills.

This is our challenge, valid for people from all kinds of backgrounds, from beginners to experts. I have prepared a versatile vessel, one that we will drive together, down and deep into the mysteries of human thought, creative thinking and innovation.

The journey we are about to begin will take you from the electric impulses in our neurons, deep inside the brain, through the key business decisions that shape our world, till we eventually arrive at the challenge of how to achieve the delicate balance and peace we all seek in our existence.

To get to that point we need to walk together down to the deep roots of creative thinking. It is a road that may change the way you view yourself. So let's cross that line and there shall be no turning back.

"Off we go!"

In search of a great solution

An engineer decides to explore in detail an unexpected signal, an apparently insignificant trace value that eventually helps him or her prove the cause of an important accident. A broker predicts successfully a large and unexpected change in the markets by linking two seemingly unrelated events. An artist engages audiences, virally, with an unusual kind of photographic style born from the blending of apparently unrelated creative disciplines. A couple explores creatively their interactions and finds the activity that best connects them during difficult times.

All of these events have one thing in common. Human beings face or set complex challenges, define missions in relation to specific objectives, events or communities. They gather data and information from multiple perspectives. And after incubating that data, they eventually generate unique insights, unique solutions born from the combination and incubation of a unique set of ingredients. Those solutions are then transformed into something tangible, for instance, a decision to buy or sell stocks, a report about the causes of an accident, a series of new photographs, or the decision to do new activities together.

These solutions can be prototypes or fully fledged products, services, behaviors or actions. The feedback gathered from the recipients of the previous results can be used to restart the process of further polishing or pivoting those solutions in new directions.

Isn't it amazing how these discoveries can turn entire lives, communities and even the entire planet upside down overnight? This same concept applies at smaller levels, in relationships, at your job, at any environment that is complex.

Some call this innovation, others creativity. How good we become at such processes not only influences in dramatic ways our professional life, but also our health and general well-being.

I invite you to travel with me to the depths of creativity. Join this mission and begin to unravel the mysteries of innovation while promoting a healthier and more balanced mind.

People often improve their focus when they frame their challenge as a mission. That's why I am giving a name to this mission: "Operation Free Your Mind".

Let's review some of the objectives of the mission.

- Unblock and stimulate your creative thinking.
- Understand how your creative thinking can empower your health, career and relationships.
- Provide you with tools to exercise your creative thinking skills.

And let's clarify what career, health and well-being mean in the context of our mission.

- **Career:** acquire the resources that allow you to live comfortably.
- **Health:** keep your body and mind fresh and active.
- **Well-being:** achieve an internal feeling of peace and satisfaction, one that allows you to feel peace and joy even in the absence of external helpers, which often come and go.

Above all this is a mission about human beings, about the need to move towards a better internal balance. A balance very much linked to the close cooperation and harmony between our powerful and diverse modes of thinking. Everything in this mission is oriented towards improving the parts of your life that matter the most. As such creativity becomes a way of being, a way of living.

In context, the age of innovators

Context is everything. If we are to tackle our challenge successfully, we should understand the times in which we live.

And we live in very exciting times.

"Sometimes I can hardly sleep!"

That's right, creative minds can get overwhelmed nowadays!

"I guess it wasn't always like that?"

Well, dear mind, as complexity has increased in our societies, in the way we interact with each other, in the way we work and how we communicate, the importance of innovation and creativity as tools to deal with such complexity has also been steadily increasing.

In such a complex, dynamic and constantly mutating society, previous solutions and strategies soon become irrelevant and outdated.

"Innovation becomes a key companion."

It is that tremendous pace of change which calls for new ways of thinking and approaching the world.

Today, people realize that isolating themselves from the world is not effective. The ground shifts quickly, opinions change overnight, entire communities of followers appear and go away within days; and, finally, work done in isolation may unexpectedly lose its value.

In response, professionals are learning the value of quick prototyping and iteration, agile development and lean methodologies, adapting to environments that change at the speed of thought.[1]

That's why successful ventures are those that strive to constantly innovate in response to the changing environments. They distinguish themselves from the rest by presenting, communicating and displaying their offerings in the most attractive and original way.

The best innovators are artists of life, integrating emotional, financial, technological and media solutions from both global and local perspectives; artists of life that understand the markets as well as the audiences which will share and benefit from their products, services and initiatives. At the core of this exciting transformation we find a powerful engine: technology.

On the tech highway

It is easy to take for granted what a tremendous engine of innovation technology has become. Today we have at our disposal amazing tools that accelerate innovation and business productivity and at the same time help bring about their convergence and integration. They also free our time so that we can dedicate more of it to our families and loved ones.

[Web] **torchprinciple.com/arttech**

Just consider this: for an amount of money that is within the reach of most middle class citizens, you can setup new businesses in hours or days and acquire many of the creative tools you need to engage audiences on a global scale. Let's review some examples:

- Opening a new business is faster than ever. Online websites allow you to register and setup a new company in a few minutes or days.
  Examples:
  [Web] **legalzoom.com**
  [Web] **clerky.com**

- When you create an online product, you need to host it somewhere for it to be accessed worldwide. Hosting your website or app on the cloud or in a dedicated server is becoming more and more affordable. In addition, many cloud platforms help you scale quickly and in real time in order to deal with audiences of any size.
  Examples:
  [Web] **ovh.com**
  [Web] **aws.amazon.com**

- At affordable prices you can own a photo and movie-making camera with enough quality to project your work on the big screen of a cinema. Media productions with top quality become possible for companies of all sizes.
Example:
[Web] blackmagicdesign.com

- You can outsource a lot of your work to freelance professionals for affordable prices at online locations like Upwork, Guru, Amazon Mechanical Turk, Task Rabbit, etc.
Example:
[Web] upwork.com

- The tools available to market your product and the size of audiences online have skyrocketed.

- Earning passive income online through blogs, affiliate marketing, e-books, tech apps and other means is becoming a way of life for many people around the world.
Example:
[Web] smartpassiveincome.com

- Investors and banks are not the only way to raise funds anymore. Crowd funding has become a regular way to fund businesses, projects and ventures. Success stories abound, going from as little as $2000 to millions of dollars to fund movie productions or business ventures.
Examples:
[Web] kickstarter.com
[Web] indiegogo.com

And the list continues on and on.

"Exciting times indeed!"

Today, the success of our ventures depends more on the quality of our ideas, on our productivity, perseverance and performance, as well as on the evolution of the markets, rather than on our budgets.

"Innovating has become cheap."

Certainly much cheaper. There have been many eras of innovation, but this one is different, this is an era of affordable innovation, because it involves a greater percentage of humanity than ever before.

As complexity around us keeps increasing and tools become cheaper, innovating becomes a necessity that more people can address.

"Ideas become a commodity."

We are becoming an idea-centric society. A society in which budgets, as long as we remain flexible, can be relegated to the background. The emphasis is mainly on the concepts and ideas behind our ventures as well as on their implementation.

"But you are talking here about careers and jobs, right? What about our health and well-being?"

What we are talking about here applies to all three areas. Complexity has increased enormously in our society and this affects everything we do, not just our jobs but also how we relate and communicate with each other, how we take decisions and how we live day by day.

"I see. This is about how to deal with complex challenges and those are everywhere around us."

Yes, our challenges are not only the ones we face in our jobs. They also concern how to deal with the stress of having to take decisions and how to tackle the nuances of communication in relationships. And this is just the start of it. Problem-solving is at the heart of creativity and this applies to everything we do.

In an increasingly complex world that is in rapid evolution, solutions and ideas for those challenges need some unique features to have a chance to fight and win not only in the marketplace where we face our competitors, but also in the intimate domain of our personal lives.

In regards to our career:

- They need to fit a proven market/context or demonstrate they can open a new one.
- They need to have important differentiating factors that put you above the competition.
- Some of those differentiating factors should be complex enough to constitute barriers of entry to prevent competitors from catching up too quickly.

In regards to our well-being:

- They need to resonate with your specific circumstances and personal context.
- They need to motivate you and challenge you enough, but not too much to discourage you, so that you keep engaged and working through them.

In both cases, above all, they need to be treated as dynamic living entities; capable of evolution, mutation and pivoting in response to the always-changing contexts we live in.

"Challenging requirements!"

Yes, and that's only the beginning! The implementation stages have their own many challenges.

"I gather that we will need a special approach to tackle this complexity."

Indeed, when tackling a specific challenge, working only with logical and analytical tools soon becomes slow and inflexible. We need a global approach.

To adapt to today's complexity, people and businesses need to integrate all human capabilities in their strategies, uniting creative and analytical thinking in order to combine the best of simultaneous, specific and detailed perception with the most powerful abstraction techniques.

"Integration and balance."

Yes, design, art, business, health and well-being. This is an age of convergence. That's why artists today are more entrepreneurial than ever and vice versa.

Let's explore together what this global approach means, what these different thinking strategies are and how finding the right balance between them can benefit us in incredible ways in our professional and personal life.

"Show me the way!"

CHAPTER 2:

The Electric Mind

*"Curiosity about life in all of its aspects, I think,
is still the secret of great creative people."*

– Leo Burnett

Before we begin to explore our different ways of thinking, we have to familiarize ourselves with the framework, the tool that makes it all possible.

"That amazing tool that rests above our shoulders."

Yes, understanding your tools before you start to use them sounds like common sense, doesn't it?

"I would say so!"

If you are a painter, you take good care to understand how brushes work, the different types of materials, their properties. You also care dearly for your tools so that they remain in great condition for a long time.

Why do we often fail to do the same with the most important of all the tools we have?

"We take it for granted."

Yes, but it doesn't have to be that way.

In 2011 I wrote and directed a 20 minute fiction film that emphasizes the importance of taking care of our most important tool. The film represents metaphorically our mind as a transformer of both negative and positive energy. You can watch the film for free on this link:

[Web] <u>torchprinciple.com/lightmovie</u>

It's now time to review some key points about our mind before we embark upon the mission to balance its thinking strategies. We will reflect on what learning means from a biological point of view as well as the challenges CT encounters in an adult brain. To get there we need to review some areas of our biology.

"Oh!"

Hang in there, it will be brief and it will make you appreciate much more how each one of your thoughts is literally transforming your brain every second!

Breaking the habit

Every action, every word. Everything we say and do leaves a mark behind. A mark in the context around us, a mark in our minds and bodies.

We are constantly receiving information from the world. It comes through our senses and is interpreted by our brain.

"That's a lot of information."

Yes, every moment, when we speak with a person, watch a movie, walk in the street or stare at a sunset, our senses are being flooded with data.

When you say or do anything, the biochemistry in the brain is altered. The patterns of activation through our neurons reflect our behavior.

"So the connections in our brain mirror our behavior over time."

Imagine your mind, when you were a baby, as a smooth surface that is barely scratched. As we live and experience things, we create dents and marks on that surface. The more you say or do something, the deeper those dents or marks become.

"Sounds to me like you are talking about habits."

Indeed. Continuing with the metaphor, whenever your mind needs to act, the activity in your brain will tend to flow through routes that have already been carved, deep channels, deep marks on your brain that have already been traversed hundreds or thousands of times. Routes that are easily reactivated.

For the sake of efficiency, learning has the side effect of producing habits. It tends to fall back on behaviors and patterns that we have already used before.

"It kind of makes sense."

If we had to explore things in depth every time we interact with the world, life would be unbearable, very hard to manage .

"Is there any downside to this process of forming mental habits?"

A side effect of this habit formation scenario, is that as we accumulate more knowledge and experience, innovation and creativity can become challenging.

"You mean that opening new routes in our mind becomes harder because it's way easier to reactivate existing habits and patterns of thought?"

Yes, if you want to experience something fresh and different, if you want to behave in ways that differ from your common experience, you need to encourage your brain to get out of its typical patterns of activation.

"It seems this will require some effort and/or a different mental strategy."

You need to put some effort and help your mind process information in a different way. By flexing your creative muscles, you open new avenues of thought and new channels of activation, instead of falling back on the typical ones. This requires determination and effort, especially at the beginning, because our traditional mental strategies are the result of the biochemical organization of the brain and creativity requires challenging those strategies in strong ways.

"And the trick to do that is…"

The trick is in fact to trick the mind, to turn things around by transforming the problem into the solution.

The brain is constantly creating and making use of habits. We can also make a habit out of being creative. A habit out of looking for the fresh and unexpected. In time, constantly challenging our perspectives, behaviors and responses, will come to us naturally and effortlessly. The more we exercise our creative muscles, the more we will approach a healthier balance between our different thinking strategies.

It can seem daunting at first. It certainly requires courage, but you will be surprised at the incredible capacity of our mind, when motivated, to transform anything, including itself, its own habits and the way it's been working for years!

Facing the other side

Let's now continue our exploration by travelling to the source of it all, energy.

Human brains require huge amounts of energy to function. They work thanks to the glucose and other fuel that comes with our food.[2]

"No food, no mind!"

Indeed. And as we will discuss later, child and adult brains have different priorities.

A child's survival depends on the parent's support. The child's brain is mainly concerned with learning about the world. It is creativity in its purest form. It's all about exploring, connecting and learning. The future survival of the grown up child depends on how much quality learning happens before. So the child is by nature spontaneous and creative.

The adult brain has other priorities and responsibilities. It tries to be as efficient as possible with the available energy. Its priority is its own survival, maintenance and efficiency. Creativity is very often the last thing we have on our minds when faced with a new situation.

It can take some effort to convince adult brains to deal with the unexpected. Dealing with the unexpected means having to spend precious fuel to interpret it, to figure out something new.

"Extra effort and extra investment of precious energy."

Realizing what the main priority for adult brains is can help you gather the courage to face the reactions of other adult brains when you behave in unusual and creative ways. Behaviors outside the conventional norm can feel, to the typical adult brain, like a wasteful expenditure of energy and resources.

"Being creative requires courage."

Courage to challenge the ways of comfort, which are the ones adult brains prefer to walk.

"Those are the ways trodden upon by most minds that surround us daily."

Yes, so when we take the step to challenge our minds, we are very likely to bump into the expectations of other minds around us about how we should behave and act.

Facing those minds is like facing your own mental habits. You are challenging yours, but what happens with those around you?

Most adult minds stay in the comfort zone, looking for and expecting patterns that are already known, and, therefore, easy to track and interpret. When they interact with you, they expect and in many ways wish to encounter something they can quickly recognize.

"So most of the time, depending on context, they are not expecting to hear or see something unusual and different."

Yes, anything out of the ordinary requires their brain to work harder to make sense of it. Remember, our adult brain likes security and comfort. Efficiency is its mantra.

It seeks to quickly make sense of the world, being as economical as possible with the energy it gets from the food.

Of course the way others react to creative and out of the ordinary behaviors depends a lot on context.

Sometimes, people find themselves in environments where creative and innovative behavior are the stars, the main attraction in that context. In those cases, people's minds are ready and willing to engage on interpreting and dealing with creative processes. Examples are artistic performances (theater, circus and opera), business brainstorming sessions, etc.

It is in other situations, environments where AT dominates, that you have to gather the courage to face the reactions of brains that are interpreting your behavior through the rigid and inflexible analytical glass. Examples include typical business gatherings, traditional education frameworks, etc.

So keep this in mind. The brains of most people around you are, by default, not interested in creativity or innovation. They are interested in efficiency and survival.

"Which means in repeating patterns and behaviors already tried and tested."

When you become aware of the way you react to other people's behaviors, how much you let yourself be influenced by their responses can change dramatically.

Remind yourself that the creative potential of an adult remains active, and as we face the complexity of today's world, it becomes essential for our brain to innovate.

Innovate in the face of the challenges we encounter, not just in the face of danger, illness or catastrophe, but also in the day-to-day problem-solving situations that arise when we interact with others, both at work and in our personal lives.

"Complexity is increasing the need for innovation and creativity."

In the old ages, innovation was rarely needed by the average person. The world moved and changed slowly. Most people lived predictable lives. Just a handful of unique individuals invested the mental effort necessary to move beyond predictability and help advance our societies.

Thanks to them, today we live in a world that is constantly changing and reshaping itself, where our lives are anything but predictable.

"And this process seems to be accelerating."

Things have changed dramatically in the last decades and our biology struggles to catch up with the speed of that change. It is up to us to make the effort to adapt to the current context.

In today's world, creativity is not an option, it is the way of life that fits our complex world.

Let's now understand why the way the brain deals with that raw complexity is at the root of the obstacles we encounter as we try to work with today's challenges.

Saving energy, simplifying life

Bringing to our conscious attention every input that reaches our senses would overwhelm and paralyze us.

"I imagine the amount of information flooding our senses must be enormous."

In order to increase efficiency and save energy, the brain attempts to simplify the complexity of the world around us.

"And how does it do that?"

By abstracting, simplifying and filtering that complexity.

The advantage is efficiency, being able to deal with the world faster, spending less energy, re-using our existing knowledge, avoiding wasting our time with the very fine details around us.

"Hold it for a minute... that last one you mentioned, that could also become a disadvantage sometimes, right?"

Right. The disadvantage becomes obvious in connection with the innovation and creativity skills that are so essential in today's world. In order to innovate we need to get past those filters and abstractions and get in touch with the fine details and complexity of the world. And that will require new strategies to change the way we manage our thinking.

Let's keep exploring the way our brain works.

High level view

The brain, combined with the spinal cord, makes up the central nervous system, which together with the hormonal and immune systems, coordinates the functioning of all of us.

This is our framework, this is us.

And this amazing brain is the master controller that interprets inputs and produces outputs, making sure that the different parts of our body, from the organs to the senses, work together and act as they should.

Our master organ is divided into two hemispheres which communicate through a dense set of nerve fibers called the corpus callosum. Communication is a key foundation of life, right from the start, right from our essential biology.

Diving in

Let's go deeper. The brain is composed of two types of cells. Glial cells are responsible for housekeeping tasks.

"What would we do without some good housekeeping!"

The more famous ones, the neurons, are in charge of providing processing power. And we have one hundred billion of them![3]

"One hundred billion!"

Yes you heard right. One hundred billion right there above your shoulders.

Neurons

Each of these neurons can be thought of as a little tree, with branches called dendrites, and a trunk, the axon.

The functional core of this metaphorical tree consists of bursts of electric current moving between their ends.

"It is our electric mind."

Electricity indeed. Neurons are packed densely and come into contact with each other at points we call synapses. It is at those synapses that key elements of the magic of learning, memory and habit formation are taking place.

"We are getting closer, I can feel it."

Hang in there. In general, neurons send impulses through their single axon to the dendrites of other neurons (there are exceptions to this rule such as neurons that have no axon or connect axon with axon. The variety and complexity of our human bodies is staggering).

The potential in perspective

Now think about this. Each of these neurons can receive inputs, i.e. stimulation, from up to 20,000 different sources. Overall we can have over one million billion connections just in the outer mantle, the cortex alone!

"One million billion, talk about complexity."

And the way these neurons work together is not necessarily connected to their physical closeness, but their functional one. We are still learning the intricacies about how and why they connect with each other.

It's now time to explore what shapes how and why we learn.

The threshold, how we learn

An increase in electrical activity in a neuron will increase the chances that neighboring ones will become more active as well.

"And when and how does a neuron become active?"

This is a very complex topic and we will simplify it at a high level for easier understanding. Before a neuron can fire it needs to receive enough stimulation from a number of neighboring neurons.

Once stimulation reaches a threshold, it can then send new impulses along its axon and dendrites.

The key thing comes here. Once you reach it, the threshold is lowered, and that effect will last for some time.

"This means that next time it will take less effort to reach that threshold again."

Yes. So it takes effort to reach that threshold and activate a neuron, but once you reach it, it becomes easier to activate it again. This is how we learn, how we create habits. This is the reason why once you do something enough times it becomes easier to repeat it.

"But also why changing and modifying habits and behaviors is so difficult as well."

Yes, the existence of these thresholds contributes to the formation of patterns in the activation of neurons and ultimately the formation of habits in our behaviors.

All of this relates to the effort that it takes to change the way we think or behave, and to the strategies we can employ to bypass these obstacles when we need to.

"I sense something exciting is coming…"

Shaping the mind

Everything you do, each one of your experiences is changing the electrical communication between all of these neurons.

How your brain behaves, thinks and looks changes constantly according to what you do, moment by moment, thought by thought.

Who you are with, the things you say, what you listen to, what you do, where you are, where you go, all of it is constantly shaping your mind.

Rich and stimulating environments create more connections and denser jungles of neurons in the brain and vice versa.

So if you are what you eat, you also think the way you live.

Carving electric channels in the mind

Now we know that learning and experience can be directly correlated with the way neurons work. Let's take a closer look at the very key thresholds we talked about.

At the core of current research on learning and the brain we find something called: Long-Term Potentiation (LTP).[4]

Remember when neurons touch each other at places we call synapses. When neurotransmitters (chemicals that transmit signals) are released into the synaptic channel that connects an active and an inactive neuron, some of the pores in the membrane of the inactive downstream neuron will open easily and let charged ions cross. But others, called NMDA receptor sites (N-methyl-d-aspartate) are tighter and will open only if they are stimulated strongly for a long time. However, once they open they are easier to activate the following times.

"Learning is happening!"

Yes. They will respond to weaker signals for some time after having received strong stimulation.

"For some time you say. So if we don't reinforce our learning, it could fade away."

Does this sound familiar? To simplify we could say that whenever you activate a neuron strongly and for a long time, it will take less effort to reactivate it again for some time after that.

"This has huge implications in relation to learning and habit formation."

We can begin to see that as we do things in life and accumulate experiences we are creating what we can call "paths of least resistance". These are patterns in our networks of neurons along which activity will tend to flow because of this long-term potentiation effect.

The fact is that the stronger and longer something occurs in our brain, the more likely it is to happen again next time.

This has advantages and disadvantages on a practical level.

The advantage is that this mechanism allows us to learn, memorize, create habits and internalize knowledge and behaviors that we can then recall faster and faster.

The disadvantage is that damaging habits that become ingrained in our minds are hard to change or eliminate.

"Give me a simple example."

Think how hard it can be to stop humming a musical tune that got entrenched into your mind. Or how hard it is to stop thinking of a person that you have feelings for.

"When that happens I have to force myself to listen to other tunes or meet other people, and even then it's hard!"

We try our best to encourage our brain impulses to flow along different channels. Let's connect that to innovation and creativity.

Opening completely new avenues of activation in the brain takes effort because brain activity will tend to flow along the tried and tested channels that are already over-sensitive to stimulation.

But the good news is that now that we understand how the brain works, we can devise strategies to preserve the advantages and bypass the disadvantages of this process. We will be working on that throughout this book.

This will allow us to deal in much more effective and quick ways with all sorts of challenges, from finding new ideas for a business venture, to dealing with a romantic breakup or with every day stress.

The illusion of life

We are arriving at the end of this chapter. Let's do a quick summary as we get ready for the next stage.

The amazing ability of the brain to simplify and filter the inputs that constantly bombard our senses is one of the key factors that makes our species so advanced. The brain interprets these inputs and finds the most efficient way to respond to them. To do that, our mind uses abstraction, reducing reality to symbolic interpretations that preserve the essence of the information. This allows us to process, connect and decide faster and more efficiently.

But in behaving this way, the brain necessarily separates itself from the specific richness, details and variation of what surrounds us.

On the other hand, innovation and creativity need to go beyond those simplifications, go deep and access the rich and specific details of the world.

"So how can we solve this conundrum? How can we preserve that efficiency while still being able to access and work with the complexity of the world when we need to?"

As we will see in a bit, the brain is able to process information in different ways. We will call those ways, thinking modes.

In adults and in our society one of these modes often dominates. Balancing our thinking modes will allow us to preserve all the potential of abstraction while maintaining the capacity to get closer to the complexity of reality in order to feed our innovation and creativity processes.

"Thinking modes! Tell me more!"

CHAPTER 3:

Two Powerful Friends

"When the 'weaker' of the two brains (right and left) is stimulated and encouraged to work in cooperation with the stronger side, the end result is a great increase in overall ability and… often five to ten times more effectiveness."

— Professor Robert Ornstein, University of California

I t's time to explore the main two complementary but different ways in which our mind can process information and how each can help us in different ways.

Everything we face in life, from job challenges through conversations with our loved ones, to music and art, can be explained in terms of information and information processing. All of it is made up of data that our mind has to make sense of and work with.

"Too much data around us, how do we deal with it all?"

Beyond instinct, which is automatic, we can explore other ways of dealing with and processing information. Some of these ways are about simplifying inputs and interpreting them quickly and with minimum effort. Others are about fully engaging with them, to grasp them in all their richness and complexity.

"Let's simplify."

Yes, for simplicity's sake we want to focus on two strategies. These two strategies used to be called left and right modes, after their presumed origin in the left and right hemispheres of the brain. It was soon found out that these modes of thinking didn't correspond exactly with their supposed locations in the corresponding hemispheres.[5] A good amount of physical overlapping exists between them.

So even though each of these thinking modes does seem to favor one of the sides of the brain more than the other, we prefer to focus on what really matters, their functionality.

"Sounds reasonable, let's give them names."

It is complicated to choose a good name to symbolize these two thinking modes. They are complex and their boundaries are not sharply defined. We will pick the two words that symbolize best their essence. The first one we will call the "Analytical Mode" because analysis is one of the central features of that way of thinking, very related to logic and language. The other one we will call the "Creative Mode", because it is the mode that encompasses features that are key for creative thinking.

As we explained before, we will refer to analytical thinking as AT, and to creative thinking as CT.

"Awesome, tell me something about AT."

The analytical mode is very much connected to speech and language, to analysis and logic.

"Therefore to abstraction as well."

Yes, it likes to work with the simplifications, abstractions and labels that the mind creates to work quickly and efficiently with information.

"I imagine it is very active in communication as well."

It is involved in reading, counting and recognizing language. It is a key information processing mode that serves us very well, helping us to express and translate the insights and perceptions produced by the creative mode.

It also helps us to gather information, communicate and plan actions as well as carry out operations whose complexity is low enough to be dealt with by logic and analysis alone.

"I see, it is all about lowering the complexity around us and finding quick solutions."

Indeed. This mode simplifies the complexity of life, helping us navigate our existence in more efficient ways. It filters the inputs absorbed by our senses, manipulating sizes, colors, shapes, etc.

in order to facilitate quick identification and decision making processes.

"It makes our life easy."

In many ways yes. However, sometimes you want to go beyond these simplifications and access the richness of what is out there!

"I get you. That will take us into CT. But all this AT stuff makes me wonder how far we usually stand from the full richness around us?"

We like to think that we are aware of reality but reality is literally an illusion constantly manipulated by our minds.

Vision offers many examples of this. Sizes, distances, all that you see around you, arrives as raw information to your subconscious. This information is then simplified and filtered by the brain, delivering a different version to your consciousness.

"That would explain why conscious analysis during creative processes can really mess things up!"

Sure. We see this in many areas. That's why learning to draw involves a process of bypassing these filters to access the unfiltered versions that wait beyond these manipulations.

"So AT wants to make things simple and easy. Why is this so important for our minds?"

Closure, the sooner the better

For most people and most minds, closure is a way of life. We want answers and we want them now. We don't want to spend more effort or energy than necessary in achieving our objectives, be it at our jobs or in our interaction with others.

"So much urgency. What is it all about?"

It's all about efficiency. Our energy is limited. The adult brain tries to make use of past experiences and memories to interpret new inputs as quickly as possible. Closure, arriving at definite answers and reasoned interpretations, is a priority for our AT processes.

"So AT assumes that we can find solutions to our challenges based on past knowledge."

Yes, and it assumes that we can do that while working with simplified, symbolic and abstract representations of those experiences and that knowledge.

"Sounds like a good strategy for predictable scenarios."

Indeed. This way of thinking helps us in dealing with our daily lives and routines in efficient ways. But what happens when we need to come up with new ideas, with novel solutions to challenging problems?

"Seems to me that we will need to balance AT with a different and in many ways opposite way of thinking."

Yes, we need to engage with the complexity of life while encouraging a free flow of information. Incubating the information gathered, we generate new connections and insights. This process has to take place away from the tyrannical pressure of time.

It's what we call the Creative Mode.

"I'm already excited."

This way of processing information is highly perceptual. It manipulates information in many ways, sometimes spatially, other times through visual processes. It is nonlinear and simultaneous instead of sequential. It likes to wander and explore, it thrives in uncertainty and fuzzy contexts, enjoying the ambiguous, the vague and the unexpected rather than the precise and predictable.

"It sounds bold and daring."

CT sees confusion, absurdity and apparently useless details as an opportunity. It enjoys uncontrolled environments in a playful way.

"Sounds like a good anti-stress attitude."

Good point. Creative processes welcome uncertainty and bring us closer to reality in a way that dissolves our ego, our network of comparison and preoccupations. We enter a mental state where time loses its meaning, boredom dissolves and just like a cat, we relax in a broad and diffuse state of alert concentration.

"Sounds healthy to me!"

CT is also involved in processing and recognizing patterns, learning not by rules but by osmosis, by being exposed to a variety of rich patterns.

"Looking for harmony…"

Einstein liked to think of great formulas as something beautiful.[6] CT is all about perceiving the harmony in patterns of all kinds as well as grasping both their totality and details simultaneously.

"The harmony hidden within complexity, that's quite a beautiful mission…"

Yes, CT helps us identify the harmony and beauty that surround us, be it in the complexity of business strategies, in the design of a new vaccine, in the behavior of our loved ones or in the combination of video, audio, lighting and performance in a work of art.

"CT is almost a beauty sensor. I want it!"

And to sense and explore, it has to listen and observe. That's why CT is a receptive mode, specialized in observing rather than explaining. It likes to be specific and concrete rather than abstract and symbolic. It is therefore more exploratory than purposeful, and enjoys exploring without needing closure or reaching any specific goal.

"A great balance to our AT then."

Yes, it's a great complement to our AT, providing patient imagination, intuition, observation and perception, enhancing our ability to detect those magical bubbles, the subtle insights that pop in and out of existence within the unpredictable, fuzzy and complex world we live in.

"A patient mode that enjoys exploring. It sounds like CT will be comfortable delaying closure?"

Sooner or later?

Indeed. Achieving closure early on or letting the process simmer on its own can have a profound influence on the depth of our experiences.

Experiments have shown that interacting with complex contexts without trying to reach closure can produce a quality of understanding that goes much beyond analysis and logic.[7]

"So the more we wait …"

Confusion and uncertainty are often felt before great discoveries. It is as if we need to marinate our brains in the complexity of life in order to trigger an evolutionary process of connections and combinations that can eventually end up in a phenomenal insight.

"No great dish is cooked in a minute…"

Masters of creative thinking

Children are natural masters of creative thinking. Analytical thinking processes haven't fully developed in their brains. They learn by engaging deeply with the complexity of each activity, by trial and error, picking up language, walking and other abilities in a way that is beautifully organic and gradual. Osmosis is a good analogy to describe this process.

"How lucky, their creative impulses flow so freely…"

Think of learning a new language. Children often learn faster and easier than adults. Part of the reason is biological, but a significant part is related to how we think.

"So you mean that even as adults we could change our strategy when we learn a language?"

As adults we often try to learn a new language by using the brute force of AT. Of course, that hardly ever works too well.

"There must be other ways, even for adults."

When as adults we travel to a new country and we immerse ourselves in their culture, learning as we go, permeating ourselves as children do with the vocabulary and phrases that surround us every day, something extraordinary happens. It is not the gradual learning that may amaze you. It is the feeling of integration, of gradually blending with that language and culture, the feeling of how your brain slowly changes to adapt to the new world and context you are inviting it to explore.

"I need to travel more."

Remember, every one of your thoughts is shaping your mind constantly, regardless of you being a child or an adult. There is an opportunity behind every corner, behind every thought, to keep shaping your mind in the direction that you choose.

I have experienced this myself in multiple locations in the past few years. It is a way to discover that as an adult, not only do you preserve the ability to learn and grow, but by blending both thinking modes your capacities are stronger and deeper than you can possibly imagine.

"Every one of my thoughts is shaping me…"

To conclude on a fun relaxing note, watch this video in which I practice saying hello in Korean to every person I come across as I hike through the beautiful natural park of Seoraksan in the north of the country.

[Web] **torchprinciple.com/koreanhello**

"That was insane!"

Coming together

Both these modes are essential and the suppression of any one of them can trigger a variety of issues.

"I can imagine, give me an example."

Think about music for a moment. Music is a great example of an activity that when approached with mental balance produces extraordinary results. But what happens when the balance is not there?

"You mean when there is too much AT or too much CT going on, right?"

When a music performer overemphasizes one of these modes, results suffer. Performances that are mostly analytical lack in expressiveness, emotion, originality and uniqueness. Performances that are too spontaneous may suffer due to inadequate technique, timing and other analytical parameters.

"So we need both, we need a balance."

Yes. Intellect vs emotions, logical analysis vs metaphors, rational vs poetic thinking, abstract vs concrete and scientific vs imaginative. Both thinking strategies are powerful and much needed. Unfortunately this balance is hard to reach.

On the extremes, the reign of reason

In the past, historical personalities (like Homer, Plato, Descartes...) associated the greatness of humans with reason, analysis, consciousness and control. In trying to emphasize the unquestionable merit of analytical thinking and logic, many went too far, as far as crushing other modes of thinking that balance and complement the former.

Biologically, the adult brain favors strong analytical thinking skills, which provide great support for our brain from the point of view of energy spending and efficiency. And society, traditionally, has also strongly favored analytical thinking over creative thinking in educational programs and schools.

"So nowadays the balance between these modes is clearly tilted towards the analytical side."

In schools, exams have traditionally been based on the ability to analyze and work with data under the pressure of time. Contemplation and timeless processes, typical in CT, have long been considered inferior.

In addition, in the past complexity and competition were not as keen as today. Nowadays, innovation is a must to overcome competition and CT is essential in dealing with complexity.

On top of that, our personal well-being benefits enormously from finding a better balance between AT and CT. In the health chapter we will go deeper into this.

The lack of that balance can prevent us from realizing our full potential, from understanding fully the complexity around us, and indeed, from enjoying life to the full.

"Is there hope? Can this change?"

Fortunately, both in education and in business, people are beginning to acknowledge the shortcomings of a life centered mainly on analytical thinking. Today, creativity is the most sought-after skill by CEOs around the world.[8] And new education programs, such as Montessori, offer balanced approaches to the way we use our mind.[9]

"Things are finally changing!"

Yes, they are. The rising complexity and competition, together with the surge of mental illnesses triggered by unbalanced minds, is fueling a renewed interest in changing the way we think.

Our mission is to help creative thinking shine as it deserves, complementing our powerful AT capabilities.

This will put us on track to achieve balance and success in our personal and professional endeavors.

"I feel the importance of this balance."

AT copes poorly with high complexity. It can only label and barely grasp the complex patterns that surround us.

"Logic can be constraining."

And stressful. When AT becomes too dominant, it can generate anxiety and stress. Narrow focus and premature closure can produce bad decisions and wrong strategies.

"Rushing too much for closure can become an obstacle."

AT, being so focused on finding answers is a very impatient friend. It gets annoyed if answers don't appear quickly. It tends to hold onto past interpretations that are often misguided.

Dealing with complexity needs time. Most great discoveries have to first travel through fuzzy, unpredictable and confusing stages before we arrive to novel connections and insights.

"I miss CT, I can see why it's so needed."

Most real life scenarios, in business and in relationships, are made of imprecise and fuzzy data. In such contexts we need the opposite type of attention, a broad diffuse awareness that is open and alert to all potential connections and avenues of thought.

"I can see how a narrow focus could make us miss great potential opportunities and connections."

Think of when you are trying to recall a word. If you furiously insist on finding it, consciously and intensely narrowing your focus, you find yourself further and further from your objective. It is as if you were using a tiny beam of light to search for the word within a huge land of darkness.

AT's focus is too narrow. The complex scenario is too large to be reached with just analytical tools in a short span of time.

And yet, the capacity for abstraction of AT can sometimes provide shortcuts that speed up our search. But when those fail, it is much better to leave the challenge to our creative thinking processes. In general, analysis is highly correlated with language and symbols. So AT is suitable for tasks that can be broken down in discrete parts and worked with in sequential, linear ways.

"I see how using just AT is not going to take us to that forgotten word too fast."

The word you are searching for often arrives when you stop trying so hard, when you give space to your mind, entering that other wider, more relaxed mode of thinking, effectively changing that tiny beam into a broad diffused one, a much wider light that takes us to our destination so much faster.

So one of the biggest problems of AT and logical reasoning is that it is hard to make big leaps, to widen that focus, to create unexpected connections. Often the conclusion of an argument is already part of the premise.

CT, on the other hand, is all about triggering the unexpected, creating remote associations and combinations that move unpredictably and in nonlinear ways.

"I get it. And with AT it is not hard either to fall into overanalysis, isn't that right?"

Yes. Overanalysis is another challenge for AT. Analytical thinking tends to ignore non-verbal, sensorial or emotional inputs and overestimate logical and cognitive ones.

"So we are focusing too much on certain clues and ignoring many others."

The more we analyze a situation, working with abstract and simplified models of reality, the easier it is to find arguments that fit with all positions. Overanalysis often ends up on stalemates that may drive us to take wrong decisions.

"I know that feeling, thinking over and over and agonizing about a decision. It is so hard to let go and stop comparing over and over the different possibilities."

Indeed. AT can be very stubborn, preferring to look for yet more data or prolong the analysis, rather than give a chance to our creative thinking processes.

"Stubborn AT can take over our mind! I know that feeling!"

An overanalytical mind, constantly engaged in verbal activities and comparisons, makes it hard for subtle new insights to be noticed by our consciousness. Those insights are born from the organic complexity of reality, which cannot be reached by the simplified abstractions of AT.

"And what about... what happens when CT dominates too much?"

Creative thinking challenges

When creative thinking dominates too much, different issues happen like inefficiency in daily life and problems in planning, organizing and communicating effectively. Difficulties arise to translate useful insights into words and abstractions. And we need those words to communicate with others.

Also CT can sometimes enter processes of trial and error that can be bypassed with the help of logic and analysis. Because just as we can overanalyze, "think too much", we can also "think too little", evaluate and prove too little in our creative processes.

"All extremes, I see, are dangerous."

The main challenge of CT lies in its most powerful trait. Being so engaged and close to the complexity of life, creative thinking is highly specific.

"And that means that acquired knowledge is not so transferable to other domains (i.e. other areas of our lives)?"

Yes, not impossible but more difficult. That's why we need the support of analytical thinking, which can allow us to translate the know-how of creative thinking into symbols, words and explanations. We can then transfer and apply those in other areas of life.

"So CT has its limits."

Of course. CT excels in situations that are fuzzy, uncertain or highly complex, across all domains and disciplines. And yet it can certainly make mistakes. That's why analytical and logical thinking can help by overseeing, evaluating and validating the findings of our creative thinking processes.

"Working together, they produce the best results."

That's right. This means that in order to innovate and tackle the complexity of today's world, including its markets and relationships, we need:

- Logical analysis, but also the metaphors of creative thinking because metaphors can connect us to unexpected insights faster than logical analysis.

- Strong intellect and rational thinking, but also emotion because emotion is what drives customers and audiences to our products and services, creating strong bonds in relationships.

- To increase efficiency by simplifying and abstracting reality, but also to be specific and detailed when we need to dive into the complexity of life.

- To be factual and realistic, scientist like, in our analysis, but also to use our imagination to produce large leaps of understanding.

- To work in methodical, linear and sequential approaches when needed but also to employ the power of simultaneous, nonlinear, global processing to quickly grasp and understand complex patterns.

- To communicate insights and concepts through language, but also to visualize, as a whole, the subtle patterns that arise from the complexity that surrounds us.

- To manage time in order to fit the temporal requirements of analysis but also the non-temporal, meditative processes of creative thinking.

"So we need both, but can they both actually overlap?"

Incompatible friends

We arrive here at an interesting paradox. These modes are meant to be good friends, meant to cooperate and work together for the good of our mind. And yet they cannot be fully active at the same time.

"Their requirements differ so much!"

A typical example is the use of language. Language activates AT processes. When we are engaged in speaking or processing language, it is hard to activate creative thinking.[10] Analytical thinking strongly interferes with creative thinking.

"So we need both, but not necessarily at the same time."

Yes. Another area in which these modes show clear differences is in the kind of focus and awareness they require. AT is more focused and convergent whereas CT is the opposite, divergent and broad.

Both types of attention are important and useful, yet they can interfere with each other.

"So how can they still complement each other if it's hard for them to be active simultaneously?"

What we need is to train our mind in the ability to come and go between them. As we will see later, creative processes use a combination of these 2 modes at different stages. And what is key is being able to switch between them easily.

"Without any overlapping?"

We don't intend to say that when a mode is active the other one is fully off. Overlapping is possible and typical. One of the modes dominates the picture, and the other is still there although it recedes in the background until we switch things over.

Let's further reflect on this from the perspective of our biology.

Creativity on the waves

In the previous chapter we explored the biology of our brain. Now that we have presented these two key ways of processing information in our minds, let's return there for a moment. What is happening in our brain when we engage on creative processes?

When people are more alert and awake, we detect high frequency brainwaves in the brain, and the dynamics of these waves are quite random.[11]

"Sounds like a noisy environment to me."

As people relax while still awake, brainwaves slow down and get more synchronized. It is what we call alpha and theta waves.

When CT is happening, for instance, when you are in the process of illuminating new insights, people are in a more relaxed state. This state becomes more alert during the phases of implementation of the insights (which are more AT focused).

Therefore, creative processes require being able to move and switch between focused and highly articulated analytical thinking and a more relaxed, dimmer, broader form of awareness - creative thinking.

"A dance of brain waves!"

Indeed. A dance of waves that exciting tech startups are beginning to work with nowadays. Some of these startups are working on providing biofeedback that will help us better understand and optimize the way we think. One example is Interaxon, the startup directed by Ariel Garten.[12] Their headband, Muse, has the potential to reduce stress as the user monitors his/her own brainwaves in different ways.

It's now time to focus on how to achieve a better balance between these ways of processing information in our minds.

Too much of either thinking strategy can be detrimental to our health. Some creative geniuses that spent most of their time in the depths of their creative explorations ended up with mental illnesses, removed from the world, unable to cope and interact with the daily demands of society and their peers. Likewise when the situation is reversed.

"We need both ways of looking at the world."

Yes, we need AT to live our daily lives efficiently, and we need CT to go beyond AT simplifications and access all the richness and detail whenever we need.

That's why we like to overemphasize the need for balance.

"Although we put more emphasis on CT."

Yes, because our society and adult biology is strongly biased towards AT and we need to compensate for that. In order to innovate beyond typical solutions, CT is essential.

"Depth requires effort but pays off in the end."

Innovation in any field is often linked to the ability to explore a subject deeply and in a sustained way.

It is too easy to remain on the shores of abstraction. That's what our often hyperactive analytical mind encourages for the sake of efficiency. When we look deeply at something, it is still easy to do so for just a moment and quickly revert back to our default behavior.

To really unlock the complexity of any subject you need to descend onto the depths of its details and remain there for quite some time. And that requires courage in a society that rewards efficiency and high levels of abstraction.

When you are able to sustain depth for long enough, you access a phenomenal richness of detail and data, the springboard of innovation. This is why skilled artists, engineers, scientists and creative persons of all kinds are becoming more and more valuable in a society where complexity is increasing day by day.

The mission

These modes of thinking represent very different perspectives, both essential for our productivity and general well-being. AT and CT are two ways of looking at the world. The verbal vs the visual, the analytical vs the perceptual. Ideally, both should coexist in harmony but achieving balance between them is not easy and it is natural that some of us may be more analytical and verbal and others more perceptual, intuitive and visual.

"Total balance is never achieved."

Establishing a comparison between language and visual perception can help us understand more about the contrast between these two strategies.

- Words (language) vs edges (perception).
- Context (language) vs negative spaces (perception).
- Grammar and syntax (language) vs relationships and proportions (perception).

Genius is in the balance

Achieving this delicate balance is also in general the path to excellence.

For example, the best musicians are those that master the methodical and analytical sides of music while being able to trust their faster subconscious processes. This way they can achieve high levels of expressiveness and originality that are grounded on stable and firm foundations. They internalize the best knowledge and experience gathered by music professionals throughout history, and once those have reached the deepest layer of their minds, they let themselves go, trusting their subconscious blending processes until new insights emerge, which are then incorporated into their mental framework, restarting the process again.

Unfortunately, in most people one of the modes dominates much more than the other. For the reasons discussed earlier, most people's thinking is biased towards the analytical side. This is understandable. The development of language skills in humans was one of the revolutions that took human intelligence to the next level, allowing us to communicate and organize society in very efficient ways.

To achieve such efficiency, language and analysis work with abstract symbols, separated and removed from the specific complexity of life.

"The word flower does not tell us anything about a specific real flower."

Right. It represents in an abstract way all the possible flowers we may encounter. This is efficient and powerful in many ways, but limited in others. Because sometimes we need deep and detailed information about a specific flower, in order to absorb and blend rich data about it, data which can eventually trigger novel insights.

But our minds tend to be dominated by analytical processes, which interfere with other modes of thinking.

"I can see how this makes it hard to access our CT processes."

AT is like a very generous, attentive friend that sometimes goes too far and often doesn't want to leave us alone. It tries to simplify matters, rushing the interpretations of whatever hits our senses, looking for quick fits into categories and labels it already knows so that we don't have to waste our time looking into the fine details of whatever we are facing. This is a friend that enjoys the conceptual level, abstracting, simplifying, labeling and staying away from the intricate details of life.

But like all good things in life, the good can become too good.

"It can become a constraining prison."

Yes. Creativity is problem-solving with a different approach. It is all about getting out of the conventional strategies, exploring without limits and combining unusual ingredients to produce something new.

Finding the right ingredients and materials to kick start that process requires being able to perceive the complexity of the world at a deeper level.

"Which can feel inefficient to our AT."

Creative processes can feel like a waste of time on the short-term scale of things and waste is not an option for our analytical thinking. Efficient management of the food we eat and the air we breathe as well as the energy we spend is a must. So for our analytical friend, creativity is a bit of a waste of resources.

Uncertain exploration? An endless amount of details to perceive? No way! Says this analytical friend.

And here he comes ready to sabotage any attempt to exercise our creative muscles. We may be trying to contemplate and dive deep into the harmony of a unique moment and there it is with its impatient reminders.

"That's just a face, come on, a face, yes, a face! That's it, leave it. Move on! It's just a face!"

What can we do about this interference? There are ways to tame this friend in order to bypass its filters and access the complexity of our world. Only then we can stand out from the crowd by innovating and producing something different.

First, we need to train our mind to recover the balance between both ways of thinking. And we need to put more emphasis on CT precisely because most minds are biased towards the analytical side.

Becoming more creative in today's world is about exploring and empowering that other part of the mind we have neglected for so long.

The essential effort

To combine the best of both worlds, we have to make a special effort to open new avenues of thought in proactive ways and stop relying so much on tried and tested patterns.

Spending too much of our time on the conscious analytical thinking kingdom interferes and deactivates the more relaxed, patient and silent creative thinking processes.

"I feel how this may decrease our creativity and general intelligence."

The solution lies in achieving a good balance between the focused and purposeful analytical mode and the playful and patient creative one.

Henry Poincaré, French mathematician, theoretical physicist and engineer, said it best: "It is through science that we prove, but through intuition that we discover."[13]

"That's a beautiful way of expressing the key cooperation and balance we are searching for."

AT without CT is too slow to work effectively with the complexity, uncertainty and fuzziness of life. CT without analysis and logic is unable to prove, evaluate and communicate novel insights.

"How can these two then work together?"

A distanced cooperation

We have spoken previously about how interference can happen between these modes.

"Why is that happening?"

Research indicates that the brain can be active at any time only in a range of areas, not everywhere.[14] This partly explains why it is hard to use analytical and creative thinking at the same time, given that they activate different centers of the brain (with a certain amount of overlapping of course).

Different modes for different tasks

Imagine a team of professionals delivering a television show. Anna is a dancer. Peter a presenter. At some points in the show Peter speaks to the audience. At other times Anna dances on stage.

When Anna is dancing, Peter doesn't storm the stage and starts speaking at the same time. When Peter is delivering information to the audience, Anna doesn't appear dancing behind him, distracting the viewers. Wouldn't that be funny? Such a show would probably not last very long on air!

"So we are talking about cooperation without too much overlapping."

Analytical and creative thinking are also like two co-workers that need to be polite to each other. Just like Anna and Peter, they are each suited to different types of tasks. We cannot pretend to use analysis to solve tasks that require intuition, visualization and patience, tasks that take place within contexts that are confusing and uncertain. Nor use creative thinking to handle tasks that are all about tight focus, communication and debate.

For example, it is not easy to draw when speech is happening around us. Visual interpretation of patterns and verbal skills each require a different way of processing information in our minds.

So these modes are meant to be polite co-workers, ready to pass the spotlight to each other, depending on the job at hand.

Harmonious cooperation

When we manage to balance both ways of processing information, we are able to switch between broad, relaxed, diffused attention and concentrated and precise focus.

"I can see how each of these has its own time and place."

We are able to patiently absorb the world, contemplating it without judging it. And we are able as well to efficiently analyze and reach logical conclusions at higher abstraction levels when needed, which enables the transfer of information to other domains.

"Able to wait, able to pursue. Able to be silent, able to verbalize. Able to visualize, able to articulate. Able to be scientific, able to be poetic."

Like day and night. Like the poles that enhance contrast and polarity. Like the dualities that constitute the base of our existence. Like the particles and antiparticles that keep quantum reality in balance. Like analytical thinking and creative thinking.

CHAPTER 4:

Race for Survival

*"Every child is an artist, the problem is
staying an artist when you grow up."*

– Pablo Picasso

Now that we have learnt about these 2 ways of processing information in our minds, let's take a look at how the balance between them changes from childhood to adulthood.

And for that, let's start with the key driver of life, survival, and continue later with the issue of habits and how to break them.

A tale of survival

Under normal conditions, priority number one of any living entity is survival.

From the simplest life forms to the most complex ones, life is driven by this very powerful force: the drive to stay alive.

From the genes to the ideas

Survival can be interpreted from the perspective of the information encoded in our genes. This is related as well to human reproduction.

Survival can also refer to our ideas, our culture, concepts, teachings and other contributions to society.

Many humans want to leave behind an imprint, something that helps or influences future generations. Some have called this cultural evolution.

CT, supported by our analytical thinking processes, is a key tool to innovate and create something new that can contribute in positive ways, be it in business or at a personal level, to the present and/or future of humankind.

From the child to the adult

Returning to the strong drive to survive, this is something that behaves differently depending on the stage of development we are at.

"It is different for a child than for an adult."

A child's brain is like a blank canvas. Devoid of knowledge, the child is vulnerable, surrounded by many potential dangers. The child's brain contains too few skills and expertise to fall back on. Survival is fully tied to learning about the world and its dangers.

In order to survive the child depends primarily on the family. But that's not enough. The child needs to proactively explore and learn from the surroundings, and, by trial and error, discover the skills and tools needed to thrive not just in the immediate environment, but also in the dynamic society that is waiting around the corner. This is the fastest way to grow and enrich the brain in order to become independently able to face the challenges and dangers of our uncertain world.

So every child is creative by nature. Every child is an innovator, an explorer of life, wired to discover and rearrange the known in order to find the unknown. CT dominates in the child's brain. Survival is the main motivation; curiosity and confidence are the weapons.

As the child grows, the brain matures and its analytical and logical thinking skills become stronger and more dominant.

By the time a child becomes an adult, the accumulated knowledge and skills provide the child with the ability to comfortably navigate society, socially and professionally. At the same time the adult has to deal with many responsibilities from relationships to career, all of which need to be managed efficiently.

Resources to deal with all these responsibilities are limited. Money, food and other essentials cost time and effort. We invest our childhood in accumulating knowledge and skills and as we become adults, we naturally want to protect that investment and make the most efficient use of it.

Priorities change. Exploration and discovery are not so important anymore for survival. Survival is now more tied to making efficient use of the accumulated knowledge. Simplifying and abstracting the complexity of the world becomes important. It's all about not wasting precious resources.

"Resource management."

Every interaction with the world forces our brain to spend some of its valuable fuel and energy to make sense of it. Simplifying and abstracting the tremendous complexity of information that reaches our senses becomes a must for the efficient adult brain.

The brain filters inputs and outputs with that goal in mind. It attempts to interpret inputs by relating them to already known symbolic abstractions. And it tries to conform outputs to already known and easy to recall patterns of activation, in order to minimize energy expenditure.

This anti-creative perspective does make sense in many ways. Having to do an extra effort every time we interact with the world would make daily life impossible. If our brain was to bring to our attention every piece of information that arrives through our senses, we would be literally clogged with data and unable to function.

We become conscious of some of these inputs, but for the sake of efficiency we are not aware of most of them. The brain brings to our attention what it considers to be essential. The rest, though, does not disappear. It is absorbed by our bodies and minds and becomes part of that mysterious internal pot that we often call the subconscious.

It is there, deep within the subconscious, where the complexity of the world we interact with blends and combines. It is from that special place that all sorts of insights and revelations can arise.

The question is: How do we access that subconscious, how do we tap into it? In the next chapters we will go deep into that.

Let's now return to the permanent push and pull between generic, abstract and shallow processing vs specific, personalized and deep processing. This is a battle typically won by the more abstract and generic contender, because our energy supply as adults is limited and therefore an efficient use of our energy is considered a key priority.

Think of what happens in society in so many fields. In medicine, treating all patients with generic drugs is cheaper in every way. Treating each patient in a personalized way, taking into account specific behavioral and biological patterns works much better, but it's much more expensive.

"What about education?"

Evaluating all students with the same parameters and criteria is faster and cheaper, but of course it is not only unfair, but also absurd in many ways. Evaluating and working with each student in a different way, depending on the specific abilities and drives of that human being is the fairest way to go about it and the more effective long-term solution, but it's also more expensive and inefficient from our typical short-term analytical perspectives.

"So creativity can feel like a waste of time from an AT perspective."

But is it really so?

If we think about the examples above, we may begin to realize that what looks inefficient in the short term can become the most efficient solution in the long term.

Treating all patients with generic solutions may produce benefits in some of them. But those medicines will either not work or even harm a large percentage of the patients, which will drive up the costs enormously in the long term.

Education that is rigid and inflexible will produce flawed human beings, and those will cost much more to society in the long term than what is being saved in those early years.

CT is not like sugar. It is not about producing a short-term quick rush or gain that, just as quickly, fades away. CT is good nutrition for your mind. It stays and produces good metabolic changes that transform the way you think in positive ways.[15] It is a long-term solution that is as comprehensive as personalized education and personalized medicine.

CT is also the best strategy to go beyond the known to get to the unknown.

It is the tool of choice as soon as we need to exit our abstract bubble and face the real complexity of the world out there.

Unfortunately, most adults find it very hard to activate their CT because of the predominance of AT processes in their minds. These often interfere, block and prevent CT processes. Because of this, people often take decisions based on analytical abstractions.

"Which are very removed from the reality out there."

Yes. And this has profound implications connected to relationships, business, health and our well-being.

In an ideal world we would balance analytical efficiency with creative skills, which can enrich and add meaning and value to our lives. In practice, encouraged by a society that rewards methodical logical thinking and planning over uncertain fuzzy explorations, the analytical centers of the brain soon take over most of the adult's thinking efforts and slowly banish creative thinking to the sidelines.

AT and the simplifications of logic provide a useful illusion of permanence and efficiency. Things get done in a logical and methodical way. Logic justifies actions. Days proceed in an orderly fashion.

However, as the weeks, months and years pass, problems begin to appear. Even though the adult is managing resources correctly and material goods are readily available, something is missing. A certain void fills the spaces in between the noise and distractions of life. And yet we cannot understand what it is that is missing.

Sometimes, as the adult interacts with children, moments of joy fill those spaces, and remind him/her of childhood. But of course we think, that's just kid's stuff…

Maintaining the openness and fluid contact with life that children have can feel risky and inefficient. But the problem is that living permanently in the world of AT is what is truly risky. It depletes our energy. We collapse under the weight of stress and anxiety. Plus we miss all the benefits that a balanced mind can bring us.

CT is a positive experience that helps sustain our energy. AT brought to the extreme often affects our emotions to the point of impacting our general energy levels and well-being.

The transition from childhood to adulthood is not meant to be a brain replacement process. This is a key point we need to bear in mind.

"So, it doesn't mean that we replace CT with AT."

The transition is a growth phase. Our CT capabilities get augmented and complemented with new ones. These enhance our abilities in areas such as analysis, logic, planning and others.

"We are growing, not replacing."

Ideally, as we grow, we integrate new capabilities into our system and find a harmonious balance between them all. A balance that allows all our skills to complement each other for the good of the mind and the organism as a whole.

"And yet, our society encourages AT to dominate and be in charge."

It's like tying one of our arms to our back. The other arm may be very skilled, but you will soon start to feel tired and anxious. You will need to overcompensate your loss by stretching your single arm further than it can reach.

This is what we often do with our logical, analytical thinking. We attempt to use it for all purposes, dealing with situations whose complexity goes beyond its range of action. And we can feel that. Be it in a job/career scenario or when dealing with our relationships, we sense it. We get anxious, nervous, depressed. We find it hard to take decisions because we are using the wrong tool to process the complexity that we face. We have forgotten that we have other skills. Skills banished to the sidelines of our minds. We take decisions based on the narrow and abstract perspective of language and logic. Whatever the outcome, our mind is the loser. It accumulates stress, tiredness and anxiety, having to do all the work with just that one arm while the other one looks helplessly on.

Overtime, our AT, like a muscle constantly exercised, becomes powerful and strong. But just as when we use the wrong muscle for the wrong action, it also becomes tense and overstretched. On the other hand, our forgotten creative muscles become weak, risking atrophy.

And yet, there is hope. Just as we can slowly rehabilitate our body muscles after surgery and long periods of immobilization, we can do the same with our creative thinking in order to move towards a better mental balance.

A balance that makes an optimum use of our mental resources, and by balancing our thinking processes, balances as well our health and well-being.

"This balance makes us deeper as well."

Being creative means engaging deeper with the world. Going beyond the simplified interpretations of the analytical mind and penetrating into the actual richness and complexity of life.

The process to balance our thinking modes can start right now. Of course this involves taking a risk from the point of view of energy management and efficiency.

"I get it. CT requires a bigger effort for adults."

Yes, the brain will try to resist and fall back on its comfortable routines and behaviors. But let's not forget. Creative thinking was effortless when we were children. As we became adults we made a habit of doing the opposite. Changing habits is always hard, but it can be done.

What may look to the brain as an unnecessary investment of energy, becomes over time, if done correctly, an investment with a large return. A return in the form of better mental health, better professional career prospects as well as better relationship management and general well-being.

"It cannot be easy to get out of the habit of relying mainly on AT processes."

Indeed. In many ways it is just like training any weak muscle in the body. The beginnings are hard but after a while, the training itself becomes a habit.

"A habit?"

Yes, exercising our creative thinking skills, going deeper and being more in contact with the world around us become a habit. It gets easier and easier and it also sharpens our perception skills, our awareness and the general performance of our brain.

In fact balancing our thinking will improve our performance in every area of our lives because we are reinforcing our foundations with a more solid base, stronger and deeper.

The best of both worlds

In summary, a child's creativity is intuitive, born out of necessity. An adult's creativity has to be encouraged and requires effort. At the same time, an adult's brain is full of experience and connections whereas the child's brain is a blank canvas.

We naturally want the best of both worlds. A child's attitude, fresh and ready to explore, and the support and foundation provided by all the experience and connections we have developed as adults.

A strategy

To balance our minds and use our full potential, to correct the bias towards analytical thinking and innovate in our careers and lives, we need to do two things.

First we need to tame our analytical thinking and conscious chatter. We need to calm down our minds and create space where our creative thinking can thrive. This involves learning ways to prioritize different modes of thinking while avoiding analytical trickery. The chapter on health will cover a lot about this.

Second, we need to train and exercise our creative thinking muscles, opening new avenues and channels in our minds, in a mission to rearrange what is known in order to trigger novel insights and solutions to the challenges we face. The next couple of chapters will go deep into this.

CHAPTER 5:

The Torch Principle

"There is no doubt that creativity is the most important human resource of all. Without creativity, there would be no progress, and we would be forever repeating the same patterns."

— Edward de Bono

Now that we understand what AT and CT are, let's explore how to combine them to find great innovative solutions to any challenge we may face personally or professionally.

After this chapter we will move on to practical exercises to train our creative muscles. You don't run a marathon without first training appropriately. In the same way, you can't innovate like a master without first exercising your creative muscles regularly.

In these next two chapters you will gain deep understanding about how to find great solutions to your challenges and how to train your creative muscles to become better and better at implementing your ideation processes.

Let's begin with a metaphor that crystalizes what we have covered till now. The metaphor also emphasizes the importance of CT as the key driver when we wish to produce innovative solutions for our challenges. Welcome to the torch principle.

The torch principle

When we face a challenge and need to find an innovative solution for it, what we don't know is always larger than what we know. So we can imagine that at the start, we are surrounded by a huge ocean of mental darkness. This ocean holds infinite solutions to infinite challenges.

[Web] <u>torchprinciple.com/torchprinciple</u>

"I wish I had some light in there."

You do. Somewhere within that ocean of mental darkness we are standing holding a little torch. That torch can throw some light onto the challenge. The torch represents the information, the knowledge we currently hold about the challenge.

"That's a start."

Around us, within that ocean of mental darkness, there are solutions to our challenge. Some of those solutions are typical and predictable and are therefore located closer to where we are. Other solutions are more innovative and original and are therefore located further away from our current mental patterns.

Our objective is to find those innovative solutions that are hidden in the darkness.

"That can't be an easy task."

It is not. One approach would be to use mainly analytical/systematic strategies. If we do that it will be as if we took our torch and started walking around, step by step, hoping to somehow bump into one of those innovative solutions.

"That's going to take some time…"

Yes, and our time is limited. So it is likely that we will end up finding one of the most typical/predictable solutions, the ones that are located closer to where we started. Or we may even walk in circles and end up right where we started. This typically happens in political or business negotiations that tend to overemphasize analysis and logic.

"There must be another way…"

A different and better approach consists of combining analysis with creative thinking strategies. In this new approach, we first diverge before we converge.

"Diverging before converging. It sounds powerful."

We jump instead of taking small steps. We gather more torches and plant these new torches on different parts of this vast space of mental darkness.

"What are these new torches?"

They are information, sometimes apparently unrelated to the challenge and at other times more obviously related. We focus on diverging right from the word go, which is why we end up, at times, throwing torches on areas that apparently have nothing to do with the challenge.

"And then, how do we connect those torches together?"

We need some glue. That glue is our brain.

"The great connector!"

Yes! Our brain is designed by nature to connect and interpret any information pattern we present to it, under the right circumstances.

"What do you mean with under the right circumstances?"

Our mind requires four key things to function as the great connector that we know it is. I call it DITS, depth, ingredients, time and space.

"I'm all ears!"

1. **First, the depth elevators**
   We need to be working at the right depth. The information we have given to our subconscious needs to be neither too shallow nor too deep and complex. You have to take the depth elevator right down to the complexity level that matches the complexity level of the solution you are looking for. There is no right or wrong depth. You have to decide what your depth should be in each process.

2. **Second, ingredients**
   Those torches, those lights, need to be of the right quality and depth. And they cannot be too few neither too many (specially when they are too obviously connected to the challenge). Think of a cooking pot that is too empty (it can burn) or too full (ingredients cannot move and don't combine well).

"Too many will blind us, saturate us, or drive us to a premature closure. Too few won't throw enough light to take us to those innovative solutions."

3. **Third, time**
We need to give enough time for these lights to combine with each other, for new connections to happen.
"We cannot rush the process. The mind needs time to incubate these new ingredients."

4. **Fourth, space**
We need to have the right attitude, the right sensitivity to notice when this process generates something special.
"Our mind cannot be full of noise and chatter. It needs space."

The incubation context

The mind will combine and recombine all that new light, all those ingredients we throw into our subconscious. This is what we call incubation. Eventually some of those combinations will knock on the doors of our conscious mind. For us to notice those delicate insight bubbles, we need to have enough space in our minds. A mind that is constantly dominated by noise, chatter, anxiety and stress, will not be ready to receive these calls.

"So under the right circumstances we may hear these calls."

Yes, this is what we call an illumination, a leap of understanding and clarity. Suddenly we feel the solution is within us.

"What is really happening behind the scenes?"

The accumulated light, an aggregate of all the torches we planted (information gathered at the right depth), in combination with the connecting abilities of our brain, is incubated for as long as necessary. All of that, in the context of a mind that has enough space and sensitivity, allows us to eventually find one of the innovative solutions located within that vast ocean of mental darkness. We can then evaluate that solution, consciously translate it into words and implement it.

To succeed, therefore, we need the right kind and amount of torches and lights, that is, the right kind and amount of information collected at the right depth. We then allow those lights to combine and connect for as long as necessary. The result of that process is brought to the attention of our conscious mind, which needs to have the right amount of sensitivity and space to become aware of those insight calls.

"Depth, Ingredients, Time and Space, DITS."

Diverge before you converge

The most important part of the torch principle can be encapsulated in this phrase.

"Diverge before you converge."

This is really the cornerstone of creativity and innovation. Diverge before you converge. Imagine before you analyze. Expand before you contract.

Move away from premature closure and from the typical solutions by first going wild and far, before you later converge onto specific solutions which will then have more chances of being innovative and different.

Diverging before converging is like a fractal. It is a process that keeps appearing at different scales all around us. It appears in the way natural selection works in biology and in the way startup incubators function. It is part of the process investors use to take their decisions. It is, in summary, present in so many scenarios.

"But it is hard to implement."

It is. Because we are all conditioned to want results and answers straightaway. We want closure now. We want to converge immediately. We find it hard to give ourselves the chance to diverge before we converge. But in there lies the secret of great innovations and of a mind with fit and healthy creative muscles that balance our AT capabilities. In this chapter and the next I will give you strategies, exercises and tips to become great at diverging in intelligent ways before you converge.

The model

Let's now move on from the metaphor to a more formal model of the creative process. Over the last century there have been many models created to describe innovation and creativity processes. Processes that can happen in an instant or take a lifetime.

Some of these models have 4 stages, other 5, 7 or even 9!

As any model, one that describes innovation or creativity cannot be an accurate description of such an incredibly complex process. It is, however, a useful exercise to explore one of these models. It will help us understand where we need to improve and what we need to focus on.

"Bring it on!"

Most creativity models proposed agree on a number of key stages. We will call these with our own names: seed, nurturing, incubation, illumination, implementation and iteration.
[Web] **torchprinciple.com/creativitymodel**

Stage one: Seed

A challenge is identified. This challenge is often associated with a specific community or group of people, a specific target audience. A deep understanding of that community is often a precursor before a challenge is identified. This is the stage from which the rest of the creative tree springs out. Understanding the community, the audience, the people related to the challenge is a key part of this phase and the next.

"In the torch principle, this is the part where we set our initial position in that vast ocean of mental darkness. Where do we start? What do we know about our challenge at the beginning?"

Stage two: Nurturing

A process of gathering data and information about the challenge and often the related community takes place. The objective is gathering quality ingredients. Metaphorically, think of a subconscious child getting toys to play with or of a subconscious chef getting quality ingredients to cook with. It is an essential step if we want our seed to grow and develop.

"In the torch principle this is the part where we plant more torches and lights around us."

Stage three: Incubation

We let go, we give time for our seed to grow. Time is needed for us to absorb and process the information we have gathered and for our subconscious to play with the quality ingredients we have brought together. Incubation is the time for our quality ingredients to combine in order to potentially generate new insights.

"In the torch principle, this is when we give time to our mind to combine and blend the new lights we have planted."

Stage four: Illumination

The incubation stage will eventually produce interesting combinations, delicate fleeting insights that may reach consciousness and be noticed if our attention and focus is broad and sensitive enough. This is the key moment when new understanding arises in our conscious minds.

"In the torch principle, this happens when the accumulated light of the new torches combines, under the right circumstances, to illuminate one of the innovative solutions around us."

Stage five: Implementation

A new insight needs to be evaluated, proven and if found useful, transformed into a product, service, message or action. This new clarity and understanding is therefore transformed into a tangible and stable trunk with solid branches.

"In the torch principle, when our mind has enough space and sensitivity, we become aware of a new solution being illuminated by our torches. We can then proceed to evaluate it and implement it."

Most importantly, the implementation stage is not the end. The creative process is iterative and often nonlinear.

Stage six: Iteration

We can continue nurturing our seed with new ingredients, incubating them, evaluating new insights and implementing them. The name of this stage expresses the importance of the dynamic flow that keeps solutions evolving, mutating or pivoting at any time.

Seed, nurturing, incubation, illumination, implementation and iteration are ways to represent key stages we identify in typical innovation processes.

We could name them in many other ways. We could subdivide some of them into further stages. But the essence of the model remains. Identifying challenges, gathering information about them, allowing that information to blend and combine with our own existing knowledge until new insights arrive, which are then evaluated and implemented.

"How much do these stages overlap with each other?"

It is key to understand that the way these stages relate to each other is often very loose. Nurturing can be bypassed by utilizing our existing knowledge. We can redefine our challenge, our seed, multiple times through prolonged nurturing. Incubation processes can last milliseconds, as when a pianist improvises, or years in the case of the writing of a novel. Multiple illumination stages can feed back into seed and nurturing stages in a dynamic mixture that evolves over time, shaping our ideas as we discard some of our insights and encourage others in a process that may remind us of natural selection in biology.

"So the model is totally flexible, it is a tool, not a rigid guideline."

Yes, understanding these example stages and imagining new ones will help us devise strategies to empower our creative thinking even more.

"You spoke about a chef, I like that analogy."

Metaphors can help us a great deal in describing processes as complex as creativity.

One of the metaphors I like to work with is the one of the creative chef. That's us by the way!

"We are on our way to a tasty metaphor!"

The creative chef, that's us, decides on a dish to cook, gets ready with the preparations and then starts to gather quality ingredients inside an extraordinary pot that we shall call our subconscious pot. **[Web] torchprinciple.com/subconsciouspot**

Let's remind ourselves that I will be labeling as subconscious those processes of whose existence we are not consciously aware. Processes that happen out of the radar so to speak, away or below consciousness. They are therefore subconscious. What exactly is the nature of our subconscious is something that experts continue to investigate. For the purposes of this book, all that matters is that there is a fuzzy threshold that separates these two domains, conscious and subconscious.

The land of the subconscious

We could actually speak of two thresholds. The first and most important threshold is the one that separates what becomes conscious in our mind from what we absorb, but doesn't reach our consciousness. A secondary threshold would separate information that doesn't even get picked by our senses from that which does. In between those two thresholds sits this mysterious subconscious pot.

The subconscious pot is a way of representing the vast amount of information that gets absorbed into our system, but is not necessarily brought to our conscious attention.

This is a key point to emphasize. The vast majority of the information we absorb at any given moment exists in that subconscious pot. Only a small amount, an occasional spoonful, is brought to the attention of our conscious chef when needed.

All the mind is a stage!

Think of the stage of a theater. Actors enter and leave. Behind the scenes there is a hidden world of rehearsals and discussion in which interpretations and performances are way more fluid and dynamic than those that finally appear with the final costumes in front of the audience.

"A hidden subconscious world."

The final performance on stage is the tip of the iceberg of all that other reality of loose, dynamic and open rehearsals that combine and blend every parameter of the story and its performers to produce a fantastic final show.

The vast pot vs the spoonful. Subconscious and conscious.

Subconscious wisdom

"Which one is really wiser, the conscious or the subconscious?"

Is the conscious mind mainly the final communicator, the messenger carrying the valuable treasure insights elaborated below our mysterious thresholds?

What we know is that some geniuses, like Einstein, enjoyed the potential and wisdom of their subconscious CT processes during most of their work, making use of AT processes at specific moments, for example, during the implementation phase of their projects.[16]

"We are so much more than our consciousness."

When we admire great creative geniuses, beyond their personalities and creations, we are admiring the richness of that fascinating world below and beyond their consciousness. We are admiring a lifetime of processing and manipulating the rich and complex information they gathered at their subconscious pots.

The efficient bear: Store for the winter

If we were to bring to our conscious attention all the information that reaches our senses, we would quickly saturate our mental resources.

"Not to mention the amount of energy we would spend acting on it!"

So the brain brings to our attention only what it considers essential. The rest still reaches us and gets encoded into our system, joining our subconscious pot.

Just like an efficient bear, we store valuable information that may eventually be useful later on.

"I love my subconscious pot!"

You should decorate it with beautiful ingredients. And now, let's enter the subconscious kitchen!

The subconscious kitchen

The kitchen is all yours.

"Awesome! I have to choose what dish I want to cook."

What about coming up with a new type of cleaning product that provides some unique advantage over the competitors? That should be tasty. Let's begin gathering quality ingredients.

Giving birth to a new dish can remind us of human births. Our subconscious pot can be thought of as a mental womb. A womb we have to take care of and feed with the best ingredients in order to encourage the birth of something extraordinary.

"Information about cleaning processes, other cleaning products... "

Yes, but also other more apparently unrelated ingredients. Remember that at the start we want to diverge as much as possible. That implies gathering ingredients that are also very diverse and not necessarily connected to our challenge.

"Cool! Well let's gather also a bath here, a tortoise there, uh a nice colorful kayak, some ice as well, an alarm could come handy... Environment, I like that concept! Let's continue: some water..."

Keep going. Diverge before you converge. And now we mix it all together. It flows nicely. We have enough ingredients, but not too many related ones. Too many ingredients directly related to the challenge may sometimes restrict our ability to combine and recombine them in productive ways, reduce their room for maneuver and eventually drive us to a premature closure.

"Hey look, something is coming up from the pot! Is that an insight bubble?"

Bravo. I see that this mind has enough space and sensitivity. Our ingredients have combined and produced something special. A unique and fragile scent emerges from the pot. If we are sensitive enough, our conscious mind identifies that scent as something beautiful, harmonious, unique and useful.

"How can we promote the generation of more of these unique bubbles? And how can we tame our AT processes and conscious noise in order to have enough mental space to be sensitive to them?"

We will provide answers to that in this chapter and the next. The subconscious kitchen never rests. The Information, the ingredients, keep streaming through our senses and into our pot. The quality of those ingredients depends of course on what we expose our senses to.

"How we live makes our subconscious pot!"

That's why creative thinking is linked to everything you do. Every interaction, every action. You are feeding your subconscious pot at all times. And this is a complex beast. Whatever you feed it with has consequences.

"We have to treat it as gently and respectfully as we would treat our best friend."

Can you smell it? The dish is ready!

"A cleaning product that is small, portable and doesn't require water to be used!"

Great initial insight, it's tasty!

So your insight has reached our consciousness and survived, entering a process of competition and survival against other thoughts.

The evolution of ideas

"Can we speak about a natural selection process with ideas?"

You are referring to ideas that compete with each other in our minds, some fading away while others propagate to other minds. Ethnologist and Professor Richard Dawkins originally proposed the concept of a meme, an idea that spreads between minds. Memes are regarded as cultural analogues of genes, able to mutate and respond to selective pressures. If you are interested to know more about memes, check his book "The selfish gene".[17] There is also a short chapter in this book dedicated to this topic.

In summary, a great collaboration

Our capacity to collaborate and empathize with others is a positive human trait. One that we also need within our minds. AT and CT are opposite in many ways and yet they have to collaborate and work together for the good of the common goal, finding a great innovative solution to our challenge.

In summary, creativity is a collaborative effort between different ways of processing information. All of these stages combine AT and CT processes, but some of the stages favor one more than the other. We need AT to evaluate and translate our perceptions into language and gather information. We need CT to manipulate that information in faster and deeper ways.

Nurturing and implementation are very conscious stages driven mainly by AT. Incubation, illumination and the seed stage put more emphasis on CT.

Great creatives are able to switch and comfortably alternate between CT and AT, between broad, diffuse, open attention and tight, concentrated focus. We need both in this delicate dance that takes us from the initial seed to the great insight at the end of the creative bridge.

"And I guess each of those stages may have an impact in how we work as well."

Environments free from pressure, language and analysis, favor a mind that has the space necessary to be sensitive to its subconscious and intuitive processes. Some creative people go through periods of isolation to encourage the triggering of valuable seeds.

Later on, when the moment arrives to evaluate, communicate and analyze these initial seeds, group brainstorming and team work can be very effective.

We shouldn't see both ways of working as being incompatible, nor as sharply separated processes. They feed on each other all the time. In my work, I quickly switch between them. For example, I may leave home on my own and walk for hours incubating ingredients until an initial insight comes to mind and then immediately communicate that insight through language to other people, evaluating it and analyzing it.

That, in turn, may trigger another creative thinking stage, which I may work through on my own, at the studio or away from home, until the moment arrives again to brainstorm in a group. We will go over this in more detail later.

On to the details

Let's now review each of the stages in more detail. A fascinating journey from the tight focus of conscious analysis to the wide, fuzzy and flexible world of creative thinking.

"I'm ready for a wild ride!"

Seed

Where are we going today?

Most creative processes begin with the seed stage.

Einstein once said that the process of setting up or formulating a challenge is often more important than its solution.[18]

At the seed stage we establish a direction, the challenge we want to work on, the problem we intend to solve. A seed is an interesting analogy because when we first establish our intention to find the solution to a challenge it is as if we literally planted that first intention-seed somewhere in our minds. From that point on, the seed can begin to sprout, spread, interact with other parts of us and in time grow into a robust tree, spreading its branches further and further.

We are also finding our initial position in that vast mental space the torch principle talks about.

The seed stage can involve both conscious analytical processes involving language as well as more fluid and organic creative thinking processes involving more of our subconscious pot.

Sometimes this initial direction may arise from a fleeting feeling, a delicate bubble arising from our subconscious. An initial hunch that is hard to translate into words. Other times early impulses are quickly transformed into words and language, verified and elaborated at more conscious levels.

In summary, we need a seed that establishes the base of it all, the direction we want to work towards.

Let's reconnect with our cooking metaphor. First you need to decide what you want to cook. You need to give a direction to your subconscious pot.

If we don't set a direction, our bubbling pot will keep blending and recombining our ingredients in a random fashion, without any intention.

"Can we get anywhere without a direction?"

Do you get anywhere if you take your car and start driving randomly? Probably. Without a direction, spontaneous valuable insights can arise from the random movements of our subconscious. It is just a more unpredictable and often a more difficult process.

If you board a ship in Seville and decide to navigate randomly the oceans, you can still arrive at valuable locations. But your trip is likely to be harder, more uncertain and of course, there are no guarantees of any kind that you will even arrive at some interesting place.

Setting an initial direction helps. It makes the process easier.

So what is your direction? How complex is the dish you are trying to create? Is it about solving the world's hunger problem? Improving transport in cities? Documenting the suffering of children during a war? Exploring the robots of the future in a film?

At the following address you can find a list of themes that can inspire you to create your next seed.

[Web] **torchprinciple.com/themes**

"And how detailed should this seed be?"

The seed can be very precise or more generic. It could start as a theme, a horizon painted with broad strokes that gets more precise and targeted over time as the creative process advances.

For example we may say that we want to create a painting about fishermen, and leave it there to begin with.

"Broad strokes."

Or write a story about two robbers who decide to rob a bank to help their families.

"This is a bit more detailed."

Or we want to make a film about betrayal in relationships.

"Broad and open."

Or we plan to create a web internet venture that can help people reconnect with long lost friends from their childhood.

"More detailed."

More detail can accelerate the process and bring us faster to a solution. But it can also prevent us from discovering the most original solutions that are hard to get to if we tighten our initial focus too much.

Remember our mantra, diverging before converging. Tightening the initial direction too much can restrict our creative potential. It is all about balance. Set a direction with enough detail, but not too much.

Sometimes you quickly find out what your objective is. Other times you are not sure or you just want to work in a fuzzier and more exploratory manner. There are ideation exercises that can help you generate unique initial seeds and we will be talking about them later on.

"This is really exciting. And what attitude favors best results at the seed stage?"

To generate initial seeds faster and easier, be alert to what excites your curiosity, to what triggers questions in your mind, to that which challenges you and seems to cry out for a solution to be found.

Once you catch one of those subtle seeds, make a quick grab for it and note it down. These seeds are delicate and subtle, and they soon fade away from your consciousness if you don't register them.

Use whatever method you are comfortable with, writing it down in a journal, recording a voice note on your phone, etc.

Most importantly, don't stop on your first hunch. Generate as many seeds as you can. Later on you can evaluate them and settle on your favorite ones.

As this process advances and a seed takes hold firmly, the next stage is already beginning. It is the moment to define and explore the essence of the seed, to break it down and understand it in detail.

So get ready to start growing that seed, keeping it alive with quality ingredients. Before we go there, let's reflect further on the psychology of this initial stage.

The everything in the nothing

Beginnings are hard. It is frightening standing in front of a void: staring at a blank page, an empty canvas or a computer screen. But is nothing really nothing?

Recent research in quantum mechanics concludes that even a vacuum is not really empty.[19] What looks empty is actually teeming with particles that pop in and out of existence. It is a nothingness that in a way contains infinite possibilities within it.

"An infinite potential."

Staring at nothingness is like jumping into an apparently empty and wild ocean. It is very frightening at first. But gradually things change. First, you realize that you float! You don't sink, you are still there. You can move around, you can explore. Second and most importantly, details come into focus. The ocean wasn't as empty as it seemed. In fact, it is swarming with activity. You start to find logs you can hold on to, small islands, boats and other animals.

"Courage seems to be key…"

Exactly. CT and the seed stage require the courage to jump into that apparent nothingness. Sometimes you quickly find out what your direction should be. Other times you don't even want it to arrive quickly. You want to dive into that ocean and let the waters take you where they may.

"The lack of direction contains all possible directions."

Yes, and of course, as we explained before with the analogy of the sailor, such exploration risks getting nowhere. But for an avid explorer, even nowhere is somewhere.

Let's show an example from one of my experimental films where I began the process without a direction.

But first let's clarify that the direction, even though it can be more or less detailed, must have some detail at least. The intention to create a business, a story for a film, to write a book or help the world is just an intention, not a direction. So we shall not consider this baseline intention as a direction, but just as the obvious motivation to kick start any creative process.

In that film project, I decided to first dive into a musical ocean, using a large pool of random music tracks.

"A musical ocean…"

I simply listened to random music, not looking for anything specific. I allowed the music to blend with my subconscious pot and I waited. And waited.

After some time, a track came on the speakers. As the music played, I started to visualize a character very clearly. I gradually saw more details. The character was dressed in a certain way, standing in a beautiful square. I could feel his mood. As the music kept going, the character and the story, in other words, the seed, started growing. Details fell into place. It was a fascinating process that felt right. It felt harmonious.

"What was really happening there?"

By entering into a relaxed, contemplative, open and diffused state of awareness, devoid of language and analysis, I was letting my attention become as broad and loose as possible.

"Expanding our mental radar so to speak."

I was absorbing and bathing my awareness in the vast complexity of the information encoded in the music, blending it with the one already present in my mind.

"AT was not interfering."

Yes, so I wasn't trying to figure out anything specific in the music. I wasn't judging it in any way. Closure was not an objective. I was leaving all options open and simply allowing things to fall in place by themselves.

"Diverging before converging."

Throughout this process, a massive collection of quality ingredients was interacting with my existing repository of information.

From the combination of all of those ingredients arise potential insights, some of which are picked up consciously when our mind has the right attitude, a gentle alertness devoid of conscious chatter.

"When we are sensitive to those subtle bubbles arising from our subconscious pot."

This is raw creative thinking at its best. Swimming in uncertainty and confusion, relaxed yet alert, like a cat, broad and diffused, yet watchful. It is such a state, which often precedes the discovery of a great insight.

Let's get back to the process. The seed is planted. Now we have to grow it!

Nurturing
Strengthening our seed

To nurture our seed, first we need to understand it. Our key objective is to metaphorically become the seed. Understand it really deeply. Expand it. Enrich it by diverging before we converge.

Einstein used to visualize himself being part of his challenges.[20] Imagining that he was chasing after a beam of light and through many other visualizations, eventually he arrived at his relativity theory. Like Einstein, we should also try to blend with the seed.

"Becoming one with the seed, that's fascinating!"

The better we understand our seed and the more we enrich it, the more it grows. Every seed needs nourishment to survive, as every dish needs ingredients to be cooked.

Without nourishment, without ingredients, without information, seeds perish and eventually disappear.

"Gotta feed that seed!"

You feed it with information. Einstein told us that energy is not created or destroyed, it merely changes form. In creative processes all we are doing is repackaging and recombining existing information into new configurations that we sometimes identify as insights.

Resonating data

Information is at the core of everything, from the DNA in our cells to the way we interact with each other. At the core of the creative process is the combination of two information sources.

The first source is the new information we gather in connection with our challenge. The second source is the past information that is already encoded in our minds.

When these two sources of information are brought together in the chambers of our mind and allowed to resonate, combine and recombine, new information is generated. If this new information is found to be useful, it may be perceived as an insight.

"And how much information do we need to gather during the nurturing stage?"

There is a delicate balance. Too much information too closely related to the challenge can minimize divergence and movement, constraining our incubation stages. Too little can lead to shallow, useless or erroneous insights.

This fascinating tension between the nurturing and incubating stages of creativity, between the need to care for our seed and the need to give it space to breathe and expand, is one of the most interesting aspects of this journey.

Analogies can be drawn in many ways. Too much love or too little love in any relationship often signals troubles ahead. Too few ingredients in a pot can burn it. Too many ingredients can saturate the pot and prevent any blending and combining from happening.

"Delicate process indeed!"

Nurturing requires patience, confidence and courage. So once you decide on a direction, a dish to cook, a seed you want to cultivate, you begin to research and gather as much information as possible related to your challenge. You also gather other information apparently not related, for the sake of diverging. These ingredients join your subconscious pot where a continuous blending process is taking place.

And the process of gathering information has to begin with the people, the community connected to that challenge.

Who is it for?

As creative people and innovators, it is easy to forget that our challenges are almost always connected to a specific community of human beings. You are connected by an invisible link to the community that will be the recipient of your product, service, movie or e-book.

That community lives within a context, socioeconomic, technological, etc. That context constantly changes. A flow that influences and shapes the responses of that community to whatever you are working on.

That's why understanding your audience, becoming aware of their current trends, is so important. It is as if you were downloading the latest version of the operating system of your subconscious pot. It updates your mental context.

Would you plan a complex adventure road trip with an outdated map?

"No way, that's dangerous!"

Signs will have changed, deviations as well, unexpected obstacles may exist that we are not aware of.

Just as we can get lost by driving with an outdated map, we can also reach irrelevant solutions when working based on outdated contexts. Contexts that don't reflect the reality of the community your challenge is connected to.

"I shall update my context!"

Let's review some strategies you can implement to make sure that your context is updated.

- Visit and read the latest news at blogs that deal with your challenge. Also, for the sake of divergence, get updated on other areas unrelated to your challenge such as technology, economy, politics, etc. This will help you diverge in wide and updated ways.

- This is also the time to have a chat with any friends that may be experts in your area of interest. To encourage divergence and if time allows, speak to experts in other interesting but unrelated areas as well.

- Speak with people who apparently know nothing related to your challenge. Explain the challenge to them. See what they think about it. Sometimes these people come up with the most amazing ingredients!

"Interacting with others, connected and unconnected to our challenge, helps us diverge and find interesting ingredients."

Once you understand your community well, you continue nurturing your seed by gathering other relevant information about the challenge.

"And who is more active at this stage, AT or CT?"

Nurturing your seed requires both strategies to collaborate. It is mainly a conscious process but guided often by CT. CT helps bypass the analytical filters in order to access the complexity underlying your challenge.

"You mean that CT can allow us to go deeper and broader while gathering information?"

The ultimate purpose is to gather a good range of quality ingredients, the more diverse the better.

"Diverging before converging."

Some may be verbal, others visual, acoustic and of other kinds. It is key to enrich our subconscious pot with variety and good taste.

And as we said before, the ingredients we gather may be closely related to our seed or they may be apparently unconnected. We need both because it is so important to diverge before we converge.

"And how many quality ingredients do we need and for how long should this process go on?"

Tricky question. There are some key things to consider here. First, there are occasions in which, because of time constraints, the nurturing stage has to consist mainly of just our existing experience and immediate context.

"We just don't have time for much nurturing!"

For example, when a musician improvises at the piano, the pianist is feeding the subconscious pot mainly with previously stored experience and ingredients. We must not, however, disregard the influence of the present moment. The context and environment in which the pianist improvises has a great influence in the creative process. That fresh information is absorbed into the subconscious pot where it blends with the stored knowledge contributing to the triggering of novel ideas.

Improvising with a piano at home or at an auditorium, surrounded by friends or by strangers, in New York or in Tanzania. The context in which a creative act takes place provides in itself a massive amount of information that can change the outcome in dramatic ways. We could therefore say that in these cases the seed is being nurtured by the context and the environment as well as by previously gathered information.

Most often though, the process is longer, slower and more methodical. If we want to solve the challenge of providing clean energy to isolated homes in the countryside of Chile, we have to enter a lengthy nurturing process of research and gathering of information and ingredients related to that challenge.

How long that process should be is related to how much we already know in relation to the challenge as well as how much we want to diverge on top of that. However, we should overemphasize the danger we mentioned earlier.

"Oh, what was that?"

Knowing too little starves our subconscious pot and decreases our chances of success. But if you are looking for truly different and innovative solutions, knowing too much may be just as bad, it hurts our chances in a different way. Saturation may prevent flow and movement and drive you faster to closure, to predictable outcomes. If you saturate a pot with too many similar things, nothing moves, nothing blends.

"There is just too much stuff!"

This happens especially when most of the ingredients are too connected to the challenge. Fill a pot with many potatoes and nothing else. What do you get in the end?"

"Potatoes! More of the same."

So there is a delicate balance that you need to achieve during the nurturing process. Gathering enough quality and related ingredients to enrich your subconscious, and yet keep a fresh and open attitude in regards to information outside of the domain you are studying.

The nurturing process should be flexible, not rigid, dynamic, not fixed.

Nurturing from day one

Another perspective on this stage is to consider that the nurturing of any seed starts from the beginning of our lives. From our childhood years, we begin to gather ingredients and information, patterns that get engraved within our minds.

"The sum of who we are influences our present incubation processes."

All that you experience has an impact, it all ends up somewhere within your subconscious pot.

When we plant a new seed, at any stage of our lives, our subconscious pot already holds a set of base ingredients. Another set of ingredients is constantly arriving from your present context and through your senses.

Often, those two sets of ingredients are not enough to sustain growth. When a seed deals with a particularly complex challenge, we need even more specific and richer ingredients. It is then that a methodical process of gathering new data takes place.

If our seed is for example writing a great story about two bank robbers...

"We want to create a really great story with surprising elements, twists, suspense..."

We are going to have to go really deep into the subject to come up with a very different, original and unique idea.

Formulating our seed already gave a direction to our subconscious pot, where existing ingredients that resonate with our direction start to combine and recombine with each other. On top of that we need more. First, specific ingredients connected to the challenge. We need to understand more about how robbers behave, their psychology, the way banks work etc.

But that's not enough because you don't want to create just any story about robbers. You want to create a really original, unique and innovative story. That's why you need to combine the above with other information apparently unrelated to the challenge, information that helps you diverge, that takes you far and away from the starting point, expanding your horizons.

Remember the torch principle. Throw many torches far away and then incubate all that new light and connect it to your challenge. In the next chapter we will exercise our creative muscles to diverge our torches in many different ways.

More than words

Getting close and personal with your seed and diverging as much as possible at the start implies studying it from multiple perspectives. In order to do this, we have to transcend the straightjacket of language, which as an abstraction and simplification of reality has its limits.

"We go multidisciplinary!"

You want to explore your challenge verbally and visually, acoustically and through other sensorial means. This enriches your subconscious pot in amazing ways, increasing the chances of triggering unique insights later on.

And above all, stay fresh!

Fresh please

Would you cook your favorite dish with the very same ingredients you used last week?

As creative chefs that we are or aspire to be, we may use a few old ingredients, but certainly we don't want to rely only on them.

In the same way it is best if we don't tackle our challenges based on too many past assumptions or experiences. The world has moved and changed. So have you.

If you want to find innovative solutions, face your challenges as if it is the first time you are dealing with them. Support yourself on your past experiences but then diverge strongly to prevent early closure which may drive you towards typical and predictable solutions.

"I can see that past experience has advantages but also challenges."

Relying only on past experience and knowledge drives us fast towards tunnel vision and closure, one of the biggest foes of creativity.

Imagine yourself driving a car in search of a unique destination. Your copilot is giving you nonstop advice about where to turn and what to do. Such an excess of information narrows down the options ahead and can lead to premature conclusions. A journey that relies only on past information is in a way already moving towards a predefined range of possible answers.

Past knowledge is valuable and necessary. The magic happens when you combine new and current perspectives with old ones. By combining the fresh and the known, the uncertain and the tried and tested, your subconscious pot is empowered, increasing the chances of making novel connections and discoveries.

Driving your thoughts with an open mind and a broad attention keeps all options open, and can lead you to completely unexpected places.

The impact of tuning your perspective to the present moment cannot be underestimated. The right attitude can mean the difference between taking moments or years to find a great solution for your challenge.

So innovation is favored by a calm mind that holds enough knowledge, but not too much. One that is well informed but not constrained and overwhelmed by an excess of information related to the challenge.

"Too much can literally become too little!"

Exactly! We want to open new routes and avenues of thought, not to make the cliffs of our existing mental habits even steeper. That would interfere with the fluid movement we need in our subconscious pot.

Encouraging the blending and combining of our ingredients is as important or more as gathering the quality ingredients themselves.

"So the priority is a mix of deep understanding and divergence."

Yes, too much data could drag us down and prevent us from moving. In here lies the importance of the depth elevator metaphor that we will describe in more detail later. Getting deeper in our understanding is a natural organic process that is born from contemplating our challenge through multiple perspectives. This ensures both depth of understanding as well as the fluid movement that comes from the variety and diversity of sources that feed our subconscious pot.

"Balance is key again…"

Innovators need to achieve a calm proactiveness. They need to be ready to nurture and grow the seed without suffocating it. To provide stimulation without relentless noise and chatter. To gather enough quality ingredients for their subconscious pot without saturating it so much that movement stops. The seed must be cared for while welcoming the development of unexpected mutations and fresh angles.

It is a process that requires the systematic gathering of information, but must be complemented by the relaxed, open and fluid pondering of everything around the challenge and the gathered ingredients.

Managing this process carefully, keeping it alive for long enough, is key to eventually trigger novel and original insights.

Let's return to the importance of a multidisciplinary approach to enrich our subconscious.

Sail beyond word land

Einstein said: "Imagination is more important than knowledge."[21]

He understood the importance of diverging using our imagination and intuition, before converging through language.

Language is efficient, abstract, simple and easy to manipulate and apply to different scenarios. But it is also restrictive, inflexible, fixed and separated from the raw complexity of life.

Imagination can fill in the gaps in between words and help us plant those new torches, diverging and expanding our horizons.

So we want to take advantage of the knowledge that we already have, but also stimulate our imagination and intuition by combining our existing knowledge with other more unusual, surprising and sometimes random stimuli that can light up our mind in unexpected ways. That's why some of the greatest thinkers enjoyed using their mental imagery instead of words when manipulating insights in their minds.[22] The world of perception can help us get closer to the complexity of our challenges.

So enrich your subconscious not just with words, but through all your senses. Our exercises in the next chapter will help you to do this.

"And what are those steep cliffs that I see around me?"

The cliffs of closure, dangers along the way

Great question. As you explore your challenge looking for quality ingredients, you will have to deal with the delicate issue of premature closure. AT processes are constantly trying to make sense of things, to fit what we experience to patterns of thought previously experienced. You can imagine those as if they were steep cliffs, patterns of thought that have been traversed over and over and are now easier to activate as a result. Those deep channels can prevent you from diverging and may drive you quickly to typical and predictable solutions. Instead, make an effort to diverge and explore your subject with a combination of strategies including non-verbal ones.

"That will help us to avoid falling too early into the closure trap."

Some people wonder if it's that important to go beyond words. Words and language are great for brainstorming in groups, for evaluating and communicating insights and for many other uses. But they have limits. A word is an abstraction, a simplification. Words can push us towards closure faster than other more organic forms of representing information.

"This all reminds me of an equilibrist trying to stay on the tight rope!"

Don't look down!

Good analogy! What a delicate balance we are looking for. Like the equilibrist on a tight rope, we need to keep looking all around us, interacting with friends and audiences, absorbing the details of our surroundings, and yet ensuring we remain on the rope.

"Not falling too early on the cliffs of closure… scary!"

Fortunately the creative process is a bit less risky than walking on the tight rope. Still, you may not break a leg, but mental stress can be just as bad!

All in all, you want to keep the process alive for long enough to get to the other end of the creative rope where you can gather the cheers of your conscious mind.

"Who knows what great insights will be waiting for us at the other end…"

"And who are my friends, the allies that can help me in this nurturing process?"

Know your allies

To stay away from the cliffs of closure you need some good allies. Good allies are those that help you diverge and keep you away from predictable routes. They include randomness, fantasy, play and others. They are also the great allies of some of the greatest genius-es in history. Welcome these friends and they will make your road easier and more exciting. In the next chapter we will be working with a few of them.

"And is the process of gathering ingredients one that I should approach cautiously?"

To begin with, get wild!

In fact, it's more the opposite. Sometimes, to get up close and personal you need to go very far. Diverge before you converge, and go wild at the beginning. If you start cautiously, you will be walking too close to the cliffs of closure and it will be harder for you to approach innovative solutions. It is best to start as wild as possible to quickly move away from those dangerous cliffs. Later on you can move towards more practical and realistic possibilities. Beginning far away from the cliffs increases the chances of your final solutions being more innovative.

"Diverge before you converge!"

You can also change the level of abstraction as you explore, and the multidisciplinary approach previously described will help you with that. Using not just words, but also visuals, movement, sounds and other channels allows you to explore your challenge at different levels of abstraction.

"Riding the depth elevators."

The key is to combine strategies to prevent the mind from settling down too early.

Feel free to explore the most unusual and absurd possibilities you can imagine at the start. And for that I recommend a visit to our friend, randomness.

Randomness

In the exercise part of this book we will work with randomness to stimulate your imagination, helping you to connect your challenge with what apparently seems totally unrelated.

Randomness forces you to diverge in radical ways and it is the most powerful way to exercise your creative muscles.

Apparently unrelated ingredients take you quickly away from the cliffs of closure and closer to innovative solutions when you work at the right depth and through the right process.

"So dreaming comes first and practicality last?"

Yes, put on your dreamer and visionary hat to begin with and later transition to more realistic and practical perspectives.

"Dreamer first, realist next."

Don't stop there. After that will come the critic's moment. It will be the time to be actively critical on how the cooking process is going, relating it to your future audience, the markets and other elements.

"So Dreamers first. Critics last!"

Let's give you more tips to go wild at the start of this nurturing process.

The opposite is the wildest

Imagine you are given the challenge to cook something amazing with two apparently totally incompatible ingredients whose features oppose each other. Say banana and cucumber.

"Banana and cucumber!"

Yes, complicated. But connecting them you will have the chance to generate something really different and unique.

One of the easiest ways to go wild is by presenting your mind with opposites or with elements that seem incompatible with your challenge.

"Total divergence!"

Presenting apparently incompatible elements and opposites to your mind, stimulates your brain's connecting abilities. Remember, your brain is designed to connect and interpret information patterns. Give it time and it will find a connection between anything you present to it, even between the most unlikely companions.

"Is this a case of opposites attract?"

Consider complementary colors, which are positioned opposite in the color wheel. They reinforce each other when they are put side by side (think blue and yellow). Holding in your awareness opposite elements simultaneously, stretches your creative muscles, encouraging your mind to connect what at first appears impossible to link.

Say that you want to work on a business startup to reduce hunger in a community. Well, consider a business that aims to increase the hunger instead!

"That sounds insane!"

Yes indeed, but by reflecting on a business that aims to do the opposite you may grasp quicker key insights about what to do with your challenge.

"For example?"

A business that wants to increase hunger would likely try to increase food pricing and encourage the manufacturing of food with nutritional deficiencies.

"Aha, I see where you are going…"

This quickly inspires us to consider that in order to solve hunger we can research new ways to put together food packages/meals that include more valuable nutrients at the expense of other parameters.

"I feel my creative muscles stretching!"

Celebrate opposites, diverge and go wild!

"This is fun, give me more!"

Jump the fences

Another way to get away from the cliffs of closure is by jumping your fences and invading somebody else's space.

"Off we go!"

What happens when you change the background behind a model at a portrait session? The entire character of the production changes. That simple change can trigger a complete different stream of associations and insights.

"You are talking about changing the context around the challenge, right?"

Yes, shift the entire context of your challenge. Reflect on it in connection with totally different fields and disciplines. You will be getting further away from the cliffs of closure, diverging and getting closer to innovative insights.

"I like it!"

Jump those fences! Taste the grass on the other side!

"I'm beginning to really care for this subconscious playful friend. It feels like giving toys to a child!"

Pamper your child

As you nurture your seed, think of your subconscious as if it was your child. We are gathering toys for our child to play with.

"Our subconscious is like a playful child really."

This playful child loves to play with beautiful ingredients, blocks of so many shapes and colors.

"The more diverse, the better!"

It loves to try to connect all those pieces into new shapes and possibilities. The more diverse and original pieces we give to our subconscious child, the more chances our child has of coming up with innovative results.

"Is this a high maintenance child?"

Not at all. Once we gather the toys, we can relax and let the child play. We will keep an eye on the child, but it is not our job to connect the pieces. Our job was to go out there and gather the best materials. As colorful, original, different and fresh as possible. It is then our subconscious child who will be in charge as we enter the incubation stage of creativity.

"And when do we know it's time to leave our subconscious child alone to play with the ingredients?"

Eventually we will feel that we have given our subconscious child enough materials and toys to play with. We all know what happens when we pamper a child too much…

"Chaos and confusion!"

Yes. At that point, we have to let the child discover new things on his/her own.

"Got it. Give me more strategies to enrich this nurturing process please."

A metaphorical pond

We have mentioned some friends that can help us in diverging and staying away from the cliffs of closure. The torch principle is an example of another of those friends, the metaphor.

At its most basic, a metaphor means describing your challenge in a way that connects with a different and unrelated subject. You find something in common between both unrelated elements and then describe one of them in terms of the other.

In the torch principle, we describe the process of looking for an innovative insight in terms of the process of exploring a dark space using torches. The vast space represents our mental space. The torch is our knowledge of the challenge and so on and so forth.

A metaphor activates an area unrelated and unconnected with the original topic and establishes a connection between our original topic and that new area.

It helps us to move away from the cliffs of closure and diverge towards new routes. It widens our thinking, stimulates our imagination and enriches our subconscious pot with unusual ingredients, increasing our potential for incubating great insights.

"And how do we find metaphors?"

Life is an infinite source of them. Look around at objects, people, events, etc. Pick unrelated elements and attempt to explain your challenge in relation to them.

"Give me an example please."

Imagine that your seed is about improving transport in cities that are suffering from heavy traffic congestion.

"That's a great challenge."

You may throw a new torch from the transport area to the health area and say that attempting to improve congestion on the streets is like trying to ease congestion on the nose of a person that has a cold.

"Brilliant!"

The immune system must firstly identify the viruses. Then it uses fever, sneezing and other strategies to expel the germs from the body. What if there was a way to label and make visible those cars that are the main culprits of the traffic congestion? Special police could then fine them and take them away.

"Wow, I see the power of the metaphor!"

Start bringing more light into your challenge by switching on metaphorical torches all around your mind.

"The mind is truly a great connector and also a fast traveler…"

Travel in business class, for free!

Another way to bring more light onto your challenge is by taking imaginary mental trips to contexts related or unrelated to the challenge. You will then be alert to any connections and insights that may arise from the experience.

These imaginary trips can be a huge source of inspiration and were often used by geniuses such as Einstein.[23] In fact, you could imagine that your journey happens alongside some of your favorite historical personalities.

"I'm a fan of Leonardo Da Vinci."

Good! Find a quiet, tranquil setting where you feel relaxed. For many, right before sleeping, can be the best time to start this process.

Now imagine visiting Da Vinci at his home in Florence, Italy, and spending a great afternoon walking and chatting with him. Tell him about your challenge. Be as detailed as you can in visualizing the details of your walk. Visualize the textures in the houses, the noises in the streets, the scents, the contact of your feet with the ground, the voice of Leonardo. Let yourself be guided by his wisdom, you will be surprised at the potential of this exercise.

"I can't wait to try this!"

This exercise helps you diverge by transporting you to a completely different context, a faraway area of the vast ocean of mental darkness where innovative insights are waiting to be found.

"Diverging is all about getting out of our comfort zone, right?"

Get out of your comfort zone!

Yes, and actively pushing our imagination is a great way to do that. As we know, habitual patterns of thought are recalled faster and easier than unusual ones.

We tend to walk the streets we know, sing the songs we have heard before, repeat the words we have recently used. AT loves comfort, it's quick and efficient.

"But it gets in the way of innovation of course."

Yes. In order to innovate you need to push yourself away from that comfort. Think of filmmakers. When they use their cameras, they often avoid the typical angles. They know that we all view the world through our eyes from a certain height, with a certain depth and perspective. So they constantly try to innovate and diverge by looking for different angles to surprise and engage the audience.

"Looking for new angles..."

Yes, shake your angles. As you ponder your challenge, imagine being a woman instead of a man, or vice versa. What is your new perspective?

"Cool, how do I see my challenge if my gender was the opposite!"

Imagine being one of the objects involved in the challenge. Imagine being the challenge itself or part of it. Act your challenge. We will be working with this in the practical section of the book.

Involve as many ways of expressing your challenge as you can. Language, visuals, sounds, etc. Use them to express your challenge at different levels of abstraction, from more organic and detailed levels to more symbolic and abstract ones, and all the way in between. We will also work with this later.

"I'm feeling playful!"

Be playful. Rephrase your seed in ways that challenge your mind. Even tiny changes in the way you express a challenge can lead to unexpected associations. Try to describe your project in as few words as possible. Try to express it from the point of view of a fan, and then of a critic. See what happens.

Bottom line is the more angles and perspectives you gain on a subject, the more you diverge and the deeper your understanding of it becomes.

Einstein and Da Vinci were constantly searching for new perspectives. Einstein used to imagine himself being part of the challenge. Da Vinci would study his subjects and challenges under extreme conditions.[24]

"Extreme conditions... contrast and opposites..."

Studying extreme perspectives helps us to diverge in wild ways. It deepens our understanding. When Da Vinci was studying human anatomy he would look for the ugliest and prettiest people in town and would study these subjects. Through these extreme examples he would gather key insights into human nature.

"So many possibilities to gather useful ingredients! I sense the importance of keeping a record during this process."

A note at a time

New subconscious ingredients can evaporate quickly from the pot before they've had a chance to combine with other ingredients.

To prevent that, it is important to take notes of all the ingredients and insights you generate during the nurturing process. And the more creative languages you use to record them, the stronger the presence of those ingredients will be in your subconscious. You may write them with words, draw them or even sing them. Whatever time allows.

Annotating ingredients and insights in multiple forms engraves them deeper in your mind, triggering associations that facilitate and accelerate incubation processes.

So be alert to anything interesting that pops up on your mind. Don't question, don't judge, note them down quickly before they fade away. These are all precious and valuable new ingredients that you need to preserve.

It's your turn to be playful

You were once a child, capable of engaging in incredible ways with the world. Children make use of all their senses as they explore.

Growing up, as our mind develops powerful ways of abstracting and simplifying the complexity of life, our engagement with the raw complexity of life decreases. We create abstractions, and that builds up distance between us and that raw complexity.

Regain your engagement capabilities. Involve your sight, touch, smell, taste and hearing senses. Relate their inputs to your challenge.

Be inspired by children. Observe how they act. Children speak and communicate without inhibitions or filters. This comes across easily in their drawings. Spontaneity is their natural gift.

Access your inner child and regain an intense engagement with the world.

"Combining the best of adulthood with the freshness of childhood."

We will be exercising this actively in the practical module.

"Children love to ask questions."

Questions come first

Asking good questions is another way to stay away from the cliffs of closure. Rushing for answers drives you towards them.

Questions are like teleports on the vast ocean of your mind. A great question can take you places, opening new routes in your mind that lead you away from typical avenues.

It is a paradox that when the answer lies far away, the fastest way to get there may be to change the question. As we enrich and expand our questions, we are like sailors in that vast foggy ocean, throwing torches into the sky to try to illuminate new areas that may contain potential answers and solutions.

Yes, questions come first. Think of your creative challenge as a car competing in a race for the best insight.

What's the best strategy to win? Trying to correct potential problems when you are already on the road? Or setting up your machine, your challenge, by asking the right questions from the very beginning at the mental garage?

If you have any doubt, ask a Formula 1 Driver.

"And what if I feel like I'm getting stuck or moving too close/too early towards closure?"

If your dish gets boring, add a pinch of random!

If your nurturing process starts to feel predictable, if you feel you are getting too close too soon to the cliffs of closure, and your mental torches are illuminating terrain that is too familiar, you may need to spice up your dish.

Many dishes can benefit from a bit of salt, and every challenge can benefit from a bit of randomness.

"Randomness is our magic salt."

You wouldn't abuse salt and neither should you randomness. The right amount can take you far.

"Randomness encourages divergence and the opening of new mental routes."

Those new avenues are hard to open by conventional means because our thinking tends to follow paths of least resistance.

In the practical section of the book, we will give a boost to our nurturing phases with random ingredients produced with a variety of tools.

"How soon should I evaluate the usefulness of these random ingredients?"

We will go into the details about this in the next chapter. Face every random ingredient with an open mind. Early judgment extinguishes your mental torches.

Absorb the new information and wait for your creative muscles to react and blend the new data into your subconscious pot.

"How do I know which random ingredients are the most useful ones?"

Take notes of those random ingredients that fulfill either one of these two conditions.

1. They pique your curiosity even if they don't suggest an immediate connection with your challenge.

2. They immediately suggest an interesting connection with your challenge.

Let the rest fade into the background of your awareness.

"This is cool. And remind me, why are these random ingredients so important?"

To understand the importance of randomness think of mutations in biology. If DNA cloned itself perfectly every time, evolution would not happen. We would not exist. Identical copies would simply perpetuate themselves ad infinitum.

Random mutations are "mistakes" and you could call them the most beautiful mistakes in the universe.

"They are necessary to introduce variation."

That variation can sometimes introduce benefits for the organism or quality ingredients into our subconscious pot. Other times, mutations and randomness take us nowhere in biology and in our creative processes.

"But the effort is worth it because the potential rewards are huge."

On top of that, our minds can work in more flexible ways than natural selection does. Whereas natural selection is a slow and rather inflexible process, our mind can quickly learn from useful variations but also from those that apparently lead us nowhere.

"I can see that what randomness brings is hard to obtain in a short time by other means."

Randomness multiplies our reach exponentially. Bringing light quickly to far away areas with our torches would be much harder or even impossible without using it.

"But to get to some useful random ingredients I guess you have to keep trying for some time?"

This is another reason why productivity is so important.

"Some of the greatest geniuses in history were enormously productive."

Randomness, trial and error, mutations. All of them are essential to transcend the habits of our mind. To throw our torches into useful areas within that vast ocean of possibilities we often require multiple attempts until we reach the right place at the right time.

"So nurturing should be productive."

Creativity is productivity

The most successful innovators, inventors and creative people are typically extremely productive. They produce multiple versions of each idea, explore hundreds of perspectives and experiment with all sorts of angles. For them a new attempt is not about succeeding or failing. It is just another stepping stone in an evolutionary process of refining solutions for their challenges.

"What's more important then, expertise or productivity?"

Both. Many people think that expertise is the main key. But if you are looking for really innovative solutions, productivity and boldness are just as important, if not more.

"1% inspiration, 99% perspiration."[25]

Natural and trained abilities as well as our genes matter, but they are just the first page of a long story. The other 99% is full of productivity, research and experimentation. All of those generate quality ingredients for your subconscious.

"Productivity must require a lot of persistence."

If you give up too soon on your quest, you are missing the moments when the best insights are found.

"Patience is needed."

When facing a new challenge, you are entering uncharted territory, looking for the right ingredients that fit in unique ways with the puzzle of your current mental context. It is natural that many cycles and attempts may have to happen until we gather the right ingredients.

"Anything could be potentially useful."

Stay open. It is often those attempts which many would label as "unsuccessful", the ones which combine in unexpected ways with the soil of your mind. They provide fertile ground where key insights can arise.

So get productive, welcome "failures" and keep plowing the soil of your mind.

"And how can I increase my productivity?"

Involve all senses

Productivity is easier when you involve all of your senses. Sight, smell, taste, touch and hearing. Don't hold back, your subconscious child needs feeding!

Another way to get more quality ingredients faster into your subconscious pot is to interact with other people. Ten subconscious pots are more powerful than one.

"Bounce your mental recipes off others."

In general, to be more productive during the nurturing phase, you should study your challenge from different angles and abstraction levels.

The Depth Elevator

The depth elevator is a metaphor. It represents the importance of studying our challenges from many angles and abstraction levels. **[Web] torchprinciple.com/depthelevator**

"We can look at something from shallow, abstract angles, or go more specific, closer to its raw details and complexity."

The lower we go on the depth elevator, the closer we get to the roots that link our subject with other fields. Connecting our subject with other areas at the bottom of the depth elevators is very powerful.

"We can then understand what our subject shares in common with other fields."

A journey on the depth elevator is a journey towards the essence and roots of our subject.

"And how do we descend on this depth elevator?"

The more perspectives you study about your subject, the lower you descend on the depth elevator towards the roots and the complexity down below.

"And once you get there?"

At the bottom of the depth elevator you can connect with other scenarios and challenges through the common roots that they share. This helps you diverge and enrich your subconscious pot even more.

Instead, when you approach a challenge from a single perspective, you remain on the shallow surface, away from the deep roots that sustain that challenge, unable to link with other scenarios that share common roots with your subject.

In summary, going down on the elevator we gain deep understanding and enrich our subconscious by diverging through other areas that share common roots with our challenge.

"Many challenges that seem different on the surface, touch common ground at their depths."

It's like thinking of rhythm in music, rhythm in dance and rhythm in the brush strokes of a painter.

"It's all still rhythm!"

Likewise with contrast, which can serve to reinforce and highlight information, be it in visual arts or in marketing, business development or clothing design. Think of the law of simultaneous contrast. Opposites reinforce each other. These can be opposite colors in the color wheel but we can also refer to rhythm and stillness, light and shadow, harmony and dissonance, curves and lines, a character in a film and its opposite, or how something is presented at different timeframes.

Reaching and understanding these roots through our depth elevators and riding them back up to the surface to connect with completely different topics that share similar roots, can provide a tremendous level of creative stimulation for our subconscious pot.

"What a journey!"

Indeed. The depth elevator takes you from the surface of your challenge to the fine details, as you descend towards deeper understanding.

"I start to see more…"

While you ride down on the depth elevator, details that were invisible on the surface start to come into focus. The texture and richness of every tiny part of your challenge becomes clearer and sharper.

"Can you give me an example?"

If your challenge is finding new ways to process and understand the emotional reactions of your customers, you can take the depth elevator to the roots of human emotion.

"We research and understand that principle, human emotion."

We do that by absorbing multiple perspectives on that principle. Once you have settled at that root, which means once you have understood deeply human emotions, you can then get on board other elevators.

Those other elevators take you back up to the surface of different areas which are also strongly connected to that root, human emotion.

"Those will be areas in which human emotion also plays a key role, right?"

Yes. Examples would be acting, romantic relationships and infinite others.

"So this process is helping me to understand in more depth my challenge and to diverge again, further enriching my subconscious."

Yes, being back on the surface of a diverse collection of areas connected to those common roots, together with the deep understanding you have gained, can help you generate powerful ingredients and insights.

"Fantastic. Another example please."

If your challenge is a musical one related to rhythm, you will take the depth elevator to understand the essence and roots of rhythm.

This can connect you later with other elevators that link you with, for example, painting or dance. Your understanding of the roots of rhythm, together with these other contexts, feeds back into your challenge, providing new perspectives that enrich your subconscious pot.

"So dance and painting give me completely different perspectives on the meaning of rhythm, and that generates great ingredients for my subconscious."

And this works both ways. Understanding rhythm in a musical context helps you understand it in a writing context or in a public speaking context.

"This is powerful, let's summarize!"

In summary, study your challenge from multiple angles and perspectives in order to ride down your depth elevators. And then connect your deep understanding with different domains and disciplines to diverge and stimulate the birth of new insights and valuable ingredients.

What we said about challenges, we can apply equally to skills. But before we arrive at the skills, you should realize that the key to mastering creativity lies in understanding the deep principles below those skills, for example how simultaneous contrast works and how it can serve us to engage audiences. Once we understand that, it is then easier to apply that principle through any channel and skill we choose.

These principles apply to most areas of life. Those who go through extreme experiences, which are full of contrast, may come out stronger and deeper if they survive them. Those who taste just one side of life are sometimes shallower and weaker. Simultaneous contrast is universal.

"So talking about creativity is talking about the deep universal roots of human existence."

Indeed. This goes way beyond learning to play an instrument or to draw. The merit is not so much in executing many skills, but in understanding a variety of deep principles that support them.

You can then see poetry in a dance and dance in poetry, melody in how words follow each other and rhythm in the way voice patterns fluctuate. You see lights and shadows in people's emotions and find emotions in the way highlights and shadows chase each other.

Understanding comes first and is followed by a variety of techniques and skills that express that understanding. By exercising numerous creative languages we can arrive at a deeper understanding of these core, key, root principles that power it all.

"I want to ride down these depth elevators as fast as possible. How can I do that?"

Be like water, be like wood

If I want to understand wood, I need to metaphorically become the wood. Get so close to its complexity that I literally feel I can understand its own perspective, as if I was the wood itself.

That is the bottom of the depth elevator. When you reach the deep roots in your understanding of that challenge.

"Do I need any special gift or talent to be able to go so deep?"

Everybody can innovate by combining a series of strategies with deep understanding. Reaching that understanding requires hard work.

Some people can do this faster than others. Same with the way we synthesize information and grasp it at various abstraction levels.

In any case, our capacity to understand and go deep can be trained in all of us. Genetic predisposition goes nowhere without productivity and hard work, the telltale of the great innovators.

"So if my challenge is about wood, I have to understand wood itself."

Yes, say that you want to draw or paint a surface made of wood, or maybe represent wood with a sculpture, or photograph it, film it or write about it. Most people will focus on the technique you need to produce the drawing, photography, etc. But that is the very end of the creative process. The implementation. The tip of the iceberg.

"That is all secondary to the deep understanding of our subject, the wood."

Exactly, starting at the end of the process, the implementation, keeps you on the surface, where you can stay for years, away from truly innovative solutions.

"Because we haven't really explored our subject in depth."

Innovation starts with deep understanding.

"At the base, riding the depth elevators. In this case, the wood elevator."

[Web] torchprinciple.com/woodelevator

We need to go beyond the simplified symbol - wood - that our mind has generated to make things easy. We need to understand wood in terms of its unique features. The way light interacts with it, its hue and chroma, how it changes over time, how it feels when we touch it, how it sounds.

"Looking, listening, touching…"

Becoming it. Becoming Wood.

Wood is your seed. Nurture that seed, become that seed, understand it.

"And once I do that…"

Then you can express it through any creative language and channel you choose to transmit your interpretation of that challenge to an audience. Build a business around it. Draw it, paint it, photograph it, write about it, compose music based on it, etc.

This deep understanding applies not only to a material or a business challenge, but also to people, to our loved ones, to our interpersonal relationships.

"Understanding comes first, implementation later."

Yes, execution is critical to keep our creative muscles fit through the practice of a number of techniques. But focusing only or mainly on the techniques, we are missing the most important part of the creative process. The depth elevators, the deep understanding.

"And what are the obstacles between us and these depth elevators?"

Fighting the inertia

Getting on the depth elevators is not that easy. The logical and analytical armies of the mind are constantly pushing you away from the complexity down below. They prefer you to stay in the world of symbols, abstractions and simplifications.

"The closure foe again!"

Yes, you try to get on the elevator, but the mind wants closure and wants it fast, which takes you back up to the surface.

"How can we get past these forces?"

Only by distracting or taming our analytical forces can we hop onto the depth elevator and descend to the depths of complexity and detail, where we can access a whole different level of richness and understanding.

"Show me how!"

A transformer and connector

You own a brain. A phenomenal transformer and connector on top of your shoulders. A phenomenal tool that loves to interpret, connect and make sense of anything and everything you put in front of it.

In the practical section of the book we will explore specific exercises to diverge in powerful ways. Now we will quickly introduce some principles behind them. Absorb the concepts. You don't need to put them in practice until the next chapter.

Random hooks on a random planet

Diverge. Create unusual connections. Encourage your mind to open new routes. Perform unusual activities, note down whatever piques your curiosity in magazines, websites and people. Force connections between those and your challenges.

To ride down the depth elevators, go random in a multidisciplinary way. Involve high abstraction by using words and then involve lower abstraction levels by using visuals and other means.

Generate random concepts, phrases and words with either a dictionary or the online tools SK-Engine and SK-General that we will introduce later.[26]

Note down those that either excite your curiosity or immediately suggest a connection with your challenge. Don't judge them yet. Contemplate them with an open mind.

List the features of those you selected.

Then draw them, involve visual perception. Use lightstorming and soundstorming tools to further create unexpected connections.[27] We will go in detail about all of these in the practical chapter.

Object galore

Pick interesting objects around you, connect them with your challenge, especially if they seem unrelated and even contradictory. They will generate creative tension that can stimulate the generation of new connections and insights.

Engage the right gear with a story

Storytelling is one of the pillars of creativity. An actor would never dare to act a character whose background he doesn't understand in depth. Contexts and stories are key to developing complex understanding, to going deeper in our depth elevators.

Narrate your challenge from the point of view of different characters. Imagine a community living with your challenge. Build stories and let them blend with your existing subconscious ingredients.

A world of seeds

Cultivate an open and welcoming awareness. From time to time, pay attention to what surrounds you, the conversations, the subtle details, those puzzling sounds. Make a habit out of connecting your challenge with all that complexity.

The secret is in the details

The more specific you are, the richer you make your subconscious pot. When you visualize, get to the details. Imagine textures, sounds, smells and voices. Relive your challenge, become a virtual explorer within your own mind.

Practice makes perfect

The more you innovate, the easier it gets. Triggering new connections between unrelated stimuli stretches your creative muscles. Make a habit out of connecting the unexpected.

In the practical section of the book I will provide you with step-by-step ways to implement all of the above and more. Let's move on!

The nurturing process can be happening on and off as we go through our daily lives. At some point, when circumstances are right, when we have gathered enough quality ingredients, the incubation of those ingredients may produce the magical insight we are looking for.

Incubation
Where the magic happens

So you have fantastic quality ingredients in your subconscious pot. Awesome. But if those ingredients stay there doing nothing, if no blending and combining takes place, nothing original is going to come out of that. The final dish won't be much different. It won't be that tasty.

Incubation is the stage in which those ingredients combine, recombine, blend and mix in your subconscious. For many people, incubation is hard to understand because there is not much that you have to do consciously. You should keep your challenge at the back of your mind, but then dedicate your time to other purposes. You need to give time and space to your subconscious to play with its toys.

Einstein liked to spend lots of time just staring into space.[28] This gave his subconscious mind the valuable time and space it needed.

Incubation requires patience and a wide and sensitive awareness as opposed to the anxious behaviors that produce tunnel vision and drive us to premature closure. We have to see our conscious mind as the lucky observant, the recipient of the magic that is being cooked at our subconscious pot.

Encouraging successful incubations

To encourage successful incubations, there are two key points to consider. One is giving our subconscious enough time for the ingredients to combine and blend. The other is having enough mental space and sensitivity to notice the faint calls our subconscious emits when new insights are produced.

Passing the baton

When does incubation begin?

The nurturing stage eventually reaches a level of complexity that becomes too much for our slow and limited conscious analytical processes.

It is the moment to pass the baton to our subconscious processes.

"Let CT take on the lead!"

Yes, combining and blending the accumulated data requires a different set of skills.

"Like?"

Like simultaneous, fast and nonlinear processes that can work through all that complexity.

So when we feel we have accumulated enough pieces of information in our subconscious, the time arrives to do something rather challenging: Nothing.

"Nothing?"

The Interference problem

Nothing, because conscious analytical thinking can easily disrupt the movements of our subconscious pot. Or it can drive it towards premature closure.

"So we have to kind of consciously restrain ourselves?"

Simply give time and space to your subconscious to do its job.

Keep in mind that this nothing is not a typical nothing. It is in fact a rather active kind of nothing.

"Tell me more."

The guide

Our analytical processes work in a very sequential way. You can't expect to get too far too soon. It is as if you were walking step by step through a road somewhere in Australia. You can't expect to appear in Spain the next minute.

The paradox here is that the best way to encourage success is not to force the process in any way. Our mind is a natural and extremely powerful connector. If we have gathered enough ingredients at the right depth and we create the right incubation context, our mind has the capability to connect anything we throw at it. Once we have gathered enough ingredients, the best we can do is to turn on the heat and leave the kitchen, allowing the ingredients to mix, blend and combine on their own.

In order for the process to stay focused though, it is important that from time to time we re-enter the kitchen, take our conscious spoon and help the ingredients with gentle moves, reminding them of what the goal is.

"What the challenge is, the one they should gravitate towards."

It is therefore crucial to keep in the back of our minds the direction of our challenge, as this will increase the chances of triggering related insights.

"As well as shuffle some of our ingredients from time to time, gently move them around."

Gently, in a relaxed way. It is not wise to run around your kitchen neither review your challenge anxiously. This increases mental noise and chatter that interferes with the real voice we are seeking, the one of our subconscious pot. It is there where all the pieces are blending, mixing and reacting with each other, creating insight bubbles that eventually move up and try to reach our conscious awareness.

"So anxiety and stress prevent good incubation processes."

Anxiety and stress are great analytical activators that easily interfere with our fragile subconscious voices.

"We need mental space."

Yes, our mind needs space, not at all times, but often enough. Space for what may be waiting behind the curtains, waiting to illuminate us with our subconscious wisdom.

Eventually, if we have accumulated enough quality ingredients, the natural connecting abilities of our mind will generate new insights. These insights may then knock on the doors of our conscious awareness.

"The subconscious child comes to tell us something exciting."

Yes, and when the subconscious child comes with its tiny delicate voice to tell you about an exciting discovery, will you be there? Will your mind have space to listen to your child? Or will your consciousness be so full of noise, dealing with your concerns, preoccupations and past and future issues that you won't even hear your child approaching?

"I can feel that to be sensitive to this child, the context around me is key."

The importance of context

Yes, when is it easier to listen to our inner child, when we are relaxing in the lap of nature or when we are driving through massive traffic and chaos in the city, swimming in stress and anxiety?

The context in which we incubate insights is crucial. A stressful context easily activates our analytical problem-solving network. A tranquil context broadens our attention and increases our sensitivity.

Create the right context for your incubation processes. Keep the communication with your inner child fresh and active.

"These insights we produce really feel like special miracles."

Delicate miracles

New insights are like delicate bubbles rising from our subconscious pot. They are there now. Gone in a second. Delicate, unique, different and fragile. Subtle opportunities soon to be wiped out by the habitual weather patterns of your mind.

Way before we become aware consciously of any of those bubbles, our subconscious pot is continuously blending and integrating stored and fresh ingredients. Some of the generated insight bubbles reach our consciousness. Others never do.

"Insight bubbles of so many different types."

Some of them take years to reach the surface of our minds. Those can be bubbles that integrate multiple inputs over months or years or they can be bubbles we are resistant to face. They may contain traumas or painful emotions we prefer to avoid.

If your mind is dominated by conscious noise, racing from thought to thought, it will be very hard for you to notice those subtle bubbles. You will never know they were there. For you to notice them, you need to cultivate space in your mind. This is the reason why some of the best insights come to us when we are doing simple tasks such as taking a shower, waiting for a bus, driving or taking a tranquil walk. During those activities our mind relaxes, expands, shifts from a tight tunnel like focus to a wandering, broad, open one.

Calming our consciousness increases our sensitivity. As we relax into the drive, the shower, the bus stop or the walk, and abandon ourselves to the moment, our mind's antenna widens its reach. Instead of obsessively focusing itself on a very specific preoccupation, it becomes sensitive to our wide and expansive inner processes and their subtle voices.

While incubation takes place, you still hold your challenge on the back of your mind, but without actively pushing for a resolution.

Eventually one of those delicate insight bubbles may reach your conscious awareness. You may then feel that beautiful harmony that we call an illumination, the birth of a new insight.

"And how long will this process of incubating new insights last?"

From a millisecond to a lifetime

Incubating an insight can take milliseconds or years. Sometimes, as during the improvisation of a new music piece by a pianist, incubation processes can be happening on and off extremely fast, giving birth to new ideas almost in real time.

The nurturing process of the pianist has been going on for a long time, gathering knowledge throughout a career. In such a case, if the mind is sensitive and open enough, the incubation of the present context blended with the accumulated information can drive the mind to creative insights almost instantaneously.

Other times, like during the creation of a play, movie screenplay or novel, the incubation process may take years until the key insights appear that take the project to its resolution.

The speed of the process depends on a number of factors. We have already spoken about some of them: the quality of our ingredients and our state of awareness or sensitivity.

"I feel like I really have to take care of my subconscious, giving it space and a mixture of stimulation and tranquility."

Everybody needs love

Treat your subconscious as you would treat your best friend. Keep in touch with it regularly by keeping your challenge in the back of your mind. That helps to keep a direction, a guideline for your subconscious to follow as it works with the ingredients you have provided.

As you engage on other activities and proceed with your life, your good friend is working hard and a magical illumination could well be around the corner.

"Does any special activity help you incubate ideas better?"

Walking towards the insight

Everybody finds different activities favorable for the incubation of insights.

These tend to be activities that help your mind relax, broaden your attention and open your awareness without interfering with that delicate communication between the conscious and the subconscious.

For some it is taking a bath, relaxing in bed, waiting for a bus, painting, practicing sport, meditating, fishing, listening to music or staring at a sunset.

Engaged into any of these activities and others, the mind relaxes as the subconscious pot bubbles furiously encouraging unexpected connections to form.

One of my favorites is walking. I like to repeat the same path over and over in a sort of meditative exercise. But I also enjoy a lot hiking in nature through random and unpredictable routes.

"What about running?"

I love running, but personally it doesn't work so well for me in connection with the incubation of insights. While running, probably because of the extra effort I have to make, my mind cannot relax enough to provide fertile ground for incubation processes. Also, running fast requires me to pay more attention to the street, the people and potential obstacles, and this tightens my focus and awareness. This of course is different for each person. Many will be as relaxed running as I am walking. Find your own best environment and activity.

"Everybody is different."

Let's describe an example of one of my incubation processes. Whenever I need to find a new insight, I first make sure I have gathered a good collection of quality ingredients in my mind connected to my challenge.

"Then you are ready for incubation."

Yes, and in my case I may go out for a walk. I abandon myself to the walk. I tune into the world around me, keeping in the back of my mind the challenge. From time to time I may mentally shuffle some of my ingredients. I literally make them pass through my conscious awareness while I contemplate them in a very loose, fuzzy, unfocused way.

"That's kind of like taking the wooden spoon and moving things around in the pot."

And most of the time, after a matter of hours, minutes or sometimes seconds, new insights arrive. They pop out like delicate bubbles that come out of nowhere. When I am relaxed, they are easier to notice, because they contrast vividly against the fuzzy, blurry and relaxing mental background in which we find ourselves in our drive, walk, shower or similar activity.

"Awesome! I'm ready for a great illumination!"

Illumination
Something smells wonderful

We caught one of those delicate and unique insight bubbles. An insight born from the blending of the toys we gathered in the subconscious room during the nurturing process.

The sum of incubating our subconscious and becoming aware of these insights is what we often call inspiration or being inspired.

Becoming aware of new insights requires a relaxed mind and a broad awareness. The mind should be sensitive enough to hear the delicate voice of our inner child coming to share its great discoveries.

"And how does it feel…?"

How do parents feel watching their child running towards them in excitement, eager to share something new, different and unique?

Einstein and others have described that moment as one of joy, of clarity, of things coming together, of beauty and harmony.[29] A moment, in summary, that just feels right.

"Like when you know it's time to get that dish out of the oven!"

Yes, think of the cook that, while resting nearby, suddenly smells something special. The ingredients have combined and blended in a unique way and we recognize that scent as a beautiful harmony, the birth of something wonderful.

"Harmony."

Yes, harmony in the proportions and relationships between the ingredients that make the final dish, and between those ingredients and the challenge. There is also a general sense of unity.

"Everything feels right."

The solution fully fits what we were looking for.

Illumination is a good word to describe this moment and it's been used by many others to describe the birth of new insights, because it literally feels as if in the darkness of our mental struggle, something lights up. For a brief moment, this fleeting miracle lights up the stage and we are right there with it, eager to grab it, to hold onto it before it blends back into the shadows.

"Because if we don't grab it, it will go away!"

These brief spells of harmony and beauty are as delicate as a fragile flower in the middle of a winter storm. They are subtle fresh marks surrounded by deep trenches. Their chance of survival depends on us spotting them and managing to reinforce their presence.

That's why some of the greatest innovators in history used to carry with them at all times notebooks or some other way of quickly recording insights.

"Be ready to grab those bubbles during the most unusual and even uncomfortable moments!"

Nowadays we can use portable recorders, mobile phones, and even friends and people around us. The sky is the limit!

"And what should you do if a sudden insight strikes and you have nothing to record it on, not even other people around you?"

Short-term human memory is neither reliable nor long lasting. Your best chance of preserving the insight is repeating it to yourself regularly until you get to a place where you can save it in a permanent form.

"And these insights, do they have any special format?"

An insight can be anything that triggers those feelings of clarity and harmony we have described. It could be a word, a dream, an image, a musical theme, a formula, a verbal element or any other variation you could imagine.

Once you have secured your insight, it is the time to explore it and verify its validity and potential.

Implementation
A delicious dish

The dish is ready, and it's quite a treat!

In the hands of your mind you are holding a fragile insight bubble. The moment has arrived to verify that its potential is truly there. It is the moment to write the poem, compose the soundtrack, test the formula, write the book, implement the product or do that new activity with your partner. This is a process that can take from seconds to decades.

This stage is made of a range of tasks including verifying the validity of the insight and proceeding to develop and refine it fully. The ultimate goal, as the name says, is implementation, transforming the delicate insight into an actual product, service, action or whatever our objective was from the start.

"I feel that AT will enjoy this…"

Incubation and illumination are stages very much driven by our subconscious processes. In them, our conscious mind acts as guide and observer. The implementation stage, on the other hand, gives the controls back to AT.

"Analysis and language are back in charge!"

This is also the moment to welcome other people back into the process and get their feedback and perspective as you proceed to implement the solution to your challenge.

"I'm sure CT will still be around, correct?"

Oh yes, no stage is black or white. There is always a blend. In fact it is crucial to keep our creative thinking very much active at this stage. CT will be acting as a wise guide and supervisor, making sure the harmony of the insight is not lost through the implementation stage.

Because as we implement the insight, it is easy to lose that delicate harmony, those balanced proportions, the wholeness and unity we felt in the solution. So our creative muscles have to keep active as quality controllers. We have to make sure that the final result continues to feel right and harmonious.

"Fantastic! So we made it. Time to celebrate, right?"

Not quite! Because…

The ending is a beginning

The implementation stage may feel like the end of a process, but there is never really such an end.

We implement a solution that fits our current circumstances and context. As the context changes, and it always does, so do we and our needs and the challenge itself and the community the challenge is related to, and therefore, also the nature of the solution we need.

"A fixed and static implementation risks becoming irrelevant very fast!"

Today, more than ever, we need to use dynamic processes to keep our implementations evolving. This way they can adapt to the changing markets, events and audiences.

Let's make an analogy with the visual media market.

In the past, paintings, photos and movies were static. Once completed, they never changed even if the context around their message kept evolving.

Nowadays there is a growing acceptance of art as a dynamic experience that can constantly mutate and evolve together with our thoughts, opinions and interpretations.

"I get it! A photo, a painting, or a film, can be revisited and reimplemented."

Yes, furthermore, modern art is all about interaction. Audiences interact with the artwork or are part of the artwork itself. Emphasis is on an experience that is always different, an experience we cannot separate and isolate from the observer. An observer that is always in transition, always evolving.

"I see. Solutions fit contexts and the contexts keep changing. Therefore the solution keeps changing."

Yes, every implementation is a solution that fits the puzzle of a specific context. And as the context evolves so must the implementation.

"With so many changes, I would appreciate some help to ensure things are moving in the right direction!"

Feedback loops

Feedback becomes essential in a world of fast evolving contexts.

During the nurturing stage, knowledge of anything related to our challenge was especially important. In the implementation stage, the information we require the most is the feedback and opinion of audiences as they interact with our solution.

"I'm sure the recipients of our solution will have many useful things to tell us."

This process should be continuous, and in combination with other feedback sources, it may trigger specific actions. It is actionable feedback. Feedback that becomes the fuel and motivation behind new innovation cycles.

"Rapid innovation cycles that adapt to changing environments."

Rapid prototyping, rapid innovation, lean practices

Realizing that contexts are shifting and evolving faster than ever has important consequences.

- Feedback from users, collaborators and audiences becomes important at all times.
- Implementation stages must be flexible and short, while preserving quality.
- To provide solutions that are always relevant and adapt to the changing contexts, innovation must be a continuous process that can feed back into other stages of the creative cycle at any time.

"Feedback is crucial."

Two areas emerge as key for success. Creative thinking for the development of novel solutions and insights. And feedback to sustain the iterative process of adapting to the changing contexts.

Flexibility is a must. Feedback merges collaboration and communication in order to provide a healthy flow of information feeding back into all the stages of the innovation pipeline.

And now, time to summarize.

Push and let go, a delicate ballet

We have gone through some of the stages involved in innovation and creativity. Let's now look at the whole of it together.

You can view the creative process as a very delicate choreography in which you combine moments of more conscious control, when you decide on a direction, push ingredients into your subconscious pot or translate an insight into final products or actions, and other periods where you relinquish control and let yourself go, allowing your faster subconscious processes to work with the accumulated material, forming connections and combinations until new insights are perceived consciously under the right circumstances (DITS).

A delicate ballet, which can break down when balance fails you.

"Too much of anything is not good."

Yes, too much control and conscious management will interfere with the all-important subconscious incubation processes. But too much letting yourself go without the essential previous conscious groundwork will lead you nowhere, due to a lack of quality building materials.

"What a delicate balance!"

Remember, if you are searching for really innovative and unique solutions, there is no point in saturating your subconscious pot with too many ingredients related to the challenge, as that may prevent divergence, healthy movement and recombination from happening. But it's also not possible to combine ingredients effectively when you have generated too few of them.

So the good innovator comes and goes between AT and CT as the work progresses.

"It's a bit of a game, isn't it?"

A game of opposites

It really is a game of opposites. Keeping AT and CT balanced throughout the process is key for success. In order for this to happen, communication between conscious and subconscious processes must be fluid and smooth.

Innovators need to be very proactive at some stages and very receptive and calm at others. Ready to absorb the complexity of the world while keeping consciousness as free as possible from unnecessary noise and chatter.

They must interact actively with the world in order to feed the always hungry subconscious pot. At the same time they must know when to stop, to prevent oversaturation.

"And what's the best way to perform this process, in isolation or with others?"

With or without you

Good question. What's better for exercising our creative muscles, isolation or interaction? Or both?

It's easy to recall examples of creators working alone, deeply engaged with their craft.

But just as we need both AT and CT during innovation processes, so we need both of these lifestyles to thrive.

The different stages of creativity require more or less emphasis in AT or CT. Depending on that, the ideal scenario for each stage will be different.

For example, when we are incubating an idea and need to let our subconscious explore it in a relaxed way, being alone is often best. Interacting with others may activate our AT, which interferes with the conscious-subconscious communication and our CT processes.

However, when you are looking for ingredients for your challenge or implementing the product or service after finding your key insight, interacting with others is best in order to expand your perspectives, gather feedback for quicker validation, accelerate the process of gathering information or implementing the solution.

In general, the seed, incubation and illumination stages are biased towards CT and favor more isolation, whereas the nurturing and implementation stages are biased towards AT and benefit more from interaction and teamwork.

"This is such an interesting model, can we apply it to other fields?"

Learning, in search of clarity and understanding

The model we have applied to innovation applies to most forms of learning. The objectives of deep learning can be summarized as follows: Reaching a level of understanding and clarity that is similar to the illumination we have described. Preceding that understanding there are similar stages of seed and nurturing. Less obvious but just as important, is the need for an incubation period to happen after the gathering of the ingredients and before deep understanding is reached. Validation and implementation stages can be found in the application of the learnt material to various projects or ventures.

"Fantastic, give me an example."

Think of the process of learning to play tennis.

"I want to improve my technique."

That is your seed, the direction for your subconscious.

Good, then you fill your subconscious pot with information. In this case that means tennis practice and related activities. You watch games, practice with friends, talk to experts and read articles.

"Got it, I'm nurturing that seed!"

Yes, and gradually all that information is incubated and interconnected in your mind, until deep understanding, the illumination, or a series of many illuminations, happen.

"Aha, I may start feeling that my technique is getting better, or maybe suddenly one day something clicks."

Yes, sometimes this illuminating understanding is a gradual process, but it can also come all of a sudden. You may wake up one day and notice that your drive has that extra something that seemed impossible to reach for such a long time. Integration of all the accumulated ingredients has taken place, producing a new level of understanding.

"New mental patterns, new improved technique."

Once you get there, you need to validate, maintain and reaffirm that learning with more practice. You may also want to deeply analyze what has changed in the way you play and move, to reinforce even more your understanding and your strategies. This helps you refine and maintain these new patterns.

"Fantastic, and I guess the mental attitude will also be similar to other creative processes?"

Yes, all the points explained in the previous sections apply as well. Withholding judgment and keeping an open attitude as we juggle our ingredients during practice and study, allowing our incubation processes, under our guidance, to work their magic in integrating all the information. We must keep, during that process, a broad attention and awareness, sensitive to the multiple leaps of understanding that we can then validate and reaffirm as we iterate multiple times.

"I start to feel that these processes are happening…"

Around the clock

In fact these processes are happening around the clock within us. Anytime we search for something in our minds. When we establish a direction, consciously or not. When we gather related information, past or present. When we let go, incubating the material for a millisecond or a day, until we become aware of a new connection, a new insight, which we then express and communicate through various channels including language.

"So we could say that learning processes happen within us all the time and creativity and innovation are ways to accelerate the learning/discovery of something new, something different to the typical solutions out there."

You could say that.

"Wonderful. I wish I could accelerate as much as possible these processes."

It takes time

"Can we accelerate incubation processes by consciously thinking about the challenge as often as possible?"

Thinking constantly about our target can interfere with the space needed to catch those delicate insight bubbles, which can knock on the doors of our consciousness at any time.

"How can we then encourage the process in other ways?"

Exploring themes and experiences related to the seed while we incubate our ingredients can help keep our incubation moving in the right direction.

Still, it is a process that needs no rushing and takes its time. Be welcoming, be gentle.

And above all, have fun.

Finally

To end this summary, a final reminder. The key driver of a great creative process can be summarized in the phrase "Diverge before you Converge". Expand before you contract. Go wide before you focus on isolating a single possibility.

What is most important, though, is that you diverge under the right circumstances. For that you need DITS: depth, ingredients, time and space.

- **Depth**
  You have to be working at the right depth. You have to take the depth elevator right down to the complexity level that matches the complexity level of the solution you are looking for. It's not the same to say that we want to find a solution for cancer than to say we want to find a solution for how to

interfere with the blood supply that powers tumor cells. In the first case, you will be diverging in more generic ways and the kind of solutions you will find will probably be also generic. In the second case, your ingredients gathering phase and divergence processes will be deeper and more detailed, and same will happen with the insights and solutions you will generate.

There is no right or wrong depth. You have to decide what your depth should be in each process. Working at higher depths may be the right thing when you need to contemplate the whole of the challenge from a distance. Descending more may be best at other times, when you want to go really deep within a specific part of the challenge.

- **Ingredients**
  You need to gather within your subconscious pot enough quality ingredients at the required depth. This means that in the second case above (find a solution for how to interfere with the blood supply that powers tumor cells), gathering ingredients that are too generic is probably not going to help too much. The ingredients you gather should have a level of detail and depth that matches the depth at which you have set your challenge.

- **Time**
  You need to give enough time for the ingredients to combine and blend. This is the incubation stage, whose duration is very variable. What is important is to realize that typically some time is needed for incubation to happen successfully. Also, during incubation you need to keep present at the back of your mind your challenge and shuffle mentally from time to time some of your ingredients if possible. In summary, although it is different for each person, it often helps to not disconnect completely from your challenge during incubation and to keep making it present from time to time in your mind.

- **Space**
  You need to have enough space in your mind to be sensitive to any insights that may arise. Only then you can catch those precious bubbles that emerge from your subconscious.

Now it's time to explore practical ways to exercise your creative muscles, so that in time you can become a master at generating unique and innovative solutions to your personal and professional challenges.

CHAPTER 6:

Exercising Your Creative Muscles

"Imagination is the beginning of creation. You imagine what you desire, you will what you imagine, and at last, you create what you will."

– George Bernard Shaw

You don't run a marathon without first training your body muscles. And you don't become great at finding innovative solutions to your personal and professional challenges without regularly exercising your creative muscles. People create daily physical exercise routines for their body muscles and meditation routines for their soul. What about those other key muscles, our mental ones?

Exercising your creative muscles you will become sharper, faster and better at diverging before converging, at filling your subconscious pot with rich and diverse ingredients and at spotting interesting connections between them, no matter how unrelated they may be. Strong creative muscles will drive you faster towards innovative solutions for your personal and professional challenges.

"Can't wait!"

In this chapter I am going to show you different ways to exercise your creative muscles. You will diverge in powerful ways and generate quality ingredients for your creative processes.

These exercises are part of a creative training program I created called Springkite. Springkite is a multidisciplinary and multisensory program. It is also the name of my creativity and innovation workshop. Springkite blends two English words, spring and kite, the personal and professional perspectives.

Spring refers to the personal blooming we are all looking for in our lives. To bloom, we need to express all our potential. That requires a good balance between our analytical and creative thinking processes. To do that we need to exercise intensely our creative muscles in order to balance our typically dominating analytical side.

Kite refers to the professional expansion we are looking for. To expand professionally, we need to find innovative solutions to overcome the competition and the complex challenges we face. Innovating requires fit and strong creative muscles. We strengthen our creative muscles and empower our creative thinking with a multidisciplinary approach, focused on diverging strongly before we converge onto really unique solutions.

The objective is to expand your creative horizons and promote the blooming of a new spring in your mind.

Spring is a state of mind. A creative mind is blooming with new ideas. Kites are universally loved. They are spontaneous, free flowing, light, colorful and expansive. Exercising our CT muscles requires a welcoming attitude. Welcome the unexpected, welcome the true nature and complexity of life. A true innovator, like a kite, is always searching for the next horizon with a dynamic, soaring spirit.

Shift Perspectives

The following exercises emphasize CT because we want to innovate and produce really unique solutions to our challenges.

We emphasize processing information in ways that are more divergent vs convergent, spontaneous vs predictable.

A starting point

The first step is choosing a challenge for which you want to find an innovative solution. Choosing your challenge gives a direction to your subconscious pot.

Exercising your CT works best when linked to a strong personal motivation, the motivation to solve a challenge you really care for.

"Motivation is a key driver in life."

You can look for a new challenge or work with an existing one. Let's see some examples of challenges (these are the examples I mentioned in chapter 1).

- At my company we are working on an app that encourages people to practice sport. We need ideas to make the app useful but also entertaining.

- Our human resources department has problems identifying the best candidates for key positions in our company. How can we improve the process of identifying the best candidates?

- I want to market a cleaning product by using storytelling, creating an original story around the product. I need ideas for that story.

- My partner and I are looking for original ideas for activities to do during our holidays or during our weekends.

- Our company wants to organize team-building events that improve our teamwork. We are looking for ideas to do this.

- Our company is researching ways to interfere with the blood flow that powers tumor cells. We are looking for new creative insights based on our current knowledge.

- I want to write a fiction book about a bank robbery. I would like to develop the base of the story.

- We are an events company specialized in organizing events for seniors. We are looking to find new original and creative ideas to surprise our customers.

- We are a company designing wearable tech, making clothing more interactive. We are competing against many others. We are looking for original ideas to make clothing more interactive in useful ways.

- I am creating a song to advertise a product. I want to generate the lyrics of the song.

- I am working on the script for a short film that will advertise our company. I need to generate the story.

- My partner and I go into conflict because of our different views on tidiness. We are looking for original ways to organize ourselves around this issue.

- And so on and so forth. There is no limit to the challenges you can work on. Anything is possible. The best idea is to pick challenges you care about, either professionally or personally.

We will attack the challenge from multiple perspectives and using many creative languages, from the verbal to the visual and beyond.

Action: Begin to consider what your challenge will be. Pick something that you are passionate about. You can describe your challenge in more generic or more detailed ways. We will see the implications of each approach later.

Change is around the corner

Your challenge and direction can mutate at any time. Give yourself the opportunity to find what you are not looking for. Everything is constantly in flow, also our desires and goals. Be flexible, be like water. Follow what resonates with your mind as you keep exercising.

It's alive!

Look at challenges as dynamic living entities that are constantly evolving. Don't resist movement, join it! If the challenge wants to mutate, it is for a reason.

A creative slap

The process of regaining mental balance can benefit from an initial kick, an intensive metaphorical slap. This creative slap is all about constantly surprising your mind in order to deactivate its powerful analytical filters. It is about challenging your habitual patterns of thinking and reconnecting with your creative potential. That's why these exercises cover a wide range of creative languages, using most of your senses.

"A total creativity shake!"

The beginning of your new life

The objective of a good teacher is to translate knowledge into a form that resonates with the current level of understanding of the student. A teacher facilitates learning, guides and provides short-cuts. But in the end it is the student, the learner, the one that has to walk the path and deliver the goods. That's why, beyond the reading of this book, we will emphasize the regular application of these principles and exercises in your daily life.

Flex the muscles to avoid repetitive mind strain injury

These exercises promote a balanced mind. They will help you flex your creative muscles and avoid repetitive mind strain injuries.

Repetitive mental patterns can hurt your mind just as repetitive movements can hurt your body.

The right attitude

You don't become a great innovator in two days. Strengthening your CT muscles requires patience and a relaxed mental state. Without the right attitude, CT will be crushed by AT processes. Here you will learn strategies and techniques that, when used regularly, will train your thinking muscles in ways that will eventually make a great innovator out of you.

Growing your highway system

Imagine a series of towns spread around a huge landscape. How well connected they are will determine how much progress they experience. Trading and the building of communication routes began the process of accelerating human progress which eventually took us into the globalization era where goods, knowledge, services and people can be reached and accessed anywhere in the world fast and easy.

In a creative mind, information habitats are interconnected and interrelated at many different levels. This speeds up associations and encourages dynamic rearrangements of information.

A great engineer can design and build a road between any two towns, even if a tunnel needs to be excavated under a mountain or an ocean. In the same way, our mind should be able to connect all kinds of information patterns, no matter how unrelated they seem to be. You want to be able to build mental highways between any pair of information entities.

Building a road implies the setup of infrastructure that can be reused for other means. Creating mental highways, new connections, can in the same way improve the efficiency of your thinking processes and strategies.

Physical roads and highways need regular maintenance. Otherwise their structure starts to degrade. Workers need to reinforce the pavement regularly. Mental highways need to be reinforced regularly as well. Exercising your creative muscles accomplishes that goal.

Stability, quality of the materials and the amount of connections in the highway system are important. But what is the use of all of these highways if you cannot find them? Welcome to the search and signaling part of your mind.

Signs and markers are essential while negotiating traffic and also in your mind. It is just as important to have a great network of connections as it is to be able to quickly and efficiently find your way around it. Here is where an interdisciplinary exercising approach helps enormously.

By training and building your mental highways through multiple senses and creative languages, you set up a variety of markers that enhance your capacity to find the best and fastest routes to get to your mental destinations.

These creative languages blend speech, visuals, gesture, movement, improvisation, performance, acoustics, etc., to approach the complexity of life from multiple perspectives.

Each of them makes use of both AT and CT in different proportions. Think of these languages and channels as alternative ways to manipulate and communicate information. Instead of expressing a concept with a single abstraction, a word, you can express that concept by using lines, sounds, your body and other channels of expression at different abstraction levels.

In this chapter we are going to cover some of these channels. You can add other channels anytime, incorporating new strategies from your own experience. These are your weapons, your creative languages, different ways of processing and delivering information.

Annotating your memory

Human brains can only retain a few pieces of information at a time in their short-term storage. Valuable information will start to fade away in a matter of seconds.

Annotating interesting ingredients and insights helps preserve them and may also encourage your mind to form new connections and associations.

Establish those markers, preserve your valuable ingredients and help your mind find its way around your mental highway system.

Pay attention to both your insights and those of others. Note down all interesting ingredients regardless of where they come from. Keep feeding your subconscious dragon!

Be productive

Talent matters, productivity delivers. CT muscles become more resilient and flexible the more productive you are, the more associations, connections and variety you bring into your creative engine.

The channels

We are going to exercise our creative muscles through the following channels:

Seed, Visual, Gesture, Pattern, Emotion, Context and Meditation. [Web] torchprinciple.com/modules

Multiple channels, perspectives and intelligences

To fully understand the importance of a multidimensional approach let's review the theory of multiple intelligences. This theory was proposed by Howard Gardner in 1983.[30] It is a model that differentiates intelligence into specific (primarily sensory) modalities, rather than seeing it as dominated by a single general ability.

There is a wide array of opinions concerning this field. Our exercises are not based on it. The one point at which we connect with it is in viewing our mind and ourselves as multidisciplinary and multi-intelligent, capable of many different modes of thought and expression rather than a single one.

Gardner's multiple intelligences include: linguistic, musical, logical-mathematical, spatial, body-kinesthetic, intrapersonal and interpersonal.

A few years after its inception, the naturalistic and existential intelligences were added to the model.[31]

The fact that our modules overlap in some ways with Gardner's intelligences highlights the shared strategy of approaching our thinking from multiple angles, channels and perspectives.

Balancing the cornerstones

In these exercises we seek to balance AT and CT. The exercises mix these two strategies in different proportions.

Seed, Visual, Gesture, Pattern, Emotion, Context and Meditation

We will brainstorm a seed, visualize it, express it in multiple ways, navigate its complexity, blend emotion, gesture and sound with it, expand its context, combine it with other seeds and iterate this process multiple times.

"I'm not sure that I have the skills to do all that."

Yes, you do. Can you write your own signature? Do you sometimes sing in the shower? Have you ever invented a word? Made an unexpected gesture? Looked at a beautiful landscape while lost in your thoughts? Have you ever pretended, acted or performed in any way? Have you ever felt emotional while interacting with others? Most people have done these things one or more times in their lives. You have the skills you need.

"Any shortcuts?"

Productivity and passion are good enough shortcuts. Get ready, we are approaching the start!

Operation free your mind

Generating innovative solutions to our challenges and exercising our creative muscles requires smooth access to a rich and diverse subconscious pot.

Let's use storytelling to visualize in more depth what our approach will be to get there.

Imagine that your creative potential has been surrounded and hidden by the power of our dominant analytical thinking processes (AT) and logical forces (LF). AT has built a strong fortress surrounded by high walls, defensive filters populated by abstract symbols and deeply ingrained habits. Behind those walls lies the precious subconscious pot. This pot is able to produce fantastic insights that can transform our professional and personal lives in amazing ways. It is full of a wide range of ingredients generated by our experience and is ready to be further enriched by our nurturing processes.

[Web] **torchprinciple.com/mission**

AT doesn't mean to harm or hide our creative treasure. It is just trying to make our life "easier", filtering and classifying all the information that arrives at the fortress, helping us take conventional decisions quickly, making life efficient and organized. Unfortunately, this hides from view our subconscious pot and greatly limits our potential to produce innovative insights, as well as our access to the raw and detailed treasures it contains.

The LF-AT headquarters at the conscious factory constantly churn out pre-packaged answers and interpretations from its database of old knowledge.

"So what can we do to regain full access to our amazing subconscious pot?"

Our intention is to mount an assault on the AT fortress and find/bypass the weak points in these filters/walls in order to communicate fluidly with the creative treasure that lies on the other side. We can then enrich the subconscious pot with relevant ingredients, diverging as much as possible at the start before we later converge onto unique solutions.

We will create smooth communication channels to and from the pot so that we can be ready to catch the unique insights that may come from it.

As in any assault campaign the surprise factor is a key one. We need to catch the filters and logical processes off guard and surprise our mind in unexpected ways.

- **Massive assault**
  We have more chances to succeed if we attack from multiple positions and using multiple weapons.
  "Many creative channels and languages."
  Working in parallel with multiple creative languages can generate beneficial cross-pollination. This productive strategy will help us identify the best routes to reach the creative treasure; the ones that best resonate with us.
  To surprise the defenders of the fortress, we shall express this challenge in many ways, at different levels of abstraction and from various perspectives. This will also deepen our understanding of the challenge, triggering insights that can take us to the other side of the walls faster.

- **The importance of variety**
  We will explore in depth the terrain around the challenge and all the information we can gather beginning as far as we can from our initial position.
  "Diverge before you converge."

Our CT muscles need to be exposed to a variety of contexts and environments in order to stay fresh and ready for action. They can then gather enough strength to stay away from the usual habits and jump into the unknown waiting behind the walls.

- **Avoid traps and ruts**
  In the absence of CT, AT forces make ruts quickly and our forces may get stuck into any of those trenches, unable to reach and bypass the walls.
  The surprise and divergence factor will be essential to avoid falling on any previous habit or thinking pattern. Our creative forces must diverge strongly at first and keep moving and going no matter what.

- **Avoid premature closure**
  Symbols and labels are easily identified and manipulated by the logical forces of the mind. We shall use them with caution.

- **Befriend your partner**
  We don't intend to defeat the AT forces. They perform many essential tasks for us. We shall try to find ways to go around them, allowing them to perform their natural job while we find and secure good routes to access the deep subconscious treasures hidden below the AT fortress of our minds.

- **Be productive and realistic during the siege**
  In order to have the best chance of producing innovative solutions and finding great creative treasures, we shall incubate many options, knowing that some will be poor, and many average. Just a few will have the potential to be great. This is typical in any creative process. We will work hard because innovation is also 1% inspiration and 99% perspiration.

- **Persevere**
  Our initial attempts may still be too connected to old mental patterns and habits. They will soon be identified and recognized by our AT forces. To avoid premature closure, diverge before you converge. Persevere until you begin to find novel routes far from the habitual paths, routes that escape the prying eyes of the logical army.

- **Document it**
  The human brain retains 5 to 10 chunks of data at a time.
  We will note our insights in multiple forms. We will also
  note the ones of our fellow soldiers of life.

- **Send quality messages to the subconscious**
  Send multiple envoys to deliver rich and diverse messages
  and ingredients to the subconscious pot hidden deep below
  the fortress. Send these envoys through different routes to
  increase the odds of some of them succeeding.
  Deliver quality ingredients gathered far and close to where
  you are. Kick start the subconscious treasure pot.

- **Surprise is number one strategy at all times**
  We emphasize this again because of its importance. AT
  loves certainty, security and predictability. To bypass our
  conscious filters and AT controls, to gain easier access to
  the great treasure room, be unexpected at the beginning of
  the process, surprise yourself. The more unexpected and
  unrelated the movements of your forces and your strategies
  are at the beginning, the better.
  "Diverge before you converge!"

- **Get feedback**
  Your perspective is not enough. Get feedback about your
  strategies and insights from a variety of sources, including
  people completely unrelated to your challenge.

- **Fire to the fire**
  AT loves generating habits and relying on them. Why not
  make a habit then out of being unexpected, a habit out of
  looking for what is fresh and different.
  The more often you exercise your CT muscles, the more
  you will make a habit out of making connections between
  apparently unrelated ingredients. You are improving the
  balance with your mind's AT forces using their own strategies, creating a new habit, a healthy one.

- **Ignore the clones**
  Clones of your AT forces will try to discourage you during
  the operation. We must ignore them. It is natural that other
  people, other minds with strong AT forces, will censor
  our attempts to find novel routes. Such reactions are to be
  expected and they confirm that we are on the right path.

Keep close your advisers, ignore the censors!

- **Think outside the water (if you are a fish)**
  If you are a fish, a looming shadow could be a cloud or a human about to catch you. Think outside your usual boundaries. Outside the water if you are a fish, outside the sky if you are a cloud, outside the present context whatever you are.

- **Break the challenge into smaller parts**
  Make the operation more manageable by working on smaller tasks. Subdivide your challenge. Tackle each part with a variety of creative languages and later bring it all together.

- **Build up resilience**
  Challenging your mental habits can have immense rewards but it is not an easy task. Cultivate resilience and the ability to tolerate the frustrations and difficulties that inevitably appear in any challenging process. Don't withdraw your forces prematurely. Keep at it!

- **Know the terrain**
  The theater of operations is formidably complex. Three pounds of soft wrinkled tissue containing 100 billion neurons. Get to know your most important organ. Review the "Electric Mind" chapter if needed.

The tools

In the exercises we will be using a variety of tools, the most important being the brain itself.

In 2011 I produced and directed a film called "The weight of light". The film is a visual metaphor in which our mind represents the most powerful energy transformer we can access. This transformer is able to transform positive and negative energies in infinite ways. Watch the film for free here:
[Web] torchprinciple.com/lightmovie

Your mind is the greatest tool you have. It is naturally able to connect, interpret and find patterns in almost anything you throw at it. Think of any other tool as complementary to the main and most formidable one you carry on top of your shoulders. Your best tool is free!

Balanced tools

We are going to make use of a wide range of tools that go from the most traditional, such as pen and paper, to unique web and mobile applications I created specifically for my creative workshops and this book. You don't have to necessarily use the tools I will describe. I will always suggest alternatives. You can reach the same results either way. Of course I recommend using SK (Springkite) tools because they are custom built to experience these exercises in the best way possible. But you will reach the same results using other alternative possibilities.

Instructions for all the tools:
[**Web**] **torchprinciple.com/guides**

The tools include:

- **SK-General (Free)**
  A web app that allows you to generate ideation ingredients with words, emotion-haikus and languages (it contains SK-Words, SK-Haiku and SK-Language).
  [**Web**] **torchprinciple.com/skgeneral**

- **SK-Sound (Free)**
  A soundstorming tool that stimulates your creative muscles using sounds.
  [**Web**] **torchprinciple.com/soundstorm**

- **SK-Light (Free)**
  A lightstorming tool that stimulates your creative muscles using visual patterns.
  [**Web**] **torchprinciple.com/lightstorm**

- **SK-Engine (Premium)**
  Ideation module within the Posterini platform. It provides a powerful interface for ideation, combining hundreds of thousands of verbal stimuli together with visuals and other graphical elements.
  [Web] torchprinciple.com/skengine

  Buying this book gives you free access for a limited time to the SK-Engine tool. To request access, send a copy of your book invoice to **ideami@ideami.com**.

- **DCollab (Free)**
  A collaborative drawing tool.
  [Web] torchprinciple.com/dcollab

- **Texture Drawing (Free)**
  A tool that allows you to draw anonymous textures.
  [Web] torchprinciple.com/texturedrawing

- **Soundmap and music videos (Free)**
  Soundmaps and music for some of the exercises of this chapter.
  [Web] torchprinciple.com/soundmaps
  [Web] torchprinciple.com/music

Requirements

These exercises have very basic requirements

- A mobile phone to use as camera and to access some web apps.
- A laptop or a tablet to access some apps.
- Paper and pencils.

Technology, a useful tool.

Many of the exercises in this book make use of technology tools. They can also be done without them. I believe that the most natural way to exercise our creative muscles is by using our minds, bodies and senses without necessarily having to incorporate extra technology to that process. However, technology is an excellent tool that can accelerate enormously the process of strengthening our creative muscles. It can also help us to generate the healthy habit of diverging creatively in multiple ways.

We can exercise a muscle on our own or use a machine at the gym to accelerate the training. It's the same with technology. Once you master creative divergence, I encourage you to go beyond technology and apply these principles and exercises in your daily life without relying too much on technology tools. Most people don't want to spend all their day at the gym. In the same way we shouldn't depend too much on apps and tools.

Taking notes

You may take notes on your smartphone/tablet or with pen and paper. You may use erasable boards or mind mapping software. The key desirable parameter is consistency and durability. The information should be recorded in ways that guarantee easy access in the future.

Storming your mind

Get ready to break into the deepest chambers of your mind by taking brainstorming and ideation to the next level.

The following seven modules (**Seed, Visual, Gesture, Pattern, Emotion, Context and Meditation**) connect you with a variety of creative skills, including improvisation and performance, public speaking, pattern recognition, storytelling, drawing, etc.

In the process you reinforce as well key universal skills like observation, communication, lateral thinking, improvisation, teamwork and spontaneity.

"I am ready!"

Hold these points in mind before you start:

- All the exercises we will do in this chapter have 2 objectives: First, to flex, train and strengthen your creative muscles, and second, to generate through the exercises new insights/ solutions related to your personal/professional challenge.

- If your challenge is a business one, you may want to gradually fill in a BMC as you work through the different modules. The BMC (Business Model Canvas), created by Alexander Osterwalder, allows us to explain and present a business model through a graphic composed of 9 areas, which represent the key parts of a company.[32]

  [Web] torchprinciple.com/bmc

  [Web] torchprinciple.com/businessmodelcanvas

  As you generate new insights in the exercises, you can continue filling in the different parts of your BMC.

- Perform these exercises in a variety of scenarios and contexts. You may use music or other stimuli to accompany the process.

- Avoid communicating with others in the exercises that are more focused on CT. The use of language activates AT processes and interferes with CT.

- When we ask you to hold the challenge in your mind, we refer mainly to visualizing the challenge and/or parts of it, rather than thinking about it with words.

- For maximum divergence, encourage guided randomness. We will explain this in detail in the coming sections.

"Off we go!"

Seed

Tools: SK-Engine (or similar), paper, pencils, other note taking methods.

Video examples of some of the exercises:
[Web] torchprinciple.com/seed

This module exercises your creative muscles by diverging strongly through guided randomness based on verbal stimuli. AT processes are then used to converge to useful insights.

Windows to the subconscious

The easiest way to start flexing our creative muscles is to begin with language. In this module the process begins by gathering words and phrases that become ingredients for our subconscious pot.

"Every word is a universe."

From single words products have been born, life changing decisions have been taken. These verbal ingredients combine in your subconscious. New insights can arise at any moment and become solutions expressed verbally after being evaluated by our AT processes.

You can combine your verbal ingredients with drawings and other forms or expressions, but the emphasis in this first module is on the verbal side.

Our emphasis as always is on generating really unique, different and innovative solutions. For that we need to bypass AT controls to avoid falling into preexisting patterns and typical solutions. Guided randomness is a great ally in this mission.

Many of the amazing feats of evolution are produced by random interactions, which generate new features/capabilities that benefit the host's chances of survival and reproduction. Those features, over time, spread to subsequent generations continuing the process.

Randomness helps us diverge in big ways before we converge later to great solutions. As we will emphasize often and explain later, we are talking about intelligent randomness. Randomness applied at the right depth and in the right way (including the DITS process).

The importance of random

Imagine that you wish to write a story with similar themes to the Harry Potter books.[33]

"I will first make sure that i understand the Harry Potter books in depth."

And then you begin the ideation process and what happens? Thoughts related to Harry Potter keep flooding your mind, effectively blocking you from finding other fresh, relevant but unrelated ingredients and seeds.

Thinking about something reinforces that mental pattern in your brain, makes it deeper and easier to recall, potentially blocking other avenues.

"So we first need to get away from the habitual. What is the fastest way to do that?"

An all-out assault

Typical interpretations come to mind faster than less typical ones. We need an all-out assault and that kind of power is best delivered by the all mighty random horse.

Riding on the shoulders of random

Randomness is the horse that will take us very far, very quickly. At the start of the process we are looking for maximum divergence and we will focus strongly on it.

When working with randomness, it would be tempting to choose categories and narrow down our search in advance, but that would push us towards specific directions from the start. We really want to be open to anything and everything at the very beginning of the process. We want to diverge as much as possible.

"Daily life becomes a giant random canvas. I can pick random ingredients from the magazines I read or the movies I watch."

Asking words from a friend or picking them from a magazine or a TV show may seem random, but it is not random enough. There is already a conditioning and a context associated with those sources. While watching a film or a magazine, you are already introducing a bias that pushes your subconscious pot towards certain routes.

"What about asking a friend to tell me random words?"

Typically, your friend will tend to pick words that are found in normal conversations or related to his/her activities or to yours. It will be hard for that person to bring up totally unrelated concepts. In addition, the pressure of having to tell you interesting words typically constrains and narrows our focus.

"But isn't there a bias in everything?"

We can argue that everything introduces a bias, we ourselves do. But if we can avoid extra external influences, we should.

We need a truly random system and that's what you can achieve with the SK-Engine tool or by randomly choosing words in a dictionary.

The SK-Engine tool allows you to choose specific categories as well to narrow down the possibilities if you wish to do so. I remind you that you don't have to use the SK-Engine. You can use any kind of dictionary instead. The SK-Engine, however, is specially designed to help you diverge quickly and comfortably.

"Back to Harry Potter. Related themes can potentially block our process. How can we proceed?"

In order to find truly fresh ideas, you need to believe and trust that everything can be potentially connected. You need to embrace uncertainty and the natural power of your brain.

"Show me an example."

Here we go. Take any tool that exposes you to random words and phrases. I am going to describe the process using the SK-Engine but you can use any other tool that allows you to reach similar results.

You will find the instructions to use the SK-engine on this page: [Web] **torchprinciple.com/skengine**

- Start the SK-Engine.

- The Engine shows random words/phrases at random locations on the screen. If you just watch and don't touch the words/phrases, they quickly disappear and fade away. If you touch them, they become fixed and permanent.

- You can switch between word/phrase modes either individually or collectively.

- When you select a word/phrase, you can read its definition on the bottom status bar of the interface.

- Look at the words/phrases as they appear. How do you feel about them? Any of these random elements may quickly suggest a connection to the theme of your challenge. A connection that may later on trigger interesting insights. Grab not only those ingredients that suggest an immediate connection but also those that pique your curiosity and seem to ask to be preserved even though no connection with your challenge may be felt at first.

- You can edit any of the elements anytime by double clicking on them. A random ingredient may suggest to you a different word or phrase and you may want to edit the element immediately to change its text.

- You can also create brand new verbal elements, your own words and phrases, using the left menu.

- If you are not using the SK-Engine and instead you are using a dictionary or any other tool, feel free to do the same. Edit, delete and add ingredients anytime. Don't constrain yourself only to the random ones selected by your tool.

- If you are using the SK-Engine, you can also use the "Add" menu, located at the top of the interface, to constrain a random element to a specific category.

Remember the torch principle. The great value in planting these random torches is that they allow you to jump rather than take small steps. When a combination of these new torches, in combination with a DITS process, illuminates a new insight, you have to remember that it would have been almost impossible to arrive at such an improbable combination of ingredients in a short amount of time by using traditional AT strategies. Your brain tends to think along routes already explored. Creative leaps require taking the risk to leap into the unknown.

Remember to note down not only those words/phrases that immediately suggest something, but also others that may suggest nothing at first, but still resonate with you, pique your curiosity and ask to be welcomed into your subconscious pot to enrich your creative process in directions that later may prove to be very fruitful.

Trust your brain. It is capable of connecting anything you throw at it. Of course, the more you exercise, the easier it is to connect apparently unrelated stimuli.

"It won't be easy at first, but it gets easier the more you do it. You don't run a marathon after 2 days of training."

Your chosen words/phrases in combination with your existing knowledge have the potential to trigger associations that are really novel and different.

"In a way, everything is connected."

Yes, whichever elements you have chosen, they can eventually be connected to each other and to your challenge. They can become the creative seed and base for any goal you may have, a story, the solution to a personal challenge, a painting or a strategy for a business.

Our advantage

The effectiveness of this exercise doesn't depend just on random ingredients. Our adult brain has a fabulous network of associations and connections already in place. All we need is to trigger the initial spark and then put that entire network to good use. The objective is to combine the freshness of a child with the experience of an adult. The magic is truly in the combination between random ingredients and that network of patterns and associations.

CT focused

You may wonder how much nurturing of our challenge we will do in this exercise.

The purpose of this exercise is to train in fast cycles the stages of the creative process that put more emphasis on CT. So the nurturing stage of creativity will be mainly limited to the generation of random ingredients and we fill in the gaps through our previously accumulated experience.

"So we will rely mainly on our existing knowledge instead of purposefully gathering related data."

You can empower this exercise even more if, before beginning, you do some base research and update yourself on the current trends (social, technological, economic, etc.). They are a key part of the foundation and context around your challenge. You can also spend time gathering data related to the challenge. We specially emphasize the gathering of data related to the community that is associated with the challenge.

Still, what we really want to train with this exercise is the ability to diverge before you converge and to do so multiples times in fast cycles. So feel free to limit your nurturing stages to the combination of random ingredients and your previous existing knowledge if you don't have time to gather more data.

"And what if nothing is really clicking?"

Jump the block!

If nothing is coming up, it may be because your creative muscles are still too weak and/or your AT processes too controlling. Persevere. It takes time to grow those muscles. It is normal that during the exercises you may feel blocked sometimes. Don't keep looking harder and harder in the same direction. Doing so narrows down your focus and pushes you into tunnel vision and premature closure. Jump immediately into something different. Change your direction and/or your ingredients.

"So starting over is always an option."

If finding useful connections is taking too long, you can move on to different ingredients/stimuli at any time. Or you can even change direction if you wish. Don't obsess over any blockage as that will only further narrow your attention and focus. You want to feel wide and relaxed at all times. If the going gets tough, move on and see what you find when you swim back into the ocean of directions and/or ingredients.

The more often you do this exercise, the more natural it will become. When you feel ready, extend it to your daily life. You will be making a habit out of connecting seemingly random events, concepts and situations. A habit out of being creative and exercising your CT muscles.

"Can we do this exercise without even giving a direction to our subconscious?"

Yes. In a way our subconscious is already full of countless directions and challenges, and any of those may resonate with the ingredients we are playing with. Let's suppose that we start the SK-Engine without any specific challenge in our minds. We choose the following words, which somehow pique our curiosity or seem interesting.

Reply, hall, optic, employee, bound

Avoid any sense of urgency about finding a great idea from those stimuli. Keep it easy and relaxed to avoid AT processes from taking control. The objective is to flex our creative muscles, to diverge, to shake our subconscious pot so that in time, which could be seconds, minutes, hours or days, interesting insights can surface to our conscious mind.

The more we do this, the more we will make a habit out of connecting not just random words, but random experiences, events, things we hear around us and other information that arrives to our senses.

"Interesting, give me some examples of potential insights generated from those ingredients in combination with existing knowledge."

Interesting insights may surface in connection with just 1 or 2 of the ingredients, or with a combination of them. Don't feel that you need to connect a new insight with all of them.

Reply, hall, optic, employee, bound

- **A business related product**
  A bank robbery. Employees have been tied up by the robbers. Special optic sensors exist in the halls of the bank. These sensors allow employees to activate alarms by performing certain gestures in the direction of the sensors. The gestures trigger the immediate reaction of remote security teams.

- **The beginning of a story**
  A veteran director of an insurance firm has been bound to his desk and computer for so long that his eyesight has deteriorated over the years. He can hardly see. Like every day in the last 2 decades he shouts across the hall asking for the latest reports. But today no reply comes back. He paces around, wondering what is going on. The entire building is apparently empty.

- **The skeleton of a poem**
  Bound by the words and reports of another infinite night…
  No replies in the halls…
  Only reflections of silence…
  I, the lonely employee by the shadows of the moonlight.

We could continue using more channels to express insights triggered by these ingredients.

"I can see the potential!"

Trusting the ability of our brain to connect anything, we can proceed with other stimuli and continue gathering useful insights. Let's see more examples:

Finding, quick, farewell, remark

A technology app. An internet application that allows you to find quickly unusual and original greeting messages, remarks and quotes.

Permission, life, party

In a futuristic world controlled by a single political party, people need permission to exit their homes. An underground movement works in the shadows to return the life of people to what it once was.

As you can see, random stimuli help us to quickly diverge. They can become the base for innovative ideas related to new business ventures, industrial products, screenplays, poems, new activities or anything else.

During this exercise become aware of how you feel. Whenever you watch an exciting combination of stimuli you will feel something special. Some combinations will ask to be discarded, others will beg you to continue working with them. Be sensitive. Listen carefully and some of these ingredients will grow on you and start to branch out into other areas, taking a life of their own.

As you gather interesting ingredients and insights, make sure to record them immediately. Hold off any judgments. Don't evaluate them too soon. Let evolution take its course. Encourage combination and recombination. Do soft selection by recording those ingredients, insights or combinations that pique your curiosity or suggest interesting possibilities. Be productive. First generate many options. Later evaluate.

"Why is it so important to defer judgment?"

Because you want to produce innovative, not typical solutions. This means that you need to diverge before you converge. Our initial reaction to novel and unusual combinations will be heavily influenced by our past experiences and stored knowledge. It's normal to feel resistance at first. The more we persevere and exercise our CT muscles, the more confident and relaxed we will feel as we navigate new possibilities.

And these are endless. If tight logical rules can trap you, randomness sets you free. Now imagine what happens when you introduce a useful bias, the challenge you are interested in. A challenge you are passionate about.

You focus this powerful process in a specific direction. This accelerates the generation of interesting insights that connect with that challenge.

Setting the challenge, the importance of having a direction

Randomness without a direction can drive you to interesting but not immediately relevant or useful results. To get more value from this process, it's best to set a direction. Decide what your challenge is. This direction will guide your subconscious as the random stimuli blend with your previous knowledge.

The nature of this direction is key. Work on challenges related to something you are deeply interested in. This improves the efficiency of the process as well as the general performance.

Feel free to modify your challenge at any time. It is not a fixed direction, it is a flexible route. Let it flow.

"Can I combine my verbal ingredients with visuals as well?"

Words trigger visualizations, which in turn may trigger other verbal seeds. Sometimes we may want to express separately the visuals that words and phrases trigger in our minds.

Combining verbal and visual ways of representing information, we will further improve the seasoning of our recipe. So for training our CT muscles even more, you may draw the most interesting stimuli you've found. Some people like to use paper for a more organic and dynamic experience.

"What else can I do to explore the ingredients I gather?"

Optionally, you can subdivide or list the main features of interesting ingredients. You can also create mind maps. All of this encourages more associations to be uncovered.

While you are working consider as well the context around your challenge, the negative spaces, what surrounds the challenge. Consider adding some ingredients that reflect those spaces in between.

"And once I begin gathering interesting ingredients, how do I proceed?"

Combine to win

As your ingredients interact with each other at conscious and subconscious levels, interesting connections can appear anytime. You can encourage the process consciously although the most powerful part happens subconsciously. It is the incubation process we have talked about in the previous chapter.

As you spot interesting ingredients, imagine them to be pieces of a puzzle. Combining your ingredients at conscious and subconscious levels is one of the keys of creativity. If you want to have a chance to hit the jackpot, roll the wheels and let your ingredients combine.

In summary

Therefore in this module we diverge strongly by combining AT and CT, using language as a window to the subconscious. Our visualizations and the insights we incubate become fresh foundations for new solutions.

"We use words to initiate and trigger mental processes that involve CT."

And those eventually produce insights that can be engraved into new concepts, words and phrases.

Generate and generate again

Separate generation from evaluation. We generate many seeds and later consider which ones are the best. Enrich your subconscious pot as much as possible at the start.

"I see that productivity seems a common thread in great innovators."

Quantity, the vessel towards quality

Yes, we focus on generating as many seeds as possible, working our way gradually to a few quality insights. Productivity is the dynamic vessel that will take us to a few top quality destinations. And this productivity should begin in a bold way!

Dreamer, realist, critic

Be bold, let your imagination fly. Be open to crazy associations and possibilities. It is easier to go from the improbable to the practical than vice versa.

Think of the dreamer-realist-critic method used by Walt Disney. Begin with the craziest possibilities you can think of. Later on you will reshape and pick the most realistic ones. Finally you will evaluate them with a critical eye to identify challenges and develop implementation strategies.

Beginning with the SK-Engine tool helps you diverge as much as possible and dream without limits.

"Great! Is the objective to find completely new and totally unique insights?"

What is new anyway?

Be alert not only to new insights but also to variations of existing ideas. Most of what we think is new is just a variation of existing ideas, products or services. Whatever comes your way that you find interesting can be adapted and evolved to fit what you need.

"Once I find a good set of ingredients or an interesting insight, should I stop the process?"

No end in sight

Don't stop as soon as you find something interesting. Great insights are often the result of further developing initial ingredients or ideas. Consider any of the following possibilities, which you can apply to any seed. We will use the word seed to refer to any ingredient, revelation or idea.

- **Substitute:** Replace some seeds with others, creating new variations.

- **Combine:** Mix unrelated seeds.

- **Adapt:** Adapt interesting seeds to your context, or other's seeds to yours.

- **Modify:** Change parts of your seeds, alter their context.

- **Invert:** Consider the opposite of a seed.

- **Rearrange:** Rearrange the configuration and relationship between your seeds.

It is now time to summarize the exercise.

Wordstorm. Preparations.

- Decide on the key direction and parameters of your challenge. Is it a book? A movie script? A new startup? A specific product within an established company?

- You may establish your direction with more or less details. More details can accelerate the process but constrain your diverging potential or drive you prematurely to closure. Fewer details means potentially a slower process but with more creative potential.

- Have in mind that whatever you create has a target and that target is usually a community, an audience. Decide on which community your efforts will focus on. Will you look for new insights in relation to the impoverished communities of South East Asia? Executives of Wall Street? Young football players?

- Learn all that you can about that community. Create one or more profiles for their typical representatives. Describe them in detail and if possible interview one or more of them. Get to know them deeply. They are the final recipients of your future solution and hold the key to your success.

- Gather your tools. During this exercise you will use the SK Engine (or alternative similar tools) as well as paper and pencil. Combining cutting edge and traditional tools improves your efficiency.

"Ready! Let's go for it!"

The process

- Write a phrase summarizing your challenge at the top of the SK-Engine or with any other tool. This will help you to keep the direction present in your mind.

- Start the engine. Keep your mind relaxed as stimuli appear and disappear. With your challenge present in the background of your awareness, be on the lookout for any stimuli that puzzles you, piques your curiosity or any that you find interesting. Fix those in place by touching them or clicking on them.

- Keep adding interesting stimuli, drag them around. When existing ingredients suggest anything new, you may double click them to edit their text and change them in any way you like. You can also add brand new elements manually with the left menus.
  All of the above can be done alternatively with a dictionary and paper, or with other tools.
  If you get stuck using the SK-Engine tool, review the instructions in more detail at this page:
  [Web] torchprinciple.com/skengine

- We respond differently to digital screens and paper. If you feel like it, write the ingredients you gather on a paper. Interact with both the digital screen and the paper, and see how comfortable you feel as you play with the gathered ingredients. The digital tool gives you more power to reposition, add, delete and manipulate the ingredients but we are all different and some people will prefer committing the ingredients to paper and continue working there. Others will prefer to use only the digital screens or maybe to combine both approaches.

- **Take notes.** As interesting insights reach your conscious mind, make sure to annotate them before they fade away.

- **Iterate.** Iterate, start again, and keep accumulating interesting ingredients and valuable insights.

"Is this a process that is best performed alone or in a group?"

Working with others

Initial ideation processes can work better when performed alone. In a group we depend very much on AT processes like language to communicate with each other. AT interferes with CT. And what we really need at the beginning of our ideation are CT processes that help us diverge rather than converge.

Group interaction is very useful as a second step after the initial seeds have been generated. Interacting with others can help us refine, choose and implement the best insights we have produced.

So work on your own at the beginning of this exercise. Once you produce your first insights, feel free to evaluate them within a group or in pairs. Give feedback to each other. Let your findings resonate with other subconscious pots to further enrich the process.

- Find a colleague, a friend or a partner. Ideally your companion will have gone through the same process you have just gone through. That means that your partner will also have chosen a challenge and have a set of ingredients gathered during the exercise as well as one or more ideas generated from them.

- Show your partner your ideation ingredients without disclosing the challenge. Your partner will now incubate and generate a new interpretation/idea from your ingredients without knowing what your challenge is. What idea is triggered in the mind of your partner in response to the same ingredients you used? His interpretation may suggest in turn something new to you.

- Show your partner the ideation ingredients plus the challenge. Once your partner knows what the challenge is, listen to his/her new feedback and interpretation based on your ingredients.

- Compare the perspectives and interpretations of your partner with yours. If anything new and interesting comes to mind note it down.

- Now show each other both of your challenges and the insights you have identified. Try to merge both challenges and sets of insights to produce a brand new challenge and solution.

You will be amazed at how incredibly diverse are the interpretations coming from other subconscious pots.

Preparing to go visual

In the next module we will work with analog and gesture drawings. Using the infinitely expressive language of the line, they make visible your subconscious and the deepest parts of your challenge as well as new insights, interpretations and ideas. In preparation, consider beginning to involve more visuals in your seed exercises.

- Draw the new insights/ingredients you gather. Make them visible, visualize them. Make use of mind maps, diagrams and other visual aids to further enrich and solidify your creative routes.

- Have a bit of fun with the "New Life" visual exercise. Start the SK Engine. Fix and gather a few words that pique your curiosity. Now stop the engine, get some paper and draw a creature made of the words you picked. It should be an imaginary creature made of those words. For example: table, umbrella, train: a table that has an umbrella attached and travels in a train.

"That makes my CT muscles go Yuhuu!"

VISUAL
Making thoughts visible

Tools: Paper, pencil.

Video examples of some of the exercises in this section:
[Web] **torchprinciple.com/visual**

Visual brainstorming

Working with words can feel very constraining. Words are symbols, abstractions of reality. Language itself is slow to work with. It is sequential in nature.

For great innovators like Albert Einstein, the key parts of their creative processes were visual. Language became important at later stages when insights needed to be communicated to others. Let's remember Einstein's words:

"The words of language as they are written or spoken do not seem to play any role in my mechanism of thought. The psychical entities which seem to serve as elements of thought are certain signs and more or less clear images which… are in my case of visual and some of muscular type. These elements take part in a rather vague play in which they can be voluntarily reproduced and combined… this combinatory play seems to be the essential feature in productive thought, before there is any connection with logical construction in words or other kinds of signs which can be communicated to others."[34]

So a key way to expand the horizons of our ideation processes is through visualization and visual brainstorming. We will be using ways of visualizing and working with information that involve more flexible, organic and simultaneous processes.

"Visuals and visualization can take us deeper and closer to the raw complexity of our challenges."

Complexity. The power of the visual perceptual mode.

Life is complex. AT processes and language simplify it for us. For the same reason, language has limits when trying to access that raw complexity. That's why many great scientists and creators thought first visually and only later translated their findings onto words. So visual, perceptual processes are key to creativity and innovation.

Looking vs seeing

Reflect on this dichotomy. Looking is an AT process. It is related to judging, labeling, categorizing and filtering. Its purpose is efficiency and survival.

"I need to quickly classify and understand what this element is, just in case it is dangerous for my survival."

Seeing is a CT process. It is related to suspending judgment and diving deep into the details and complexity of reality. Seeing means engaging with a subject without labels, as if it is the first time you are encountering it. You are fully engaged with the present reality of that subject.

"Whereas 'looking' lives in the past."

In essence, we are talking about conceptual vs perceptual, separate processes linked to AT and CT. We may know that we are not seeing what we perceive and yet we cannot correct it because of a strong concept that stands in between.

[Web] **torchprinciple.com/creativekeywords**

"A battle between efficiency and depth, security and risk, simplicity and complexity."

Techniques

Working with visuals doesn't mean that we banish language. Language is always an essential tool that allows us to come back from the depths of complexity to higher levels of abstraction in order to refine, elaborate and communicate our findings.

Innovators from many areas use visuals to exercise their CT muscles in places where words struggle. For example, storyboard artists use the line to communicate and explain simultaneously multiple parameters of screenplay compositions, a process that would be too slow and complex for language. Similar advantages occur on other areas.

"Visual thinking is fast, detailed and flexible!"

To access the infinite power of the line we first need to bypass the AT filters that will insist on simplifying our perception, blocking our access to the raw complexity we are searching for.

Bypassing AT filters

Specific drawing exercises can help us enormously to understand how it feels to tame our AT processes and activate our CT muscles. Therefore, in this module we use drawing to explore our challenge visually, and also as a great analogy and training exercise on how to bypass our AT filters.

The visual ecosystem

As we work with lines to explore our challenges visually, we discover the key components of this fascinating ecosystem.

Lines form edges, around which negative spaces appear. Presence and density of lines produce bright and dark regions, which we can interpret as lights and shadows. Together, these components generate relationships and proportions, which provide detailed and high level perspectives.

Edges, negative spaces, lights and shadows, proportions, relationships and perspectives invite you to explore a challenge from a more organic, open and fluid point of view.

[Web] torchprinciple.com/visuallanguage

To understand these components of visual languages, we can compare them with verbal ones.

Negative spaces in perception relate to context in language.

"The spaces around our challenge."

Challenges cannot be separated from the environment they exist in. Be mindful of those negative spaces, the context that constantly affects your challenge.

Edges can be thought of as words, separating and delimiting the space. Finding the boundaries of your challenge helps you identify its different parts and components.

Relationships and proportions can be similar to grammar and syntax in language. By understanding and manipulating the relationships and proportions of your challenge, you can find new perspectives and solutions.

"These principles, edges, spaces, proportions, they all seem useful and not just in relation to visualizing…"

Yes. Remember the depth elevators and the universal roots?

Many of the principles that we can access in drawing can be found in other creative forms of expression, and vice versa. For example, rhythm and harmony, essential in music, are also present in the contours and shapes of the figures we draw. We can also establish parallels between proportions in drawings and pitch variations in music. A beautiful music chord would be equivalent to harmonious proportions in a drawing.

Continuing with this parallel between music and drawing, there is a very important distinction between them. Music has a beginning and an end. It depends on time. Drawing is different.

Similar comparisons can be established with other creative forms of expression. For example, poetry delivers its content sequentially, word by word. Its harmony develops over time as well, whereas drawing shows it all at once.

"So the time dimension doesn't matter in a drawing?"

Yes, it does. Time is still present in a drawing. Fast and slow lines look different because their speed, their time dimension, is encoded within themselves.

Additionally, a drawing is one of the forms of expression that cannot be copied exactly without using special tools. It mirrors life's complexity, which is unique and impossible to precisely reproduce in all its infinite details. Drawings are able to express infinite variations that can only be labeled with a few specific words.

All of the above confirms that drawing is an ideal channel to communicate with our subconscious pot and to access the deep complexity of our challenges.

Translating the complexity of life

As we said previously, the abstractions of logic and language are very limited when dealing with high complexity. Visuals can work much better with it. They encode reality in an analog fashion, in an infinite combination of subtle variations expressed through shapes and lines. Even time is subtly encoded within these visual representations.

What can often be only expressed with a single word becomes infinite interpretations in the visual arena.

"Reality goes way beyond words and language."

Your conscious knowledge is the tip of a treasure hidden deep below. A treasure of information that constantly bombards our senses.

Visualization gives us powerful tools to transport part of that treasure from our subconscious to our conscious mind.

Accessing the visual language

Somebody puts a hand in front of us and asks us to draw it. Typically, we won't draw the specific details in front of us but a mixture between them and a generic representation of the symbol "hand". What we draw is mediated by the knowledge and typical parameters of all the hands we have known in the past. Looking at the result, we get frustrated.

What happens is that AT, in trying to help and simplify our life, ends up interfering with our capacity to access the real complexity out there. The real "hand".

The key to access that raw complexity rests on finding ways to bypass the AT filters. These filters help us in our day-to-day life. But they become an obstacle when we need to go beyond abstract and simplified interpretations and get down to the detailed richness and complexity of reality.

This applies to everything: understanding a specific hand, the current fluctuations in the financial markets or the current state of a relationship.

To draw a hand, not any hand, but that specific hand that is right there in front of us, we first have to learn to see it, to truly see it. We have to calm down our typically hyperactive AT processes, the part of our mind that is constantly analyzing, interpreting and simplifying the inputs that arrive to our brain. Only then we are able to truly access the vast richness and complexity out there.

To truly "see" that hand, you have to go beyond the "hand" concept. When you go beyond the symbol, be it a hand, a tree, a man or anything, you find out that visually all things are made of curves, lines, textures, shadows, highlights, proportions and relationships, analog elements that can express infinite variations and as such infinite concepts.

"Aren't lines, curves and textures also abstractions of a deeper nature? And if so, shouldn't we also go beyond them?"

If you keep going deeper and deeper eventually you arrive at atoms and elementary particles. However, as humans we cannot work with atoms (not yet) unaided. But we can deal with edges, shadows, relationships, proportions and negative spaces.

"We need to stop at a level that suits our capabilities."

Yes, the point is to go deep enough to reach the level that allows quick access to the unique traits and features of reality and of that specific entity, while still being able to manipulate and work with those features. In a way, we are finding the right level of abstraction, one that is deeper than what AT typically offers and at the same time fits with our capabilities of manipulating the information we are dealing with.

"So in the case of drawing a hand… "

If we go beyond the "hand" symbol and understand that entity in terms of its shadows, highlights, lines, curves and textures, we will then be able to see the unique features of that entity (that specific hand), and also to manipulate and work with those features in any way we want.

That's where we want to be. Right there.

Because when we draw with our pencil or brush on the surface of a paper, a canvas or a digital screen, we will be working, expressing ourselves and visualizing at that same level, using those same principles: lines, negative spaces, shadows, highlights, textures, etc.

By reaching that level of abstraction and understanding that specific "hand" in terms of its lights, shadows, textures, lines, etc. we are interpreting that entity in the same language spoken by our pencil and brush.

This is key. We cannot express this specific hand through drawing if our brain is not accessing and understanding the language of shadow, light, textures and lines, the language which our brush and pencil understand and use.

So in drawing there are two key stages. One is understanding, seeing at the right abstraction level. The other is the technical execution at that same level.

"Both parts have to speak the same language."

Regarding execution, we need to produce lines, curves, shadows, highlights, textures, etc. with our brush or pencil. These are methods, techniques that we can learn, some of us faster, others slower, some with more refined results than others, but everybody can eventually get there.

"I see where you are going. We can be trained to express concepts in various ways and with different languages, but even more important is to learn to first see and absorb reality through those same languages."

Yes, technical skills become really meaningful when we first learn to understand our challenge in terms of the same languages those skills use. For example, we need to see, not a hand, not a door, not a flower, but a universe of hills and valleys, lights and shadows, curves and lines.

When that happens, at that magical moment, brain and pencil are literally on the same wavelength. We are seeing right what our pencil and brush understand. We can then grab a line with our eyes, channel it through the brain, and deliver it via the brush or pencil onto the paper or canvas.

We can absorb that highlight on the doorknob and again deliver it through the brain to be rendered onto the canvas by the brush.

The importance of matching our level of understanding with our level of expression and execution applies not just to drawing but to everything in our lives.

For example, we can best express ourselves genuinely from our hearts when we first become sensitive enough to feel others around us. Or we can best design a new product when we first are able to understand in depth the field that product is related to. And so on and so forth.

Creative visualization is therefore the process of accessing deeper and more complex abstractions of reality. It becomes especially powerful when coupled with execution skills that are able to manipulate the gathered data at the same abstraction level we have accessed.

And to access those deeper levels, we need to bypass our AT filters. Bypassing them, be it while drawing a hand or when interacting with our partner in a relationship, requires courage. It is not easy. Once we see a hand as a rich universe of hills and valleys, textures, angles and lines, or once we truly "see" our partner beyond any past judgements, we may feel at first intimidated.

"I do."

It is natural. We are challenging our brain to deal with something completely new. It is not anymore the generic "hand" concept. It is now a whole new universe contained in that specific entity, a whole new universe which is not pre-stored in our memory. Something totally new that we are now exploring deeply, fully engaged with it.

Now replace the hand with any other challenge. A relationship, a business market, a mobile application. In order to truly understand any challenge, we also need to bypass our AT simplifying filters and access the raw complexity in front of us. Only then can we gather quality ingredients to empower our innovation cycles.

"And how can I make it easier to bypass the simplifying controls of my AT processes in order to access those deeper levels?"

Bypassing the filters

In order to get to those deeper levels of understanding, we first have to deal with the powerful mental forces that insist on simplifying our lives by keeping us at higher levels of abstraction.

As we have indicated, AT and language are some of our most powerful mental assets, but all powerful things are to be enjoyed in moderation. AT becomes an obstacle when we want to temporarily activate the deeper CT processes needed to explore the finer details of reality.

I am going to show you ways to tame your AT filters and access your deeper CT processes.

"I'm all ears!"

Going beyond restrictive words and making thoughts visible makes them stronger and deeper. In order to prevent AT attempts to label and simplify everything, we need to make its life uncomfortable.

"Switch AT off for a while!"

We need to either surprise or bore or disconcert our AT processes. In relation to drawing, this can mean drawing upside down, very slowly, very fast or at weird angles. We will make it real hard for the mind to understand what it's looking at. Your depth elevators are right there, behind the AT veils. Once you practice regularly these strategies you will be able to remove those veils at once without intermediate steps.

"So these are techniques that eventually become second nature."

Yes. Some of these strategies to make complexity visible and accessible include upside down drawing, repetitive or slow acts, rapid sketches, meditation, focusing on negative spaces...

Once you discover the feeling of bypassing your AT filters through drawing, it will be easier for you to find that same feeling in your relationships, business projects and other challenges.

What's in a line?

Before we tackle the challenge of bypassing our AT filters, let's feel it first, let's literally make it visible.

Load this online address in your computer:

[Web] torchprinciple.com/lines1

Draw the lines you see in there. Do it quickly, don't think much about it. They are simple lines. Draw them on any paper you have around you.

"All righty, easy, done."

Great. Now go to this other address:

[Web] torchprinciple.com/lines2

"Ooh!"

Yes, what you see in this second address is what you have been drawing a moment ago.

"It would have felt so different if I had first seen these second versions instead of the previous ones…"

Indeed. It was easy for you to work with the first versions because your AT processes could not recognize and label the subjects. Not being able to recognize any previous pattern in those lines, they gave you a free pass to the raw detail you had in front of you.

If you had started with the second versions, things would have been different. For those with strong AT muscles it would have been more complicated for sure. You would try to draw the real lines, but AT would interfere trying to simplify the process and drive you towards previous interpretations of the concept it identified in those lines.

"I get it, distracting our AT processes so that they cannot label what we are observing is one of the ways of training ourselves to access the raw complexity in front of us."

Yes, and this works with drawing and with anything else. We have to be careful not to label people around us, for example. If we do so, we stop seeing them for what they are now, and instead we are seeing the old label, the simplification that has nothing to do with the raw reality of that person today, in this very moment.

If you have problems seeing a person, a project or a market in a fresh way, if you suspect that you are seeing them under the heavy and distorted influence of your AT filters, change the context around them. Move them somewhere else. Change their context. Make it difficult for your AT processes to connect them with previous interpretations that will simplify your perception of them.

"Now I understand why sometimes travelling can change and renew completely our perspective about something…"

Let's see more strategies. Sighting is another way that has been used historically to both understand and bypass these conscious filters when working with visuals.[35] It has been used by great artists like Durer, Leonardo or Degas.

Sighting consists in setting up a 2D transparent surface with a grid in front of the subject we are drawing. The 3D world is projected onto the 2D grid. The grid lines give us a more precise and objective way of measuring and understanding what is in front of us.

We can study the relationships, edges, proportions, negative spaces and other parameters directly on the grid, which helps us access directly the detail and complexity that we are facing. We are then able to compare and understand relationships and proportions without AT getting in the middle.

The basic method consists in lining up 3 points, one eye (closing the other one), a small circle in the grid and a point in the subject. That way we establish a point of reference/view. Then we can begin to draw. If we move the head we can simply return to that reference of the 3 points just mentioned.

"What if I cannot build such a grid at this moment?"

A simpler variation of this technique is using a simple pencil. Hold it at arm's length (as a movable grid line) to check angles and other perceptual data.

"I get it, I can estimate sizes, angles, etc., by using a pencil as a sort of temporary grid line that I can position wherever I like in front of the subject."

Yes, practicing with this and similar techniques allows you to eventually access the complexity of your perception directly without these aids. They are a great way to train how to activate CT quickly whenever you tackle complex challenges.

Outside of drawing, if you need to bypass your AT filters, consider positioning your challenge close to objective reference points you can trust. If you think your view of a person is distorted by your AT processes, speak with people you trust that know both of you. Speaking to them could help you break thorough the influence of your AT habits. If you think that your view of the status of your business project is distorted because it is heavily influenced or constrained by AT processes, consider studying other business ventures in the same field. They can provide a good reference to compare to, helping you break through the analytical distortions.

"I understand that trustworthy reference points can not only help us in drawing, but also in relationships and business ventures. In everything in general."

Let's see yet another way, negative spaces.

The positive in the negative

If we focus on a hand, it is easy to identify it and label it as a "hand". It is harder to go deeper and see it in terms of the edges and shapes it is made of.

But if we focus instead on what surrounds the hand, it is easier not to name or label those surroundings. And yet, we are still accessing the same edges, the ones shared by the hand and its surroundings.

So another way to bypass the analytical controls of the mind is to shift our attention to what surrounds our challenge instead of to the challenge itself. The challenge may be a shape we want to draw or a business solution we want to find. Whatever it is, our mind's analytical processes feel at ease when confronted with recognizable entities.

That's why changing your focus to the fuzzier spaces in between or to whatever surrounds your challenge, is a useful way to avoid past labels and judgments, and access fresher and more updated perspectives.

"I can see how this can help me prevent falling on the cliffs of closure too fast."

Yes, seeing the negative spaces of a challenge helps us avoid tunnel vision, the narrowing of focus that intense analysis of your subject can provoke.

"I'm enjoying this, give me more strategies please."

Depth gets real

AT doesn't have an easy personality. It is impatient, rather square and inflexible, and does not like to waste time. We all know some people with similar personalities. They can be highly efficient at their jobs, but you wouldn't enjoy living with them 24/7. It is the same way with AT. It is great at what it does but you don't want to be hanging around AT 24/7. You really don't.

So how do we get rid of this friend from time to time?

Analysis and language work at high abstraction levels, away from complexity and extreme detail. That's why one of the best ways to go beyond the constraints of analysis is forcing yourself to study any subject in great depth and detail, and for a long time. The longer the better. The deeper and longer you stay on the details of a subject, the easier it will be to "deactivate" your analytical filters as your subject gets fragmented into multiple parts, which are harder for the mind to label.

"So one of the ways to tame AT is to literally bore it to death!"

You could put it that way. When you look at any subject that is easy to recognize, such as a face, AT processes get to work immediately. But what happens when you go deeper, when you focus your attention on a part of your subject, and very, very slowly begin to observe its details?

"Give me an example."

Let's return to drawing. Take a paper and a pencil. Put your attention on an object nearby, maybe your hand. Focus on a small part of it and begin to draw its contour, but really, really slowly. It is not important how precise you are. What matters is that you keep moving very slowly. As you keep moving through the contour, AT finds nothing to label and it enters uncharted territory.

"It is as if we are starving AT..."

AT slowly fades away, disconnects and turns off (metaphorically speaking of course). You begin to feel more and more connected to what is in front of you. It is not a hand anymore. You now observe the specific curves, shadows, highlights, hills and valleys that your eyes are moving through, the specific concrete "reality" of that subject.

Staying on a subject facilitates the decomposition of that subject into its parts. It opens the gates to deeper layers of complexity.

"I can really feel a shift as I practice this."

A great way to train your CT muscles and emphasize this experience is by not looking at the paper while you draw. Don't worry at all about the actual result, it does not matter what the final drawing looks like. What we are training here is how to see beyond the analytical filters, how to access the raw complexity in front of us. Keep your eyes on the object and move eyes and pencil at the same time.

"It feels as if the pencil, the eyes and the point in the object I'm looking at, are all one and the same."

Experience that amazing feeling of connection, of being in close contact with something you cannot label because its complexity is unique. It is truly a special moment, the one you are now exploring. EyeDriving is how I like to call this experience.

And even though the result is not important in this exercise, you will notice that the final drawings have something special. They are very genuine, expressive and connected to the complexity that surrounds us.

"It feels so special, freeing myself for those moments from the controlling AT processes."

Beyond drawing, you can apply this strategy to anything. Interact slowly and in detail with a human being to go beyond AT simplifications and access the true complexity of that being. Work slowly and in great detail with a part of your business venture to deactivate AT simplifications and swim in its raw complexity.

Another way to go beyond AT is to not give it time to act. AT is sequential and slow, the opposite of the spontaneous and fast CT processes. If you engage with your subject in very quick and spontaneous ways, AT has problems processing and labelling the information, and this can allow you to go deeper, beyond the AT filters. We will use this strategy in one of the exercises of this module.

"Lots of ways to bypass the AT filters!"

The more we do these exercises, the faster we learn to transition between AT and CT. Drawing is just an example and a great way to practice these transitions. But this can be applied to any creative challenge. In the end, it is all about accessing and understanding complexity by shifting our thinking from higher to lower levels of abstraction, from the more abstract and generic to the more specific and raw, before we return to high abstraction when we need to refine, evaluate and communicate our findings.

In summary, innovating with complex challenges requires that we first go beyond the simplifying abstractions of AT.

Let's pick another example, relationships. It is comfortable and deceptively efficient to judge another human being from the heights of abstraction, logic and past memories. But memory and logic are anchored in a past that is no more. We are oversimplifying complex scenarios, and that often leads to mistakes.

What happens when we tame AT by giving CT a chance? When we observe not a "person" filtered by past memories, but that specific person, our partner, right now. And we hear, see and experience the full complexity in front of us, truly engaging with the reality of that unique human being at this very moment.

It's our choice as adults if we want to make the effort to exercise our CT muscles and engage life in deeper ways. If we do so, we will often find that beyond past judgements and labels there was a lot more to discover, extremely valuable information and insights that can change and influence our view of that person in very powerful ways. Ways that shallow logic can never dream of.

Visual brainstorming

Let's use two visual brainstorming techniques to explore new insights connected to our challenge. We will be working with gesture and analog drawings.

You can apply these two exercises to any kind of challenge you have, personal or professional, linked to another human being, a business venture or anything else.

Gesture drawing, flying past the filters

We spoke previously about quick drawings as another way to go beyond AT.

"Engaging with our subject in quick and spontaneous ways can help us go beyond slow AT processes."

- Let's try it with a drawing. Prepare a blank paper or screen (if using a digital brush). Visualize your challenge and then draw as fast as you can.
  "And what should I draw?"
- The key is not to analyze or think about what you should draw. You should visualize your challenge or parts of it, and

then let your hand move as it wishes. Let it move spontaneously, without concerning yourself with what is being
created.
"This requires trust and belief."
Yes, it requires trusting that something exists beyond
conscious analytical thinking. It requires letting go. And
as you let go, you begin to feel your subconscious and your
CT processes gradually coming to life.
"I visualize, I let go, I trust!"

- Let the pen flow without restrictions. AT will eventually
disengage. At quick speeds AT finds it too hard to perform
its slow processes. You have to trust that powerful way of
processing information that requires trust and space to
perform its magic.

- Insights may come to your mind as you perform the exercise or after you finish, when you evaluate your drawing.
Make sure to note them down.

Quick spontaneous reactions remind us as well of the power of
our intuition when interacting with other human beings, with business projects or any other challenge. Before AT has time to simplify
our scenarios and contexts, our initial hunches can provide raw
unfiltered information that is powerful and crucial.

Another way to take advantage of the power of visuals is
performing analog drawings.

Analog drawings

Betty Edwards introduced a lot of readers to analog drawings in her
excellent book "Drawing on the Artist Within".[36] Analog drawings
are visual expressions of our challenge. They create a visual analogy
of the challenge we are working on and allow us to visualize and
manipulate complexity using the power of visual languages.

We want to illuminate what is present in our minds of which we
are not aware consciously. We will be looking for things that puzzle
us, seem out of place or pop into focus.

- To create an analog drawing, first hold your challenge in your mind. Visualize it. Grab pen and paper, or your graphic tablet.

- Think of your challenge in terms of its boundaries and edges. What are the different areas and parts you can identify? What are the boundaries that separate them?

- How much space is occupied by the challenge itself and how much by the negative spaces? Can those amounts change? Think of the relationship of the whole of your challenge to its parts and vice versa.
  Think of the negative spaces. What can you see in those areas? Sometimes it is easier to reflect on the negative spaces of the challenge rather than on the challenge itself. Negative spaces are harder to categorize and label by the mind, so they provide a fresh perspective on the situation.

- Now reflect on the lights and shadows of the challenge. What is fuzzy and unknown, hidden from view? What is clear and obvious? Reflect as well on what you consider positive and negative in the challenge.

- Study the proportions and relationships between the different areas, the global and local perspectives. Let your pen flow, let it draw whatever it wants. Don't attempt to control the process too much. You don't want AT to take total control of the exercise, restricting the potential outcomes. The trick is to let CT be the main driver while using AT to evaluate our findings. Be courageous. Let your creative mind speak for itself.

You should visually communicate all of the above through the drawing.

"How precise should the drawing be?"

Not precise at all. A person can be represented by a line, a circle or any other shape. You don't need to actually draw a person. Same applies to any other concept.

Explore the challenge leaving words behind, using your perceptual and visual skills to grasp the challenge as a whole as well as its different parts. And within those, the different areas, edges, negative spaces, proportions, relationships, lights and shadows that you find.

"I will need to use words and language to evaluate and record conclusions and insights."

Yes, AT is essential to record, refine, evaluate and communicate any insights that you find during this process.

As you evaluate your drawing, go further, challenge your results and introduce glitches and what-if questions. Put the drawing upside down, try to find different interpretations for what you see. Remember Alexander Fleming, he saw a cure where others saw just mold.[37]

In summary:

- **View the challenge as a whole** made up of many parts.
- **Go beyond words and concepts**, open yourself to your perceptions and visualizations.
- **Identify the space occupied by the challenge** and the negative spaces around it. Can they change?
- **Identify the relationships** between the whole and the parts.
- **Challenge your visualization**, change the angles and introduce extra elements.
- **Look for new interpretations** of your visualization.
- **Explore the lights and shadows** of the challenge. Try to go deeper in the areas that are clear and bright in order to reach insights about the areas that are in shadow.
- **Look for, identify and explore** the unique traits of the challenge. Pay attention to anything that puzzles you, seems odd or draws your attention.
- **Finally, think of sighting again.** Find the constants in your drawing or other reference points connected to your challenge (your virtual grid lines). Check the drawing and

your challenge against those constants, just as you would do when sighting.

- **Evaluate relationships and proportions**. At all times look for harmony and resonance.

After you are done, bring back AT to analyze the results and note down any new insights. Visualize the picture you have created. Remember it, let it settle on your mind. Notice the whole and the parts. Now you can wait for incubation to keep providing new insights.

Gesture and analog drawings possess a special kind of beauty. They are very deep and genuine, and are very connected with the complexity that exists beyond the AT filters.

The resistance effect

While attempting these exercises, your mind will resist at first.

"I definitely felt that."

We are pushing our mind to deal with something truly new, unique and specific. Something that we don't want to interpret as a generic symbol, but as a complex reality which we can express with the infinite language of visuals. Dealing with reality at this level, when our CT muscles are weak, requires some effort and the mind will resist. You must persist in these processes until they begin to become habitual. Re-educate your mind.

The target is to find a harmonious balance so that you can efficiently go through your daily life with the help of AT and innovate, create and work with complexity with the help of CT when needed.

Gesture
Improvising your way to new insights

Tools: Our body, paper and pencil.

Video examples of some of the exercises in this section:
[Web] **torchprinciple.com/gesture**

In the previous modules we have exercised our CT muscles through language and visuals. Now we will be adding movement, gesture and improvisation/spontaneity to the equation. Involving our body while exercising our CT muscles is very beneficial. Our thoughts have a direct impact on body posture and health. And vice versa. Working with our bodies we can help our mind find new insights about our challenges.

The potential of spontaneity and expressiveness

Spontaneous performance and expressiveness can surprise AT and provide other ways of bypassing the censors of the mind. In this module we will cover different exercises that will empower your spontaneity and expressiveness.

Some of the exercises require that you move around. Therefore, we recommend that you find a large enough space to do them in.

Celebrate failure

We begin with a great exercise for loosening up and shaking away any fears that could block our spontaneity.

"I have some of those, I get worried about what others will think of me…"

Many of our fears are centered on what our perceived failure may mean to others. So what happens if we embrace this so called "failure" in front of them?

"Embrace it?"

Did you know that making yourself laugh even when you don't feel like it can have a dramatic impact on how you actually feel? The body can influence the mind as much as the mind influences the body.

"Forcing ourselves to feel or think in a direction can actually begin to move us in that direction."

Yes, so let's put a twist on the word failure. Let's celebrate it!

- This exercise is best done with a group. Gather friends, or even better, people who don't know you well.
- Tell yourself and those around you how happy you are because you have failed. Explain how many opportunities this "failure" opens for you.
- Start slow and quiet and build it up until you are shouting it, singing it, declaring it with all your energy.
- Channel your energy with enthusiasm. Declare how happy you are that you have failed, because failing opens so many new doors to you.
- Keep building it up. The more intensity you put into it, the more liberating and refreshing the experience will be.

Do this exercise whenever you feel that fear is preventing you from exercising your full spontaneity.

And now it's time to move that body.

Acting your challenge

Einstein used to visualize himself being part of the challenges he was working on.[38] The best way to understand something is to be right in the middle of it.

In this exercise you are going to act your challenge. You will pretend to be your challenge, part of it or involved with it in some way.

"Exciting! Tell me how!"

- Find a wide space where you can walk and move freely.
- Visualize the challenge in your mind at all times.
- Don't speak during this exercise. We will only use movement and gesture. We want to avoid triggering AT processes too much.
- As you visualize the challenge, let your body move however it wants. Imagine that you are the challenge itself or part of it or that you are inside of it.
- Move, let your body express the challenge.
- Be alert to any insight that comes to your mind and make a note of it.

Ideation dynamics

When we expand the previous exercise to involve a group of participants, the results can be spectacular.

- We first select a challenge and enlist a group of participants to work on it.
- We typically adopt a circular configuration for a start. Then we represent different parts of the challenge through the movements and performance of the participants.
- A director and moderator can intervene at different points to add or eliminate elements and to pose questions or change the context.

Imagine that our challenge is finding out an idea to create a mobile application that connects runners with each other while promoting healthy sport to the masses.

Two or three participants will represent the runners. Another will represent a sedentary person at home. Another will represent a reward located somewhere in the city. Another will represent a mobile phone. And so on and so forth. Once we have all the important parts of the challenge represented, we can start to act them.

The fine details of the process go beyond the scope of this book, which is focused on individual exercises and your interaction with others, but if you are interested in this deep form of ideation I recommend you join one of our workshops. Contact us anytime on **ideami@ideami.com**.

Let's now review other ways to exercise your spontaneity.

Accept and build

It is easy to keep repeating old patterns instead of innovating. It is comfortable to stay in the safe zone, judging and overanalyzing new possibilities, finding excuses and obstacles with anything that is different.

As you may recall, closure, arriving to premature conclusions, is one of the biggest enemies of innovation and creativity. And one of the easiest ways to tighten and paralyze your creative muscles is by rushing to judge things, to find issues with anything new that comes our way. We call it the "Yes, but…" behavior.

"Yes, but…"

You see? There you go. Instead we should train ourselves in the art of the "Yes, and…"

"Yes, but…"

Wait there. What if in order to train our CT muscles, we made a habit out of always adding to things, always saying yes, always contributing in constructive ways.

"Yes! And I can see how this could accelerate the finding of new insights!"

Exactly. "Yes, and...", means focusing on adding something constructive to whatever comes our way.

"It feels challenging to have to find always something to add..."

A philosophy of adding can feel scary at first. We feel that we will soon run out of ideas. But when you try your best to add something interesting within all sorts of scenarios, you need to improvise solutions quickly, and that stretches your creative muscles and makes them stronger and more flexible.

With time, your CT muscles will find it easier and easier to come up with interesting additions to whatever is thrown in front of you.

"It gets easier the more we do it. It's just like training any other kind of muscle."

- Find a friend to do this exercise. Do the exercise in either one direction or in both if your friend is also working on a challenge.

- Explain your challenge to your partner.

- Your partner then asks you questions about your challenge. To help you diverge and stretch your creative muscles, these questions should be as shocking and even as absurd as possible. Your partner will try to ask the most unusual questions he/she can think of.

- No matter what your partner asks, you must answer with a "Yes, and..." as fast as possible. It is important that you answer immediately. This stops AT processes from interfering.

- Then suspend all judgment and follow with whatever comes to your mind. You are improvising a way to connect in a useful way the question to the challenge.

These absurd questions surprise your AT and contribute to activate your CT, forcing you to open new avenues in the mind, transforming the questions into doors to potentially useful insights.

To push our CT muscles even more, the key in this exercise is that we have to react as fast as possible to the questions. Similar to the gesture drawing exercise of the previous module, this fast reaction prevents our AT processes from engaging. Instead we force ourselves to diverge and move away from typical solutions.

Note down any interesting ideas and later evaluate them and refine them with your AT.

By combining unexpected questions and fast reactions to those questions, we are stretching our CT muscles, diverging in big ways before we converge to useful insights.

The invisible gift

Excitement and motivation shake up your mind and help trigger new connections. In this exercise we give each other an invisible gift that contains seeds for new insights. You will work with a friend or partner.

- Choose a random word, one as unusual and unconnected to the challenge as possible. You can use the SK-Engine, the SK-General tool, a dictionary or any other way to generate it. Write it on a paper and transform the paper into a ball or something similar so that the word cannot be seen. Then give it to your partner. The paper represents your unique gift.

- When preparing the gift, imagine that it contains something really special. Wrap it with care and give it with intention.

- When you accept a gift, imagine this is the gift you had always been waiting for. Express your joy and excitement. Open the gift and call out loud what is written on the paper.

- Immediately explain why the gift is so important for you. Establish a connection between the gift and your challenge, and celebrate it. Stimulated by the mysterious gift, embrace the risk of jumping into the unknown. This process forces you diverge and to come up with something unexpected and original connected with the challenge.

It is again essential that we react as fast as possible after we find out what the gift is, to prevent AT from interfering too much.

Note down any interesting ideas triggered by the process.

By combining unexpected gifts and fast reactions to those gifts, we are again stretching our CT muscles, diverging in big ways before we converge to useful insights.

Story exchange

The very same story can take on a completely different character and meaning depending on the way it is delivered and on who is delivering it. What happens when somebody else takes temporary ownership of your challenge?

- Work in pairs again. Take temporary ownership of each other's challenge.

- Explain to your partner his/her challenge as if it was yours. Explain also any potential solution to the challenge that comes to your mind. Be enthusiastic as you explain it. This enthusiasm is key. It will quickly make you feel that the challenge is yours.

- Add new details as you speak. Let new insights join the process as they happen. Do the same the other way.

- If you are in a group, switch partners and repeat the process with more people. The more, the better.

This process encourages cross-pollination of insights. Your ideation process is being enriched through the perspectives of your peers.

And once again, speed is key in order to bypass AT filters and habits.

Now or never

Imagine you are trying to sell your challenge to an invisible investor. Your life and future depend on it. It is now or never. By being invisible, this investor will activate your imagination.

- Throughout the exercise, focus on being spontaneous. Don't overanalyze, go with the flow.
- Visualize your challenge and the invisible investor. Speak to the investor as if he/she was standing right in front of you. Make your best to impress him/her.
- Explain to this invisible investor why this challenge is so important.
- Explain to the investor what solutions you propose to solve the challenge.

As you keep doing the exercise, you may find yourself bringing up unexpected angles and finding new insights. Note them down quickly!

Fairy tale

Fantasy and fairy tales stimulate our imagination. They shoot for the stars. They are a great way to diverge through originality and creativity.

- Tell your challenge, solution or idea to your partner or to the group as if it was a fairy tale. Involve fantastic characters, improvise the wildest possible angles. No boundaries, it is supposed to be a tale after all!
- If you have problems to begin, you may use the traditional fairy tale structure:
  "Once upon a time, everyday… But one day… Because of that… (repeat), until finally…, ever since then…, and the

moral is… (optional)". But you don't really need to. You may deliver your tale in any way that feels best.

Blind driver

Life is full of distractions. What happens when we focus all our attention in just one of our senses? In this exercise your partner blindfolds you. Contextual music is played in the background. You can use sounds of the sea, a jungle, city streets, etc. Any ambient track related to a specific location or context will work.

- As you listen to the sounds, imagine you are being driven in a car, a boat or a plane, searching for solutions for your challenge.
- Describe what your mind visualizes. Connect it with your challenge. Let the sounds speak to you and guide you towards novel insights.
- Your partner will take notes of any insights that arise during the process.

We are diverging before we converge, by combining unexpected contextual sounds with visualization and storytelling.

Create soundscapes

Storytelling improves information retention and recall. Good stories stimulate as many of your senses as possible. Soundscapes are a great way to influence your thought processes in unexpected directions.
"What is a soundscape?"
A soundscape (or soundmap) is a soundtrack that contains ambient sounds from a specific scenario or context. For example, a jungle, rainfall, ocean waves, cars on the streets, people chatting at a market, etc.

Great soundscapes enrich CT processes. Involve soundscapes in some of the exercises of this chapter any time you feel like. Create and switch contexts while you exercise your CT muscles. Go from a jungle to a beach, from a war zone to deep space. Unexpected contexts can help you diverge more and bring tremendous value to your creative processes.

Other variations

Here are some suggestions to further exercise your spontaneity and improvisation capabilities.

- Use extremes to encourage novel and original combinations. Set your challenge in extreme environments or involve extreme characters with it.

- While you go about your life, keep exercising your CT muscles with this exercise: wherever you are, in a street or a bus, look at people around you. Imagine their life before and after that moment. What is their story? How does it relate to you and/or your challenge? Allow your imagination to take you to unexpected places.

- Whatever your current context is, imagine that it is taking place within a film. Who are you in this film? What is happening? What could happen next? How does it relate to your life and/or challenge?

Pattern
Navigating complexity

Tools: For this module you will need any kind of camera. A mobile phone is good enough.

Video examples of some of the exercises in this section:
[Web] **torchprinciple.com/pattern**

The power of texture

Textures and patterns are very important for creative thinkers. They offer infinite variety and unpredictability and excite our visual centers and by extension our mind. Texture shakes our subconscious pot.

"What do we mean by texture?"

In this module we are especially interested in what I call anonymous textures. We define an anonymous texture as any visual detail captured up close that doesn't trigger an immediate process of labeling and categorizing by our AT processes.

"Visual detail that we cannot immediately name or identify."

If you can immediately name it (rose, door, hand, tree), it is not an anonymous texture. If you cannot call it anything at first, you could find yourself in front of a texture elevator.

The texture elevator

Do you remember when we talked about the depth elevator? I want to introduce you to another fascinating elevator: the texture elevator.

We have all at some point looked at beautiful clouds trying to guess what character, form or shape they reminded us of. Likewise with coffee stains or scratches on a wall.

Looking at anonymous textures of any kind is like getting on board an elevator that takes you down to the roots of all visual stimuli. Once there, it is possible to connect with other elevators that take us back up to a whole new different set of figures and concepts.

Just like random words, these textures help us to diverge strongly on our way towards new insights. You can see them as analogs of wormholes in physics. Ways to quickly diverge, to connect with far away conceptual locations.

Which insights are triggered depends on the combination of your stored knowledge, your subconscious processes and your current context.

"New insights are around the corner!"

Delivering texture through light

Even though we can speak about texture in connection with all our senses (hearing, touch and even taste), visual textures offer the greatest flexibility and power.

Einstein preferred to use mental images rather than words when working on challenges.[39] For him, the fuzzy and open nature of visuals was a great analogy to the complexity of life and its challenges. Words were too constraining. They had a fixed and static nature.

Leonardo Da Vinci enjoyed immersing himself in the stains of walls and similar textures, using them to trigger novel connections in his mind.[40]

An image has infinite interpretations. In the Seed module we went from words to the wide subconscious and back. Now we will swim in visual textures and connect them back with language. Words will help us communicate and evaluate the insights triggered by the textures.

Walk your way to new insights

In the first stage of this module, you will work on your own. While interacting with the textures avoid language, as it can interfere with your CT processes.

Working with anonymous textures can be hard at first. So we will get there gradually by working first at higher and more conceptual levels before moving down to the deepest and more perceptual ones.

Paint seeds of external light (conceptual level, recognizable textures)

In this first exercise, you will use your camera to take photos of objects that suggest interesting connections with your challenge. We begin with objects that you can recognize and label.

- Scout the spaces around you, go out to the streets or to interesting locations.
  "The more diverse the better!"
- Visualize your challenge as you do the exercise.
- Paint the sensor of your camera with the most interesting light you find around.
- On this first stage, focus on large areas and objects that you can name. These objects can quickly be categorized and labeled by your mind.
- Capture anything that you find interesting or anything which directly suggests something about your challenge. You are using reflected light to paint your digital sensor with visuals.
- Be alert to any insights triggered by the process and note them down.

Now we go deeper to the really exciting and powerful stuff. Get ready to swim in the beautiful uncertainty of anonymous textures.

Texture spree (anonymous textures)

The key of this very powerful and key exercise is to focus on the type of textures that cannot be immediately categorized and labeled by your mind.

- Pick your camera, work on your own.
- Visualize your challenge as you do the exercise.
- Go on a texture spree wherever you are. Focus on the small details that cannot be named or categorized by your mind.
- Capture ashes, stains, strange shapes, anything that seems peculiar, unique or interesting. Whatever you capture may quickly suggest a connection to your challenge. Or, instead, it may just excite your curiosity, asking to be recorded and preserved for later analysis.
- Be alert to any insights produced during or after the capturing process and note them down.

Ride down the texture elevators with an open attitude. Keep your challenge in the back of your mind and let those anonymous textures shake your subconscious pot.

On your computer

You may also use the tools **SK-Light** and **Texture Drawing** to explore anonymous textures from your computer or tablet.
[Web] **torchprinciple.com/lightstorm**
[Web] **torchprinciple.com/texturedrawing**

Paint seeds of internal light

This is an optional variation of the first exercise in which we will use our own brain as the sensor that will capture the internal light generated by the mind.

- Close your eyes.

- Visualize your challenge as you do the exercise.

- Activate soundscapes. Play them in the background. Optionally, a recording or another participant may also utter random words in combination with the soundscape.

- Let the soundscapes (and optionally also the words) trigger images in your mind. Visualize freely. Your brain is painting with light triggered from your subconscious.

- Be alert to any insights triggered by the process and note them down.

Gesture photography

In this exercise we diverge even more by using randomness to capture textures.

- Pick your camera, work on your own.

- Visualize your challenge as you do the exercise.

- Take pictures randomly. Close your eyes or don't look in the direction in which you point the camera.

- Move your body as you take the pictures and use the zoom control. This facilitates the creation of anonymous textures, textures that are hard for your analytical mind to quickly label. This encourages creative divergence.

- Contemplate the photos that you have taken.

- Select those that either excite your curiosity, asking to be recorded and preserved for later analysis, or those that quickly suggest a connection to your challenge.

- Be alert to any insights produced during or after the capturing process and note them down.

- Ride down the texture elevators with an open attitude. Keep your challenge in the back of your mind and let those anonymous textures shake your subconscious pot.

Metaphor walk

The camera allows you to capture textures and preserve them for later analysis. Now it's the time to go bold and use a different kind of sensor to capture the light around you.

- Your eyes are now your camera.
  "And quite a great camera this one is!"
- This camera, your eye, has less reliable long-term storage so you will have to connect deeper, closer and faster with the textures you find.
- Walk around, explore objects, textures and patterns.
- Visualize your challenge as you do the exercise.
- Be alert to any unexpected connections with your challenge.
- When you find something interesting, stay with it, absorb the moment, swim into the texture.
- Note down any connections.

Sharing feedback

If you have done the previous exercises within a group, it is now the time to enrich each other's interpretations.

- Work in couples, choose a partner. Switch partners every few minutes or as often as you want.
- Explain your challenge to your partner and then show your partner the pictures you captured. Listen to your partner's interpretation of your pictures in connection with your challenge. Do the same with the challenge and pictures of your partner.
- Explain your own interpretations of your pictures and listen to the feedback of your partner. Do the same the other way around.
- Note down any new insights.

Emotion

Tools: SK-Haiku.

Video examples of some of the exercises in this section:
[Web] torchprinciple.com/emotion

Understanding emotions and communicating from the heart is key to address our personal and professional challenges.

Besides, managing the emotions of customers and users is a key part of what makes a business succeed nowadays.

In this module we will use poetic writing to exercise our emotional muscles.

A gateway made of words

A poem is an emotional window to our subconscious. It is a gateway made of words, a gateway that stimulates our CT.

Beyond symbols

Poems are all about challenging our habitual abstractions, our conventional ways of looking at the world. The best way to enjoy a poem is to avoid early judgments and interpretations. We should instead absorb it naturally, involving our emotions and all our senses, riding on the emotional elevators to the perceptual kingdom, letting the poem express itself anyway it wants.

"Poems invite us to diverge emotionally."

Literal interpretations of poems constrain their potential and prevent us from riding down the emotional elevators.

We want instead to feel the poem deeply, to let it shake our emotions, triggering visualizations and challenging our habitual patterns of thinking.

In Poetry 1+1 doesn't equal 2. Words are empowered by emotions and tinted by our senses, acquiring a profound quality that touches all of our selves.

It is speech that loses its rigidness and becomes a dance of words. It takes on a deeper voice, expressing a melody and a rhythm that move beyond our intellect, touching the deepest areas of our subconscious.

Exercises

As you do the following exercises, visualize your challenge as vividly as possible. Let it speak to you from an emotional perspective.

You may want to walk while you do some of these exercises. Let your body move if it wishes to do so. Don't remain static and constrained.

Random poetry

In this exercise we use haikus. Haikus are small poems made of 3 verses.

- Visualize your challenge as you do the exercise.
- Generate random haikus using the SK-Haiku tool we provide or any other. The SK Haiku tool produces random haikus by generating random mixes of poetic phrases. You can at anytime change all of the phrases at once or just one of them. A single click changes completely the nature of the haiku. Contemplate what comes out in a relaxed way, while you navigate as many random haikus as you like. You are diverging emotionally by bathing your subconscious pot with a diverse mix of emotional ingredients.
- Read the generated poems aloud. Allow the haikus to speak their emotional voice freely. Avoid overanalysis. Keep feeling the haiku until an insight arises. If nothing comes up, switch to a different haiku.

- Don't focus literally on the words. Instead feel the emotions triggered by the phrases.

The haikus help you diverge emotionally. Each combination of phrases/words can trigger many different emotional waves on you. Let those waves move and mutate freely.

Be alert to new insights that may connect your emotional waves and the challenge.

If your creative and emotional muscles are not strong enough and nothing comes up, you can try a more systematic approach.

- Attempt to express what the haiku is making you feel by means of a word or a series of words.
- Try first with a single word. Reducing the poem to a single word is a powerful and useful exercise in synthesis.
- Attempt to connect the haiku and your verbal interpretation with your challenge.

You don't need to connect the entire haiku with your challenge. It may be just one part of the haiku or a part of one of the phrases that provides an interesting connection.

Be patient. It takes practice to bypass your AT filters in order to fully access your emotional centers. Wait and notice any insights that pop in your mind connected to your challenge. Don't question them, welcome them.

In some cases, you may need minutes, hours or days of incubation to trigger interesting connections. Note down your haikus and/or synthesis words and return to them later on when insights pop up in your mind.

Innovators and creative people are proactive. In the next few exercises, we gradually begin to take the lead in the process of generating these haikus.

Follow the lead

- Visualize your challenge as you do the exercise.

- Generate a random poetic phrase, just one, using the SK-Haiku tool or any similar tool. The SK-Haiku tool always shows three phrases but you will pick just one of them for a start.

- Choose a phrase that somehow piques your curiosity, one that you feel drawn towards intuitively.

- Begin with it and continue the haiku by yourself, improvising the next phrases in ways that connect with your challenge.

- The phrase you picked becomes the first one of the haiku. The next two come from you.

- Feel the first phrase, don't overanalyze it. Let it speak to you emotionally. Then continue the haiku.

- Think of the "Yes, and" exercise. Voice the first phrase and quickly and immediately improvise the next two. Speed prevents AT from interfering too much. Quickly improvise the continuation of the haiku in ways that connect to your challenge. This is a great way to exercise your emotional and creative muscles, diverging before you converge onto useful insights.

- Focus on visualizing and expressing emotions, beginning from the first random poetic seed and branching out into the next phrases. Connect them with your challenge.

On your own

Now it's the moment to gather even more courage and try the whole process on your own.

- Visualize your challenge as you do the exercise.

- Generate three random words with the SK-Engine tool or any similar one.

- Choose words that you feel drawn towards intuitively.
- Construct a haiku that includes one of those words in each line of the poem.
- Feel the phrases and the emotions they generate. Relate them to your challenge.
- Note down any new insights.

Stream of emotion

Remember gesture drawing? It was a strategy for bypassing our AT filters, by bombarding our senses with quick visual gestures that were too fast for our AT to interpret.

Now think of an infinite haiku, an infinite poem. A constant stream that challenges your habitual thinking patterns through the magic of emotion.

- Visualize your challenge as you do the exercise.
- Generate haiku phrases continuously with the SK-Haiku tool or a similar one.
- Voice them with energy and intention as you move around, wherever you are.
- Keep the never-ending stream of emotion flowing, avoid judging, let it flow, let it speak. Feel the emotions it triggers.
- Be alert to any insights arising in connection with your challenge or with yourself and annotate them.

Increase the hooks

Increase the power of these exercises by involving other senses and skills. Draw some of your haikus, act them or dance them. Involve all of yourself.

Sharing feedback

If you have done the previous exercises with a group, it's again time to enrich each other's interpretations.

- Work in couples, choose a partner. Switch partners every few minutes or as often as you want.

- Explain your challenge to your partner and show him/her the haiku you selected or built. Listen to your partner's interpretation of your haiku in connection with your challenge. Do the same with the challenge and haiku of your partner.

- Explain your own interpretations of your haiku and listen to the feedback of your partner. Do the same the other way around.

Context

Tools: SK-Language.

Video examples of some of the exercises in this section:
[Web] **torchprinciple.com/context**

In this module, we combine language with performance, spontaneity and sound to produce another powerful exercising mix.

Each language we learn provides a whole new perspective on life. It does so through a unique culture, a unique abstraction of the complexity that surrounds us. The nuances and features of each language and the way it is used, shape attitudes and behaviors of entire societies.

New Scientist magazine states in his article of May 8, 2012:
[Web] **torchprinciple.com/languagearticle**

"Speaking a second language can change everything from problem-solving skills to personality."

It shakes up your personality and your perspective on life and it is a chance to look at the world through an alternative lens.

"Almost as if you were different people!"

In this module we will use a language you haven't practiced before to help us diverge and to dive into different perspectives as you shake your creative thinking.

Before going there, it is important to understand both the benefits as well as the challenges languages bring us.

Challenges and benefits

A key challenge with language is the danger of interpreting abstractions as raw data, or words as actual things.

Creative thinking deals with specific areas and domains. Within them it can be flexible and highly detailed. In contrast, analytical thinking transcends contexts by using abstractions. These can become too separated from the actual experience that inspired them.

We can view language as a consensus about the world, a way to simplify and accelerate how we classify it, describe it and explain it.

It is an approximation of reality, a way to communicate our experience that has been chosen by others and which may not fit our personal experience in the best way.

"No wonder misunderstandings may occur when we communicate with others."

Therefore:

- Language simplifies complexity and also makes it more impersonal.
- It skips detail and approximates reality.
- It introduces terms and elements that don't always match the real details of the experience.

As we have explained previously, these simplified abstractions are sometimes not the right tools to face the complexity of our world. Many challenges are best tackled through the contemplating and wider nature of creative thinking.

However, languages also bring very important benefits that can accelerate the discovery of new insights.

- They allow us to quickly partition, rearrange and recombine our knowledge in new ways.
- They encourage divergence by shifting our high level perspective to a different set of symbols. This can help in finding unexpected angles for our challenge.
- Through the combination of multiples contexts, they enrich the process of working with our challenges.
- They allow us to get closer to other cultures and ways to see the world.
- And finally, language and words provide quick windows of access between our mental strategies.

The importance of listening

Language builds meaning over time. To capture that meaning, listening is a key part of the process. In the following exercises, listening to your partners is as important as expressing yourself.

Exercises

We will work with a language that neither you nor your partner understands. You may use the SK-Language tool or any similar one. The SK-Language tool currently supports Indonesian and Spanish. If you speak both languages, Indonesian and Spanish, you may have to create your own variation of the tool in a different language.
[Web] torchprinciple.com/basicindonesian
[Web] torchprinciple.com/indonesianpronunciation

The following exercises can be enriched by having soundmaps active in the background. Soundmaps stimulate our minds and encourage divergence without interfering with the creative process.

Osmosis learning

In this exercise, we shake our creative muscles by learning new words in a new language and then connecting the learning with our challenge through gestures and body language.

After we select a new phrase in the new language, we will have to explain to our partner what the phrase means by using only gestures. Our partner will then try to guess what it all means by watching our gestures and listening to the phrase.

By visualizing our challenge while we combine soundmaps, new phrases in a different language and organic gestures, we are blending spontaneity, expressiveness and language, a powerful mix that can inspire the birth of new insights.

- Hold your challenge in the back of your mind during the whole process.
- Visualize your challenge and the culture associated with the chosen language.
- Use the SK-Language tool to pick a phrase in the chosen language. The SK-Language tool allows you to quickly choose random phrases in the chosen language together with their English translation.
- Pick phrases that pique your curiosity or suggest something connected with your challenge.
- Speak the phrase in the native language. Visualize both your challenge and the context associated with the culture and location of this language.
- Explain the meaning of the phrase to your partner by using only gestures.

- Use gestures and the chosen phrase in the native language. You cannot use any words in your own language.

- While you voice the phrase, be alert to any connection between the phrase, your gesturing and the challenge.

- If you are the one trying to understand the meaning of the phrase, be alert to any connection between the gesturing, the phrase and your own challenge.

- The following is key to understand. It is not important to guess the meaning of the phrase correctly. It is the stretching of your creative muscles that is really useful and that really matters.

- You may link an unusual interpretation of the phrase to your challenge and that may drive you to a great insight even though you may be linking the gestures to a different abstraction/concept than the one your partner intends to communicate to you.
  "Basically, we may interpret the gestures completely wrong. What matters is that we are stretching our creative muscles and any interpretation can lead us to interesting insights connected to our challenge."

- Enjoy the process. Feel yourself absorbing this new language without worrying about grammar or rules. Allow your brain and mind to explore the patterns hidden in the phrases. Learn by fully engaging with the phrase, just as children do.

Contextual travel

This is a powerful exercise that transports you to unpredictable contexts, inviting you to adapt your discourse and thinking to them, which stimulates the generation of novel insights.

We will combine soundmaps with speech, adapting our discourse to the soundmap in the background.

- A contextual soundmap plays in the background. This soundmap expresses a specific location, scenario or event.

Examples are: a war, a restaurant, flying on a plane, a demonstration on the streets, a market in a small town, etc.

- Interact with your partner and with the environment, adapting your behavior and words to the contextual soundmap.

- Explain to your partner your challenge, connecting it fully with the contextual soundmap. Your challenge and your explanation have to make sense in relation to the sound-map. For example, if the soundmap contains sounds of people chatting at a fruit market, your interpretation of your challenge has to fit with that scenario.

- Explain to your partner why it is so vital to solve your challenge and try to come up with a way to solve it that fits with the current context.

- As usual, to prevent AT closure and promote divergence, it is important to react quickly and improvise your explanations as fast as possible.

- Don't force things. If you feel inspired, great. If not, keep the dialogue open with your partner and welcome any feedback and suggestions.

- Remember at all times to keep your words related to the soundmap. If the soundmap refers to a war, you may act as a fugitive or prisoner trying to communicate vital information before the enemy troops arrive. If the soundmap refers to a luxurious recreation space like a Las Vegas hotel, you may act as if you are trying to seduce somebody with your idea.

- Interrogate your partner about his/her challenge. Try to be surprising with the angles you use in your questions. Avoid obvious perspectives. Encourage divergence by challenging your partner.

- If you both speak different languages, feel free to switch languages during the exercise in order to introduce even more contextual variation.

- Switch soundmaps at unpredictable times. You may set an alarm clock to mark the moments of change. If you are doing the exercise in a group, switch partners when the soundmap changes.

Osmosis connection

This is a subtle variation of the first exercise.

- We use random phrases in a new language and explain them to each other with gestures, just as before.
- This time, it is even less important to guess the word or phrase that is being explained to us with gestures. What is key is that we are forced to link in some way the gestures of our partner with our challenge.

This exercise accelerates the divergence-convergence cycle and emphasizes the value of connecting our challenge with unexpected stimuli.

Because as they say in (country chosen)

This exercise provides a powerful mix to further train our creative muscles. By improvising quickly, you will get used to diverge while connecting multiple information sources. The exercise is divided in 3 stages of progressive complexity.

a) Stage 1: Connect + Communicate
- You will connect your challenge with a soundmap and with a random phrase in the new language. You will explain to your partner, in your own language, the connection you created. Using both languages, the phrase and the sound-map, we exercise strongly our creative muscles.
- A contextual soundmap plays in the background. This soundmap expresses a specific location, event or scenario. Examples are: A war, a restaurant, flying on a plane, a demonstration on the streets, a market in a small town, etc.

- Pick a random phrase in the new language.

- Connect in your mind the phrase with your challenge and the soundmap in the best way you can.

- Use the phrase to convince your partner of why your challenge/idea is so important and how it could be solved. Introduce the phrase in the middle of the process of interacting with your partner. This is a great way to further improve and exercise your improvisation skills.

- As you explain (in your own language) to your partner why your challenge is so important, you mention the phrase: "Because as they say in (Indonesia, Spain, etc. depending on what language you are using)", and you add the phrase you picked. Then continue speaking, linking the meaning of that phrase with your challenge and the soundmap in some way.

- Your challenge and your explanation have to make sense in relation to the soundmap.

- Visualize your challenge, the phrase and the soundmap as you do the exercise.

- Optional: You may set an alarm clock and switch regularly the random phrase.

b) Stage 2: Listen + Connect

- You will connect your challenge with a soundmap and with two random phrases in the new language. You will explain to your partner, in your own language, the connection you created. Using both languages, both phrases and the soundmap, we exercise even more our creative muscles.

- Both partners pick a random phrase and show it to each other.

- You need to connect your challenge to your phrase, your partner's phrase and the soundmap. This requires you to reflect, communicate and listen.

- Mention the phrase: "Because as they say in (Indonesia, Spain, etc. depending on what language you are using)", and add the phrase you picked in the new language.

- Explain to your partner why your challenge/idea is so important, based on both phrases and the soundmap.

- Try to improvise a solution to your challenge connected to the phrases and the soundmap.

- Visualize your challenge, the phrases and the soundmap as you do the exercise.

- Be alert to any insights and note them down.

c) Stage 3: Combine + Build

- You will connect a soundmap with two random phrases in the new language. From that connection, you will generate a brand new challenge and you will explain to your partner, in your own language, a solution to that challenge. Using both languages, both phrases and the soundmap to generate a brand new challenge with an associated solution, we exercise even more our creative muscles.

- Both partners pick a random phrase and show it to each other.

- Mention the phrase: "Because as they say in (Indonesia, Spain, etc. depending on what language you are using)", and add the phrase you picked in the new language.

- Visualize the phrases and the soundmap as you do the exercise.

- Try to blend both phrases and the soundmap to produce a new challenge and a new solution.

- Relate the new challenge to both random phrases and the soundmap as you explain to your partner the importance of this challenge and how it could be solved.

- Be alert to any insights and note them down.

Cooling down the muscles with a far-away connection

Time to cool down your creative muscles.

- Do this exercise on your own.
- If possible, play a contextual soundmap in the background.
- Pick a phrase in the new language.
- Reflect on the phrase and connect it to your challenge.
- Speak it, feel it, taste it. Then connect it.
- Document it: Annotate anything interesting that you learn connected to your challenge.

Meditation

Tools: SK-Soundstorming. An alarm clock.

Video examples of some of the exercises in this section:
[Web] **torchprinciple.com/meditation**

The most spontaneous of human sounds are the cries of a baby at birth. From then on, sound becomes a phenomenal way of channeling emotions and stimulating our thinking.

The great catalyst

In times of difficulty, Einstein would play music that exhilarated him.[41] Music can be a great catalyst in the creative process, shifting our thinking in unexpected directions on the shoulders of information patterns and emotions.

In the roots of music we find melody, harmony and rhythm. Melody creates continuity, harmony encourages compatibility and rhythm produces unanimity. Music strives to create order from chaos, reducing entropy within the infinite ocean of acoustic potentials.

When we are feeling dispersed, music can bring order, discipline and structure while still keeping active our most intuitive sides. It is a great bridge between analytical and creative thinking and it excels when both are alive and kicking. Because it needs strong AT and

CT muscles, music requires a deep learning process of many rules and theories, being the most structured of our art forms. Painters or writers may begin ambitious works from the early stages of their careers, while musicians usually require deep and long training in advance.

A matter of trust

Music can become too complex for our AT to deal with it by itself. So music practice and performance benefit greatly from CT processes.

"We need to trust the power of our subconscious pot."

Often, when performing complex pieces of music, the least we try to consciously analyze, follow or explain what we do, the better we do it and vice versa. The slow ways of AT can interfere with our faster ways of processing information. Trusting CT and our subconscious helps us work with complexity.

Attempting to perform by consciously analyzing our actions and adapting those actions to the results of that analysis is too slow and encourages premature closure. That's why some of the most successful musicians in history performed in very intuitive ways, often unable to explain or describe what they were doing.

That's music, a wonderful bridge between the conscious and the subconscious, between analytical and creative thinking.

Exercises

Soundstorming (conceptual level, recognizable sounds)

In this sound meditation exercise, we will use the soundstorming tool you can find and use at:

[Web] **torchprinciple.com/soundstorming**

- Find a quiet place.
- Open a web browser and load the soundstorming tool.
- Sit comfortably and close your eyes.
- You can use the tool in manual or in automatic mode. You can also change other parameters of the experience. Review the instructions of this tool and the others at:
  [Web] torchprinciple.com/guides

- In manual mode, as you move the finger or mouse over the screen, short sounds start to play.
- In automatic mode, sounds start to play automatically and randomly, combining with each other.
- Visualize your challenge taking place.
- Don't analyze, visualize the challenge and feel the sounds around you.
- Your subconscious pot blends the challenge and the random sounds.
- When something interesting comes to mind, open your eyes and make a note of it.

Now get ready to swim in the beautiful uncertainty of anonymous sounds.

Soundstorming (anonymous sounds)

The key of this very powerful exercise is to focus on the type of sounds that cannot be immediately categorized and labeled by your mind.

In this sound meditation exercise, you can use the soundstorming tool or other sources of anonymous sounds that you can find at the acoustic section of the web.
[Web] torchprinciple.com/soundstorming
[Web] torchprinciple.com/soundmap

- Find a quiet place. Sit comfortably.
- Open a web browser and load the soundstorming tool or one of the videos of the acoustic section of the web.
- Load an album or video that contains anonymous sounds.
- Close your eyes. Visualize your challenge taking place.
- Don't analyze, visualize the challenge and feel the sounds around you.
- Your subconscious pot blends the challenge and the random sounds.
- When something interesting comes to mind, open your eyes and make a note of it.

Sound, emotions and challenges

In the following exercises, we will be using music to trigger moods and emotions, which we will link with our challenges.

I encourage you to walk while you perform these exercises. Walking encourages relaxation as well as openness and flexible thinking.

Use music pieces that you have available in your personal library or others that you may find at YouTube, Spotify and other music channels.

Alternatively, in the following addresses you can access musical tracks that you can use in the exercises.

[Web] **torchprinciple.com/music**
[Web] **torchprinciple.com/soundmap**

Contextual lalala

This exercise invites you to immerse yourself in specific moods conveyed to you through music.

- Find a wide open space to do this exercise.

- Music pieces are played in the background. We provide examples at:
  [Web] torchprinciple.com/music

- As you listen to the music, walk around the space.

- Hold in your mind your challenge, visualize parts of it as you walk.

- Don't think with words. Instead visualize your challenge in images.

- Allow yourself to sing along the music, voicing the mood that you feel.

- At the beginning use generic sounds or words like "la,la,la".

- Introduce specific words only when you feel like it, whenever you feel compelled to do so.

- Note down any insights or specific words/phrases that come to your mind or that you introduce in the song.

Some of the music styles you may play in the background are:

- **Celebration mood:** we sing and optionally use words that relate to the joyful sides of our challenge.

- **Funeral mood** (example: Chopin funeral march): we sing and optionally use words that connect with the conflictive or dark aspects of our challenge.

- **Melancholy mood:** we sing as we remember the good old times related to our challenge.

Soundmap exploration (in silence until verification)

In this exercise we use soundmaps and act our challenge in silence until insights are triggered.

- Activate a soundmap.

- As you listen to the soundmap, walk around the space.
- Hold in your mind your challenge, visualize parts of it as you walk.
- Don't think with words. Instead visualize your challenge in images.
- Link the soundmap with the challenge.
- Optional: Remember the "act your challenge" exercise of the gesture module. Act your challenge again but this time do it as the soundmap plays in the background. Visualize the challenge at all times. Gesture and move. Act, move and perform, linking your challenge with the soundmap.
- Annotate any insights that come up.

Voice your challenge/idea

It's the time to introduce your own sounds into the process.

- Remember the "act your challenge" exercise of the gesture module. Act your challenge again, but this time voice what you visualize using abstract sounds.
- Visualize your challenge and walk around.
- Voice what you feel and visualize using abstract sounds. Don't use specific words.
- Let your body act and move as it wants.
- Act the challenge. Voice it. Express it.
- Annotate any insights that come up during the process.

Fill in the gaps

In this exercise we pick well-known popular songs and create our own lyrics, linking them with the challenge.

- Play a popular song in the background, for example the Mexican tune "La cucaracha".

- Sing along, feeling the mood triggered in you by the song. Use generic words like "la,la,la".

- Replace some of the lyrics with new words/phrases that you link with your challenge.

- Don't overanalyze. Let yourself go. Visualize and express yourself in a loose, organic way.

- Feel the spirit and emotion coming from the song, let it drive you towards new insights as you visualize your challenge at the same time.

- As always, annotate anything interesting that you learn connected to your challenge.

Fruit mix

In this last exercise, we will randomly mix some of the previous modules to encourage more variations in the way you exercise your creative muscles.

- Set alarm clock.
- Every minute, change to a different activity, a different exercise picked from the previous modules.
- Do it individually or in a group with your peers.

Conclusion

The exercises in this chapter help you strengthen your creative muscles, involving all your potential. As you continue strengthening these muscles, it will become easier and easier to diverge strongly before you converge later onto innovative solutions. Begin using these exercises and others like them, including your own variations, with the professional and personal challenges that you face.

CHAPTER 7:

Health and Well-being

"Don't think. Thinking is the enemy of creativity. It's self-conscious, and anything self-conscious is lousy. You can't try to do things. You simply must do things."

– Ray Bradbury

F̲ew people would argue against considering health as the most important parameter of our lives. That's why discussing creative thinking and innovation in connection with it is so important.

Creative thinking can impact our health in dramatic ways, depending on how absent or present it is.

The relentless analytical chatter of consciousness, with its network of preoccupations and problems, is one of the main sources of anxiety, stress, fear and frustration in people.

Let's review some of the benefits of exercising our creative muscles as well as the dangers of underusing or overusing them.

Stress
Not all stress is equal

Let's first ride the depth elevator of mental stress, an issue that we all care about.

"Mental stress… the worst thing."

We hear it all the time. Stress kills. Stress is harmful to our health. But is that really the case with all forms of stress?

"Mm, tell me more."

There are different kinds of stresses and some of them are often necessary and even useful.

Stress is commonly defined as the organism's response to a stimulus that we can call the stressor.[42] Stated in such a generic way it doesn't sound that bad. In fact it sounds pretty neutral. But as we know, stress typically has very negative connotations associated with it.

The problem of abstracting and simplifying something as complex as what we call stress is that we end up viewing it as an all good or all bad concept. It's either you are stressed (bad), or you are not (good).

But is it really that simple?

In fact, it is not. When we start looking at a variety of scenarios, it is easy to find examples where stress is actually helping your body and mind in positive ways.

"Give me an example."

Germs are stressors for our bodies. Children who are isolated from these stressors during childhood, get sick more often and develop more allergies. The stress created by germs in a baby's body triggers the buildup of useful defenses in the organism. These become crucial both at that stage and later on. In fact, the advantages or disadvantages linked to the presence or absence of these stressors can be hard or impossible to reverse as we grow up.

"Got it. Tell me more."

For an actor, the stage and the audience are key stressors. Most professional actors recognize that regardless of their experience and expertise, there is always a certain amount of stress before a performance. In fact, without that baseline level of stress, the quality of their performance suffers! It is that baseline level of stress that stimulates them to enter their so called zone, when they are at the top of their game. It is then that mind and body feel strongly stimulated by those stressors and ready to tackle the complexity of the challenge ahead.

"So stress can literally trigger beneficial behaviors or processes!"

Yes. Some children that are born in rich families don't have to deal with too much stress or too many challenges. As a consequence, they may lack some depth as adults. On the other hand, children that have to face hard challenges and multiple kinds of stressors, often develop into more complete adults, deeper beings that are more skilled and balanced.

Stress, therefore, is not an all-around evil, but more of a wild horse, able to take you very far, but pretty dangerous when out of control.

"Like when a child is exposed to too much stress. This could become damaging and produce the opposite result."

Yes, because when this horse goes out of control, like any other helpful stimulus that is taken too far, its damaging effects can become devastating.

"So there are different kinds of stress horses. And in a way, some stress is inevitable. So how can we influence which kind of stress horse we are going to be riding?"

Different activities and mental strategies are typically related to different kinds of stress horses:

- AT encourages nervous types. These horses are afraid of the unknown, they are jumpy and hard to manage. They need to be tightly controlled with tense straps.
- CT encourages calmer stress horses. These are flexible and loose in their movements, eager to explore, easier to manage unless they become too loose. If they become too loose we can lose control over them.

Both kinds can potentially help. Both can potentially harm. But due to the emphasis of our society on AT, the AT stress horses can get out of control and turn against you way more often and with more damaging consequences.

"So we need to ride the good kind of stress horses and keep them under close watch."

Yes, do not wish for a world without stress, for you need stressors to thrive. Wish for a world without extreme and unbalanced stress. Specially the kind of damaging stress that is born from thinking strategies that are too biased towards extreme analysis and tight logical rules.

"Our stress horses can then be beneficial rather than damaging."

Yes, keep your stress horses loose and relaxed and they shall reward you with inspiring stimulation, enthusiasm and dynamism.

Exercise

At the end of each of the next 3 days, identify one useful stressor and another damaging one that you are facing currently or have faced in the past. Find ways to encourage the useful one and limit the presence of the damaging one. For example, having to study for my Italian exam stresses me, but I am really motivated to pass the exam and every day I feel more comfortable with the material. The net effect is positive so I will remind myself that this stressor is bringing me good things and I will march ahead. On the other hand, interacting with my friend X stresses me because of his negative attitude. This is potentially damaging for my health. I will either avoid this person or ask my friend to change his attitude.

Comfort
The vicious circle of comfort

The stress depth elevator connects us with the comfort depth elevator. One would think that comfort is the antidote of harmful stress. And yet too much comfort may end up triggering damaging stress.

"I like comfort."

Sure you do! Did you know that couples that rent beautiful villas in luxurious settings may have a higher than average risk of breaking up?[43]

"I will cancel my booking immediately."

Why is extreme comfort sometimes so dangerous?

By definition, comfort doesn't blend well with effort and dealing with uncertain, complex and fuzzy scenarios may require some effort.

"What is complex in a nice, relaxing and luxurious holiday?"

It is life itself that is complex. Our interactions, relationships and day-to-day actions are full of complexity.

"Aha, I guess I was being lazy, ignoring the deep stuff below the surface."

That's one of the trademarks of laziness and extreme comfort, which is therefore, anti-creative. It doesn't favor CT and therefore moves the mental scale towards AT, the preoccupation analytical network.

"So laziness and extreme comfort don't combine well with complexity."

Yes, and that encourages AT to dominate, simplifying reality and searching for joy through logical trickery, abstraction and premature judgments.

"Alas, real life is complex."

Indeed. It is made up of the other 99% that surrounds our mental abstractions. Life is uncertain, unpredictable and fuzzy. Sooner or later the analytical abstract bubble bursts.

"Oops."

And then we find ourselves naked in the middle of a mental storm.

"Therefore laziness and extreme comfort strengthen AT and interfere with CT."

Yes, think of so many talented creators and innovators that become rich and famous. Once they are dominated by fame, comfort and adulation, they often lose a lot of their creative potential.

Consider the contrast between the innovative first works of some famous pop and rock musicians and their latest works when fame and comfort have taken over their lives. When they stop opening new mental routes and keep repeating their own old patterns or those of others, innovation and creativity suffer.

"Comfort vs effort. Interesting."

Others, who become rich overnight, inheriting great riches or earning great sums of money through business, awards or other events, are in many cases unable to find mental peace soon after. Why is this so?

Extreme comfort can generate delusional attitudes. Reality is constantly mutating and extreme material comfort, which is what we are talking about, often triggers constant alertness to detect anything that can modify or change the status quo.

"We are scared to lose what we have accumulated."

Fear empowers AT, moving us away from the peace and mental space necessary to exercise our creative muscles.

"I guess spending too much time with AT can become really stressful…"

The problem with spending most of our time within our AT loops is that delusion and AT are not good friends. AT is constantly looking for challenges to solve.

"And it wants to solve them quick and easy!"

Right after you solve or pretend to have solved one of these challenges, AT insists in finding another one.

"It is a vicious circle!"

This soon becomes quite stressful. It is like having a dragon pet under your desk. The dragon keeps spitting out fire and you keep putting the fire out. Why don't we ever think of getting rid of the dragon or at least keeping it somewhere else most of the time?

Or maybe all the dragon needs is a partner, a companion.

"Something that complements and pacifies our dragon."

The fire of AT is what happens when our mind goes out of balance, when we are missing our other half.

Exercise

Describe two moments in your life. One in which your life was really easy, to the point of making you lazier, and another in which your life was challenging, so you had to put the best of yourself out there.

When did you feel more alive, excited and fired up? Which of those moments made you grow more as a person? Reflect on it.

Dominant AT

We have reflected on stress and comfort and their link to AT and CT. Let's now go deeper into why a very dominant AT can be so problematic for our health.

Find the violin in the storm

It is key to learn to bypass and calm our conscious analytical chatter.

CT is like a delicate violin in the middle of a wild mental storm. You need to find ways to calm the storm so that you can listen to this most beautiful violin.

Exercise

Become more aware of moments when your mind is dominated by analytical and logical chatter. Notice your stress levels as you enter these vicious circles. Become aware. Awareness is the first step towards regaining balance.

A world of problems

Our analytical mind is mainly focused on those things that we consider problematic. A network of preoccupations we could call it.

"Chasing problems, or inventing them!"

That's why spending most of your mental currency on AT can drive you to harmful stress and anxiety.

"Reminds me of how I feel when I watch too much news on the TV."

Yes. It is as if you were watching the television news around the clock, analyzing problem after problem. At the same time you try to find solutions for those problems using tools that are often unable to cope with their complexity.

"Most challenges are too complex for logic and analysis to deal with them on their own."

We need help. CT balances AT, taking us away from those vicious circles towards calmer waters, where we can engage with the raw complexity of the situation, staying away from premature stressful judgments.

A vicious circle

AT generates pressure, the pressure to solve the "problem".

"I know that pressure… it can feel like a never-ending circle…"

When we work under pressure, anxiety joins the party. Urgency arrives and we consciously try to rush solutions employing AT processes. These are always linked to the network of preoccupations.

"I can't imagine CT being very happy in this situation."

Indeed, such an environment inhibits creative thinking. We enter a vicious circle in which stress triggers AT, which in turn inhibits CT, pushing us to feel more stressed, which further reinforces AT processes.

Stress and extreme AT. Together they drive us away from creativity and innovation.

Patching the problem

Spending most of our time in the abstract and narrow world of AT, we miss the richness and vividness that life's complexity can offer.

For AT, perception is always meant to be simplified, abstracted, packaged, categorized, judged and evaluated. Is it useful? Is it dangerous?

"Hanging too much around AT makes me feel rather empty."

Yes, living too often in a flat and shallow mental world, surrounded by judgments, trapped in the constraints of language, symbols and abstractions, can make people feel that something is missing. To compensate they often engage in adrenalin fueled activities, such as violent games, park rides, drugs, wild parties, pornography, etc.

"Maybe it could be fun for a while…"

Just like sugar, this is a temporary high that soon crashes back down and fades away, returning people to their usual feeling of emptiness.

"Something deeper is missing."

That something is half of their potential. The half that brings them closer to the never-ending richness and complexity of life.

"So the solution to the feeling of emptiness is not necessarily out there…"

The solution is right here, inside of our minds, beginning with encouraging and nurturing our creative thinking processes.

Exercise

For a full day try to observe your own thoughts anytime you get worried about something. Observe your AT processes at work as they go around your issues trying to find solutions. How often do you find yourself in this state? And how do you feel through it all? Raise your awareness. Note down any anxiety, stress and other emotions you feel.

Healing
Beginning to heal

Finding balance in your thinking begins by realizing and acknowledging that you are more than your network of preoccupations.

"I don't have to be controlled by it."

Learning to contemplate and view your conscious thoughts, judgments, concerns and fears as imprecise abstractions of reality and not reality itself, helps us escape from the vicious circles and distortions generated by AT. Observing our own network of preoccupations at work can soften its influence.

"Cool! And what else can we do?"

Empower your CT to move away from harmful mental habits. Creative thinking moves you away from your ego, your sense of self and your network of concerns.

"That should bring me more peace…"

Yes. Let's explore why that's the case.

Understanding as part of the healing

The first step on the road to mental freedom is understanding what is happening and why. Understanding how habits are born and how they evolve can help you work with things like phobias, traumas or depression. At the heart of all of those are patterns of thought that have become deeply entrenched in our minds.

"I can't stop thinking about it!"

These patterns are so entrenched that any potential alternative faces great difficulties to displace them.

"I guess persistence is needed."

An idea that is carved deep in your mind can be displaced by new alternatives. These alternatives are weak at the beginning, but may find ways to survive if their contributions are appealing enough and if you are motivated to push them.

Exercise

Whenever you catch yourself unable to stop thinking about a challenge you are facing, take a paper and write down an alternative scenario where your challenge is solved and you have moved on. Write it down and read it as often as you need. Slowly your subconscious will start working in the direction of this new scenario. You are slowly pushing a new mental pattern into your mind. This will gradually drive your attention away from the previous pattern. It is not easy. It requires effort and perseverance. But it is doable in almost every case.

You need a new frame
Challenges vs problems

Moving on from phobias and other extreme mental states to our daily routine, we continue to track other sources of anxiety and stress.

How you frame things has a huge impact on your mental well-being. Think of challenges, not problems.

"Wait, I see a problem with that. Oops, I mean a challenge."

Challenges are positive invitations to come up with novel solutions. Problems are negative invitations to panic.

"Thanks for the reminder, I was starting to panic!"

When you think of something as a challenge, you take on a constructive attitude focused on growing and evolving through the process. This is positive regardless of the final outcome.

Thinking of problems often reveals more about the personality of the observer than about the nature of the challenge itself.

"I get it, seeing problems everywhere is saying something about my personality…"

The word problem has defeat written all over it.

"I guess it's not a good way to begin the search for a solution when defeat is part of the premise itself."

Instead, a challenge is a door to new teachings and learnings while a problem is an obstacle that stops you in your tracks.

"I get it. Challenges push me to become a better person all around. That is positive regardless of what happens in the end."

It's the dynamic vs the static, the natural flow of life vs the paralysis of fear. Life vs death, challenge vs problems.

"You got me. For the sake of my health, I choose challenges!"

If you choose challenges, you are also choosing to empower your creative thinking.

CT, by its own exploratory, dynamic and highly productive nature, teaches you to view life positively, as a series of challenges.

"I understand. CT is all about working through a series of challenges that become stepping stones on the way to innovative solutions."

Yes, finding innovative solutions requires constant experimentation and sustained productivity. A series of challenges that push you to be positive and enjoy the process of working through them.

Exercise

Think of something you view as a problem in your life. Reframe it as a challenge that invites you to grow and evolve in positive ways as you tackle it.

Failure
You need to fail

The need to reframe problems as challenges is essential for our health because as innovators we need to "fail" and we will "fail" often and regularly.

"It is only possible to survive those so called failures if we don't take them as dramatic setbacks."

Indeed. Some of the greatest achievements in history were born from what many would consider a "failure". Let's reflect on the concept of failure itself.

Considering something a failure is possible if we look at events as static entities, unconnected to past and future, dead ends without branches or alternatives, part of a static and inflexible world.

"I see. A failure hurts even more when we feel it in isolation, separated from past and future events."

But what happens when we look at the whole picture in temporal terms?

"You mean connecting the dots forwards and backwards?"

Imagine yourself lost in the middle of a mountain at night. A storm surrounds you. You are lost and you need to get home.

"I try different routes."

You are disorientated and can't find the sign that points towards home. You fall many times and you injure yourself. You feel fear and panic.

"I've been there."

Will you give up? After one of the falls, still bruised, you realize that from the position where you fell, from that angle, you can see a sign in the distance, a sign that points towards your home.

"Lucky fall!"

Yes. And so, when in the end you make it home, how do you feel about the fall that bruised your leg? Do you consider it an unfortunate event? Or do you value that it accelerated the process of finding the way home? Your fall helped you prevent worse consequences from happening, allowing you to find a sign that could otherwise have been hidden from view for too long.

"So we shouldn't separate any event from what is about to happen afterwards."

Yes, and although we cannot control what has just happened, we can control most of what is going to happen from now on.

"And then one day we may trace back the dots and realize…"

That it was all for the best in the end.

Misery lives in the word "failure". Eliminating it from our dictionary will improve our health in every way.

"Failure? I have never heard that word in my life."

For the great inventor Edison, a failure meant arriving at a different place, a different answer, which was not only valuable in itself, but could be even more valuable than the intended one.[44]

"Because of the unexpected connections and insights that it could bring…"

Remember one of the stories at the beginning of this book: you have crossed the snow field in a different direction and arrived somewhere else. It is your attitude that will transform your new destination into something useful and memorable, or an empty void.

Think of some of your holidays, of those moments in which you got lost during a trip, when because of losing your way you found something completely unexpected, something interesting or valuable.

"I love it when that happens!"

You could frame the "losing your way" with frustration and anger if your mind is obsessively focused on your initial goal.

"That sounds very AT to me."

But when your mind functions in an open and balanced way, you may discover in the unexpected destination something just as valuable or more than what you were looking for.

"I can feel how CT can help us relax when the unexpected happens."

Balance, as usual, is key. Some people eliminate the word "failure" from their dictionaries, but go too far and become something else: delusional.

"When we ignore these events and simply carry on as if nothing has happened."

What separates successful innovators from delusional people is the ability to learn from previous events. If you see the so called "failures" as opportunities to learn and improve, you are on the right track. But if such learning does not take place, if you simply ignore the consequences of your actions and the feedback you receive, then you are being delusional, not creative.

Exercise

Think of "failures" you had in the past. Think about positive things that happened after any of those failures. How did your attitude contribute to that? Now think of negative things that happened after a so called failure. How did your attitude contribute to that as well?

How many of your past "failures" seem from today's perspective events that were positive and necessary?

Change
Your attitude towards change

Accepting the so called "failures" as something positive has a lot to do with our attitude towards change.

"I'm comfortable as I am, thanks. No change needed."

Hold it for a moment, mind. Think of your life as a car on a road full of millions of other vehicles. All of them, including you, are moving fast. From inside your car, looking at the cars around you, everything seems quite stationary and comfortable.

"That's because all cars are moving at similar speeds."

Yes, so it is hard to realize how fast your position is changing.

"Mm, true. But if I could stop for a second…"

If you could stop for a second and look at things from the outside, you would gain a much better perspective on the situation.

"If everybody is moving so fast and the road is packed, it is not going to be that easy to stop though…"

Indeed. Stopping your car requires a big effort. Everybody is moving fast and it is not easy to escape the constant flow of life. But when you finally manage to stop your car on the side of the road and get out for a few moments, your perspective shifts dramatically.

"I will notice how fast everything is moving…"

Yes. You quickly notice how constant the change is. You grasp how much the context shifts moment to moment and you come to accept that change is something natural.

"It is part of the driving experience."

And you are the driver of your life.

"But what if I don't want or I can't stop and get to a position where I can understand what is happening?"

That doesn't modify the fact that the change is happening, all the time, fast and constant.

"This constant change makes me feel a little bit anxious…"

Many people equal change with instability, but it doesn't have to be that way. Change itself is inevitable.

"I get you. It is how we deal with it that matters."

Yes. Cars need good pavement and a road free of potholes and other potential dangers in order to move and change their position smoothly. Similarly, for change to be integrated naturally in our lives, we require the right attitude and a balanced mind where AT and CT work together as a team.

"A mind with strong creative muscles is a mind that accepts change as something natural."

Innovators welcome change. Not as something that they necessarily need, but simply as one of the foundational ingredients of life itself, one we cannot get rid of.

"Although you can try to fool yourself that you do."

The illusion of permanency

AT can create an illusion of permanency. By sheltering us from the fine details of life, we see the world around us as a series of generic and apparently stable entities. And we think of ourselves and our existence in similar ways.

The reality is that everything is constantly changing and evolving. From every single cell in our bodies to every one of our interactions with the world, the events we are involved in, the markets and potential audiences of our creations and all other things that are part of our existence. Moment by moment life moves on.

When we start to look at everything as if we were observing an always evolving living creature, the way we think can change dramatically. Thinking of our lives as living creatures, engages our attention, triggers our interest and motivates our actions. Conversely, interpreting events as static, permanently fixed entities, encourages inactivity and laziness.

Change is a key ingredient of life that you can befriend, to grow deeper both as a creative soul and as a human being.

Exercise

Are you afraid of change? Think of situations where you became anxious because of a change in your life. Was your mind dominated at those times by analyzing potential troubles ahead, or by taking the change as a challenge that could potentially lead you to better places in the future? Take one of those situations and write down what AT and CT would say about it. Which perspective do you prefer?

Resilience
What gives you joy?

Feeling comfortable with change requires resilience. Wikipedia.org defines resilience as an individual's ability to properly adapt to stress and adversity.[45]

"I would like to be more resilient. How can I do that?"

Resilience improves when your personal satisfaction depends on a variety of values and experiences.

"Mm, what if my satisfaction depends mainly on one thing?"

For many people, satisfaction depends on two or three very specific things. When those few things fail you, it is easy to feel extremely vulnerable, to panic and react with depression or aggressiveness.

"So what you are saying is that I have to expand the range of things that make me feel good, and I bet CT will be a big help with that."

Yes, exercising your creative muscles expands your boundaries and the number of areas and experiences that add value to your life.

"Feeling more alive and more connected..."

Feeling more alive is often related to making use of more of your potential as a human being. When you exercise your whole potential, you feel more connected to others and life itself.

"The sources of my personal joy increase... "

You become more resilient in the face of new challenges. Your creativity is a constant source of joy and motivation that can sustain you through tough times.

"I feel it. Creativity can make me more resilient, protecting me against the unpredictable changes of life."

Human beings have been creative from the very beginning. Sometimes for the sake of survival. Other times, like in the case of the ancient cave paintings, creativity was a way to record events and marvel at our existence, to explore our understanding of life and feel more connected to it and to each other.

In our hectic world, stopping this process of exploration, wonderment and connection, narrows down our sources of long lasting joy and is a recipe for mental disaster.

Exercise

Make a list of things, activities and people that bring you long lasting and intense joy and satisfaction. How large is your list? How many of the items in your list are connected to people beyond yourself and how many can be exercised by yourself without depending on others? Creativity can bring you joy even when others fail you.

Exercise
Use it or lose it

Our CT helps us increase the range of activities that give us joy. And to sharpen our creativity, we need to exercise our creative muscles just as we exercise our physical ones to stay fit.

"I'm a bit lazy to hit the gym."

It is typical to wonder if it's worth exercising our bodies and minds. Remember once again the story about the footprints on the snow at the beginning of the book. We had doubts whether to follow the footprints of others or take the risk of opening a new route.

In the same way, anytime we are challenged either by others or by our own curiosity to do something different and new, the doubt may appear in the form of: What is the point?

"I am telling you, I feel good, I don't really need that much exercise."

We think we are healthy and we think we have what we need. Why would we spend extra energy and time, which is money, to explore something whose consequences are not clear? Why would we jump into an ocean of uncertain benefits?

"Exactly, why would we?"

For these and similar questions the answer is simple: Use it or lose it.

"Mm, I know, I've been eating too much and exercising too little."

Think of your mind as a muscle that you can strengthen and make more powerful when you exercise it, or weaken and drive to atrophy when you don't. Understanding this can be crucial to finding the motivation we need to sustain our creative efforts.

"I definitely don't want my mind to end up like my tummy!"

We have been born with an amazing brain. For many people, the brain is just an organ that sits on our heads and drives our bodies efficiently and autonomously. It apparently keeps going regardless of how we treat it.

Do we think in the same way about our legs, arms or heart? Not really.

"I like to take good care of my arms and legs, and also of my heart. I exercise and I am eating less sugar and more vegetables."

Yes, we exercise our bodies and eat carefully because we know that the health of our heart and our body depends on it. We also stretch our bodies and try not to overuse our articulations because we can produce repetitive stress injuries.

And what about the mind? Do we really think that we can get repetitive stress injuries in the body but not in the mind? If you keep going over and over around the same mental patterns in your mind, you will eventually become anxious and stressed. Some people feel empty inside, they feel a lack of peace.

"Those AT loops end up becoming pretty tiring."

A mind engaged in repetitive thinking is asking for trouble just as using your arm in repetitive ways, with a computer device for example, leads to stress injuries in our tendons or wrists.

"It gets painful when I repeat the same moves too many times."

A body whose movements are diverse and flexible functions better and for longer. In the same way, exercising your creative muscles means introducing variety and richness in how you think and behave. By doing that, mind and body become stronger and more resilient.

"But what if I don't have time to exercise my creative muscles?"

Careful investment of our energy and time resources is important, but exercising your mind is one essential investment whose absence can lead to unhappiness, depression and premature death.

"Oops, I definitely don't want to go there!"

Of course all extremes are dangerous.

"You mean that too much CT could be just as bad…"

Exercising your CT processes with no restraint may lead to sleepless nights, insomnia and a whole lot of pathologies born from the inability to turn off the creative switch.

On the other extreme, lack of mental exercise dumbs down the mind, turning habitual thoughts into steep cliffs from where it gets harder and harder to climb out.

"So we are looking for that healthy medium."

And to get as close as possible to that healthy medium, variety is key. Remind yourself to regularly move away from whatever repetitive activities you engage in. Shake your body and mind with something different. This is a protective measure and one whose potential you should not underestimate.

Changing the context around you keeps your neurons busy, connecting new stimuli. It rejuvenates your mind.

So just as you can exercise your body muscles in various contexts and not just in a gym, think of ways to exercise your CT muscles on a regular basis:

- Every day do something unexpected. It could be something as simple as writing a random story or improvising an excursion after work.

- Every week learn something new. It could be as simple as researching online a new topic, something that arouses your curiosity or something you know nothing about. Or it could be as involved as joining a short course.

- Every week contact somebody you haven't talked to for some time. It could be a relative or a friend, or it could be a potential business collaborator or somebody whose work you admire.

- Every month add some spice to your life. Evaluate the direction in which things are going and add something that brings variety and a new tint to your current path.

On top of that, review the exercises in the practical chapter to train your creative muscles.

"Variety will be my new mantra!"

Variety protects us against tunnel vision, the narrowing of our perspectives and horizons that gradually tightens our views when we remain focused on the very same task or area for too long.

Spontaneity vs tightness

So when flexibility and variation are not there, repetitive mental patterns may produce tight and tense minds.

Many adults, having to deal with the daily responsibilities and obligations of adulthood, get so consumed by those processes, that they partially or completely lose the ability to improvise, be spontaneous and feel unexpected joy.

"Unexpected joy, I want more of that."

Exercising your creative muscles puts challenges in perspective and makes you more aware of the essence and beauty in life. When we recover the ability to sense that richness, potential and beauty in our existence, spontaneous joy returns.

Find the local in the global

Finding that richness and variation in the patterns of information that our senses interact with, requires being sensitive to what is unique and different.

"Sometimes finding what is unique and different in a globalized world is not that easy, right?"

Globalization can produce an effect in our minds similar to anesthesia. We experience the same things everywhere, sometimes at opposite ends of the planet.

"I can imagine CT being a great ally in order to break that sameness created by globalization."

Indeed. When services and businesses clone themselves around the planet, creative thinking is more important than ever. It allows us to discover the uniqueness of the local reality within these globalized contexts.

"Another reason to exercise our creative muscles."

When your creative muscles are fit and active, you can take advantage of the best that globalization offers without losing the richness and unique perspectives that are always there within each local context, waiting behind the global facade.

Exercise

How often do you exercise your body? Notice how you feel after exercising it. And notice how you feel when you don't exercise at all, when you spend a long time sitting in the same way or in the same place, or doing repetitive and tedious work.

The difference between both will be very clear. If this happens with your body, realize that the same will happen with your mind. Is your mind occupied always with similar thoughts? Or is your mind exposed to a variety of stimuli and engaged in the exploration and discovery of new things on a regular basis? Ask yourself that question and note down your answer.

Let's now turn to what happens when that variety and richness is lost, when we regularly engage in repetitive analytical thinking processes.

Time
The pressure ticking down

When most of your thinking currency is spent in the analytical chambers of the mind, you live under the tyranny of time.

"And time is pressure!"

Indeed. And pressure is a formidable source of stress.

"I am very aware of the passage of time when I'm analyzing my troubles."

Analytical thinking is based on logical processes that aim to be efficient. As you analyze you are very much aware of time passing, ticking down moment by moment.

"It can be exhausting. What happens when we free ourselves from those analytical processes?"

You will often hear about pianists, painters or scientists who deeply engaged with their challenges return to the "other reality" to find out that 5, 10 or 20 hours, or even days, have passed.

"I get it. CT transcends time."

Outside of time there is a special kind of peace and tranquility to be found. The pressure of what should happen the next minute goes away. All that remains is the raw reality, devoid of labels and symbols.

"I feel that even my identity goes away."

Your identity dissolves and disappears within the process. Your ego can finally rest. You feel deeply connected with your challenge.

"Sounds like a place where I would like to go often."

AT is an essential friend that can become a terrible tyrant when it becomes too dominant. So give your mind a break from time to time by locking that tyrant away and stepping into the calm oceans of CT, where a minute and an hour become indistinguishable, where perception and complexity take you deeper than words can ever reach.

Exercise

Note down any moments in your life in which you lost the sense of time passing. How did you feel? What were you doing? How active were AT processes during those moments?

Let's now dive into the effects caused by the noise that constant AT can generate in our minds.

Noise
Balancing the chatter

The conscious chatter of our minds is a very common source of frustration, fear, insecurities and suffering.

"It is hard to shut the mind up, I concur."

Conscious AT chatter is not useless. It is essential when used in the right way, for the right reasons and at the right time. It is key in order to organize our daily life, to plan activities, communicate and deliver information to others. It is also essential to engrave subconscious wisdom into statements understandable by other human beings and to transform those subconscious insights into deliverables that can serve as the seed of new creative ventures.

"I got it, it's the tip of the iceberg."

But life is complex. AT allows us to simplify it and to logically reflect on our amazing existence.

"But abstraction has limits."

Indeed. Life's complexity can be too much for the slow and methodical AT processes.

When we experience something, anything, our subconscious integrates that experience through a complex organic process of unpredictable repercussions.

Such a process has a complexity that is hard to translate into language and logic.

AT processes make humans very advanced. However, like all powerful things, AT is a double-edged sword, and one of its edges, when misused, can cut real deep!

"Thinking in circles hurts!"

Yes. AT can interfere with CT, but CT can be very useful when it comes to controlling the side effects of too much AT.

"So there is hope!"

Exercise

Try to become conscious of moments when your AT obsesses over a "problem" and keeps going in circles around it. Realize the amount of time lost in those processes. Notice how, often, at the end of those processes, you don't feel much of an improvement in terms of clarity about the situation. Rather, you feel more confused.

There are other ways to feel and understand deeply a challenge. Ways that involve more CT and less AT.

Anti-Stress
The anti-stress pill

Creative processes cannot function easily under pressure. In fact, under heavy stress, creativity collapses. Stress and pressure activate conscious analytical processes that block our depth elevators and prevent smooth communication with our subconscious.

"That's why I find it so hard to compose songs when I'm stressed."

Exercising CT produces the opposite effect, lowering our stress levels and taming our AT processes.

Balancing the poles

AT and CT are two poles that need each other in order to perform at their best.

"But perfect balance can never be achieved, right?"

Of course. Extremes are the problem. When either pole dominates too much over the other, our performance and satisfaction as human beings deteriorates.

Too much conscious chatter generates stress and anxiety. This chatter takes place in the kingdoms of language and logic, whose attempts to make sense of life's complexity often lead to frustration.

On the other hand, relying too much on our CT, constantly swimming in the complexity of life, can make us unable to function within our society: unable to communicate effectively with others, to organize ourselves, and also unable to transform our subconscious insights into the necessary structures that can be shared with, worked on and delivered to others.

"I've known a couple of creatives that went too far…"

Think about the need for striking the right balance.

In our society, strongly biased towards AT, balance begins by bringing new perspectives to issues traditionally shaped and controlled by AT.

Exercise

Think of people you have met in your life that represent the extremes of AT and CT. People that are too analytical and square in their thinking, very predictable. And others that are too expansive, divergent, chaotic and inefficient in their daily life. Notice the risks and dangers of both types of personalities. By understanding the dangers of these extremes, it is easier to set our target away from them.

Connectedness
Isolation is in your mind

CT teaches us that nothing is really isolated or unconnected. Everything is connected to everything else, even things that seem absolutely unrelated to each other. And that is liberating.

If everything is connected, there is always a route to go from A to B, no matter what A and B are, no matter how long and twisted that route may be. Suddenly the world seems full of possibilities and opportunities at all levels, personal and professional.

"I can imagine that many of the great discoveries in history happened by connecting seemingly unrelated things."

Indeed. Coming back to the challenge of isolation: the isolation that comes from excessive use of AT is also related to the many mental blocks we can bump into.

Breaking through the block

Sometimes we feel trapped or blocked, unable to proceed.

"I feel anxious."

This may be happening during our creative work or in front of important decisions in our life. All moments of blockage have one thing in common: tunnel vision, the narrowing of your focus.

As doubt starts to creep in, anxiety joins the party and quickly narrows down our focus. That's the paradox. The more we worry, the further we drift away from potential solutions. Those solutions may be very close, waiting on the edges of our awareness. But our focus tightens around the worries, unable to perceive or notice anything else around them.

These blocks are common when our AT is too dominant.

"Stubborn AT refusing to give up its dominance!"

AT is highly efficient in helping us survive in society, but its tools are abstractions and simplifications, language and logic, which are very removed from the richness and variety of our complex reality.

Feeling blocked often means being unable to go beyond our analytical filters in order to access the wider and richer information resources that lie beyond our AT processes.

"There must be a way to bypass those blocks."

Yes, throughout history people have used different strategies to tame our analytical giant. We have seen many of them in the previous chapter.

In relation to our mental health, many innovators recommend changing your context when you face a mental block. Get out of the house, take a trip or visit somebody. Change completely your environment and context. This stops the vicious circle by forcing you to focus on something else, taking you out of the narrow tunnel where your mind has been dwelling.

You can use other solutions without leaving your home. Some of the greatest innovators used music and art in order to break the dark spell and open again their awareness.

The key is that you are converging too much and you need to diverge again.

We have all experienced how taking a break or waiting till the next day was all that was needed to find the solution to the challenge that was bothering us. All we needed was to diverge a bit in order to escape the narrow tunnel of our AT.

Anything that involves CT, your wider and more intuitive mode of thinking, will help improve the situation. That's why working and living in interesting and stimulating environments can be highly beneficial for your mental health. An environment where language blends with music, visuals, drawings, scents and other rich inputs, is a constant invitation to combine and recombine information in your mind, to diverge, to expand your focus and mental horizons, to widen your views and absorb the richness of each moment. This stimulates your creative thinking skills, balances the overpowering analytical processes and protects you against blocks of all kinds.

"And what if I don't live in such an environment?"

When the block arrives, stand up, leave your house and find a context as different as possible to the one you were in. Make it your mission. Tunnel vision is like a spell that you need to break. Reset your mind, do it now.

"So diverging helps me to break the blocks."

Imagine your thinking as a set of glasses that filter your reality. What do you prefer wearing? Tight, uncomfortable and small frames, or wide and expansive ones?

There is a time for diverging and a time for converging. You don't want to be converging all the time. Converging narrows down your life. Put on the tight frames for too long and what happens?

"They start to hurt my nose."

Yes, and those small frames can feel deceptively secure. Your horizon may be tighter but you feel that at least you know where the boundaries are.

"Is that a false sense of security?"

A better kind of security

As much as we would like to think otherwise, everything in life is constantly changing. Thinking outside the box is a vital skill that helps you react faster and better to the inevitable changes and challenges that life will bring you.

"So being used to solve creative challenges trains you to face in better ways the unexpected tides of life."

Put on those wide expansive frames more often. Rigid security may give you a false sense of stability today, but unexpected events can quickly crack open that illusion, just as the tight trunk of a tree can break easily when facing a storm.

This takes us to a key challenge along the way, our ego.

"I don't think my ego is a problem."

There you go, that's your ego speaking.

Transcending ego

We have previously talked about the network of preoccupations generated and empowered by AT. This connects with our ego.

"And what is ego?"

Ego is our self-image, a distorted perception of ourselves made of symbols, labels, comparisons and judgments. It is very connected with fear, stress, comparison as well as abstraction, oversimplification and language.

"I can see that AT and ego can be close and dangerous friends."

An overblown ego, a mind racing around comparisons, concerned about potential dangers and constantly analyzing how to move above the neighbor, easily suppresses its creative potential.

Exercising your creative muscles produces the opposite effect. It tames the ego and keeps it controlled.

When you exercise your creative muscles you rely less on language and time and you tend to suspend judgment while staying in close contact with reality at a perceptual level. This state closely relates to meditation. A state where boredom loses meaning because time becomes relative. A state where concentration becomes effortless because it's driven by passion and genuine engagement, not by the fake interest of gaining advantage over others.

"But it's hard to keep our ego controlled."

It is. The first works of many innovators are full of creativity and originality. Once they become well known, their next works are often less creative and more predictable. There are many reasons for this. One of the reasons is that as people become well known, they receive more attention and this extra attention is both valuable but also dangerous.

Attention brings with it the feeling of having power over others. This power stimulates our AT and increases our vanity, the comparisons we make and also the fear of losing that sense of control. We enter a vicious circle that keeps feeding and enlarging our ego network.

As our social status improves, the ego enters a chronic state of worry. We want to maintain that status quo. Innovating becomes secondary. The main goal is to maintain our social and financial status, our reputation and prestige. Priorities change. CT is limited and suppressed under the weight of stress, comparison, fear and vanity.

The shores of boredom

Ego promotes boredom. Let's ride the depth elevator to explore a bit the roots of boredom. Our network of preoccupations and analysis tends to create vicious circles around the same or similar themes. It works at very abstract, symbolic and simplified levels. Eventually there is only that much you can do on the shores of life's ocean.

Boredom happens when you get trapped in that shore. When you fail to engage and dive into the immensity of the full experience, the one that never fails to surprise you.

Boredom has no chance to emerge when you are fully and deeply engaged with the present. When your awareness is absorbed into any activity. When you transcend AT and access the full complexity and richness of life.

That is why exercising your CT muscles, engaging deeply with reality, is the best investment towards a richer future devoid of boredom, at both professional and personal levels.

Learning new things is another strategy to stay away from boredom.

Learning to learn

The rigid ways of AT restrict learning processes as well as our personal growth.

CT encourages a free flow of ideas, an open field where learning thrives and where we gather tons of confidence in our own potential.

Exercise your CT muscles to empower your learning processes.

Spend less

The lack of exercise of your creative muscles is not only an invitation to feel depressed and empty, but makes your life more expensive as well: boredom encourages the spending of resources on external things to fill the void we feel.

Exercising your creative potential fills your life with passion and excitement through constant exploration.

"A different kind of travelling that is much cheaper!"

We all have a threshold of satisfaction that we need to reach to feel whole and joyful. Do you want to depend on your wallet to reach it? Or maybe you prefer to get there through ways that are not only inexpensive but bring you unexpected gifts?

So balancing AT with CT tames our ego and prevents boredom. To begin moving towards that balance we need to become more aware of what moves in our minds.

The right spirit

Realize that whatever crosses your conscious mind, what you analyze and judge, is made of simplifications and abstractions that are highly detached from the complex details of reality. Become a patient observer of this process. Avoid getting trapped in the ruminations and the vicious circles of your AT.

Let things flow, come and go, like winds that deliver information and then continue on their way elsewhere. Don't ignore that information. Observe it and gather it when necessary, as part of the ingredients your subconscious uses on a regular basis. It is not an absolute truth but just another piece in the complex puzzle of life.

We don't want to stay at the surface for too long. The more we exercise CT, the deeper we go and the closer we get to the immense richness of life.

Closer to reality

Creative people engage deeper with life, deeper than those that spend most of their time juggling the abstractions and symbols of their conscious AT.

And the efficient innovator is not always navigating the depths, but comes and goes between subconscious complexity and conscious abstractions and symbols.

In summary, in most cases, the creative individual has a more balanced mind than the non-creative type.

Of course, let's not forget that when things are taken to the extremes, being too creative can be as dangerous as being too analytical.

As we approach a healthy balance between AT and CT, the benefits go deep and stay with us in the long term, avoiding the damaging effects that are typical with other strategies.

A healthy drug that endures

What if the most beneficial drug in the world was to have a balanced mind, one where AT and CT lived in harmony, helping and supporting each other?

According to Wikipedia, a drug is "a substance which may have medicinal, intoxicating, performance enhancing or other effects when taken or put into a human body or the body of another animal and is not considered a food or exclusively a food."[46]

What is considered a drug or a food can change depending on the culture you are looking at. The key point is that in most of the substances that we identify as dangerous drugs, the risks and harmful effects outweigh the benefits in humans.

Almost all recreational drug use is intended to bring or replace something that is felt to be missing in our minds or to remove something that we don't want to face or experience.

Sometimes people take drugs to escape boredom, fear or stress. Other times they take them to loosen and widen their minds, to escape the tyranny of analysis and narrow thinking.

Curiously, the above matches perfectly with the effects produced by exercising your creative muscles. Exercising your creativity tames AT processes and therefore your network of preoccupations, your ego, reducing fear, boredom and stress. It also widens the horizons of your mind, balancing AT with the unique capabilities and processes of CT.

Both routes, the external drug use and the exercising of our CT muscles, would apparently seem to empower your creativity and help balance AT and CT.

But there is a big difference between them. The effect of external drugs lasts typically a short span of time and often creates chronic dependency. In general, like the boost of sugar, it soon fades away, requiring constant attachment to an external source of pleasure. And we are not even mentioning the harmful side effects.

The alternative is exercising our CT muscles. Like any other muscle training, the process accumulates benefits gradually. Its effects remain for far longer in your system and if it creates any dependency, is typically, except in extreme cases, a healthy one which generates satisfaction and a joy that comes from within. A satisfaction that doesn't depend on external sources and blends seamlessly with the rest of your being, helping sustain your confidence and energy.

There are no lack of artists that defend the use of external drugs, whichever those may be, as engines of their creativity. In the end it all comes down to a personal choice.

When you wish to grow your body muscles, do you choose to rely on gradual processes that will slowly build up your stamina, helping the body adapt to changes as they happen? These are processes that become self-sustaining over time. Or do you prefer to stuff yourself with steroids and similar quick-acting substances that can produce fast short-term gains in your muscles but later become harder to sustain at a mental and physical level? (Not even considering the other risks associated with those quick-acting solutions).

The same thing happens with creativity and innovation. Some drugs may certainly facilitate creative thinking in some situations. What you need to ask yourself is: do you really want to rely at a mental and physical level on such external aids (that are potentially a health hazard) in order to get there? I personally don't but it is a personal choice. Some would say that we already rely on many external aids, for example glasses to help our eyes focus in the case of myopia. But the associated side effects of all external aids are not the same. It is that trade off, that balance between benefits and harmful consequences that should be considered in order to decide the best route to take.

"Quick and more risky strategies vs slower and more secure ones."

The faster and higher you climb, the harder is the fall and the more difficult it is to stay alert to the potential obstacles and challenges you may encounter on the way.

The slower and more carefully you climb, the easier it is to be prepared for all eventualities, and the easier it is to set a permanent presence on top of the mountain and stay there for a long time.

Strategies that take into account our entire self, both the mental and physical perspectives, over long periods of time, are more likely to produce balanced results, balanced beings that perform well not just at a creative or professional level, but also at an emotional and interpersonal one.[47]

The best way to get there is not made of sugar boosts, of quick rushes that fail to sustain the transformation we are looking for. Instead you can use and enjoy a balanced mind, a mind that combines the best of what AT and CT can offer.

The objective is not just to produce great artists, engineers or professionals. The objective is to produce balanced and whole human beings, able to perform professionally, but also to feel empathy, to communicate and relate to others in deep ways. We get there through a balanced mind that is able to exercise its creativity in peaceful and harmonious coexistence with our all-powerful and essential analytical thinking processes.

To close this chapter, let's reflect for a moment on the issue of depth and shallowness.

From the shore to the depths and back

Pedro likes to sit on the edge of the lake, staring at the smooth glittering surface. His friend Curioso joins him sometimes. Curioso likes to imagine what is hidden beneath the surface of the lake and actively explores it.

The balance between AT and CT can also be approached from a shallow vs deep perspective. Contemplating reality from the shores of AT gives you a high level generic and abstract view, a shallow perspective that requires small effort, but also delivers little reward.

Reaching deep into life, into its complexity, requires a special effort in terms of energy, time and resources, but the potential rewards are much larger. Once you reach deep, it gets easier to return later to those depths, where the biggest potential for learning and personal development exists.

This may sound like a "no pain, no gain" scenario, but it is in fact often the opposite. Proactive efforts to get closer to the deep riches of life keep us engaged and connected, relax our mind and can deliver a constant source of excitement and motivation. In the long term we get more pleasure and joy instead of pain.

And just as divers cannot stay forever underwater, we cannot be exercising our CT muscles continuously. That would spend too many resources and besides we would be unable to perform the day-to-day obligations that are calling from the shore.

Find the balance between fulfilling your obligations at the shore and diving into the wide ocean of life to gather the riches and treasures that are waiting for you.

Second part

The following chapters are made of complementary information that expands the previous content. They are ideal for those that want to go deeper into some of the areas covered.

CHAPTER 8:

Creative Storytelling

*Without the playing with fantasy no creative
work has ever yet come to birth. The debt we owe
to the play of imagination is incalculable."*

— Carl Jung

Mijae crouched in a dark corner waiting for the troops to pass. Time
was running out. She remembered the words of her father: "Pay
attention when you open the box, it will self-destruct in a matter of
seconds… "

Silence had returned to the corridor. Mijae was breathing hard,
her leg was a bloody mess. Noises could be heard again. Mijae put
the box on the floor and opened it at once. Numbers were shining
inside: twenty, nineteen, eighteen… As more troops approached
her position, she tried to memorize what she was seeing. In the
center of the box there was a most curious engraving, an elephant
climbing a ladder and, on the top of the ladder, a spacecraft. Inside
the spacecraft there was a written code: 67-54-399. She went over
the numbers and the engraving several times as the counter moved
on: nine, eight, seven. The troops were now very close and Mijae
muttered to herself: 67, 54, 399… 67, 54, 399… As the counter
reached zero, the engraving dissolved and Mijae moved away just
before the troops arrived. She had the scene and the number fixed
in her mind. Her father would be proud.

"Quite a story, it had me hooked all the way!"

Now imagine if I tell you the code and its details without blending it with a story. Notice how much easier it is to recall the information when we surround it with a narrative.

"Why is this happening?"

We are still in the early stages of understanding how human memory works, but we know that association is a key concept.

Imagine being at the bottom of a cliff in a deep valley. Imagine that you need to climb up to get to a different valley, to another specific channel, one among a million others.

"Finding it will be hard."

If you surround that location with a narrative, you create all sorts of signs, reference points and hooks you can hold on to. They support you and guide you on your way to that new location.

"Markers, hooks and reference points."

Yes. That's the secret of the most impressive achievements related to our memory: creating reference points along the highways of your mind.

But as we delve deeper into the essence of great storytelling, we find that there is much more to it than just creating markers.

What is the essence of a story? Beyond its extraordinary usefulness in helping us recall information, why are we so fascinated by them?

We all resonate with visions of children and adults gathering around a fire, entranced by the magic that a good story weaves on the canvas of their minds.

Understanding how and why stories work can benefit you in surprising ways.

"Good stories are central to so many things."

Yes, from marketing to politics, art and science. A good story flexes and exercises your creative muscles, brings you closer to others and communicates information in very powerful and deep ways.

"What are some of the features that great stories share?"

Let's reflect about some of those and how they affect us.

Tension and conflict

Conflict attracts our attention. We are sensitive to it for the sake of our own survival or the useful information it communicates.

"Tension awakens us."

Conflicts help the mind stay engaged with the narrative. A story without tension can work in certain cases and with certain topics and audiences. But most of the successful stories out there have some kind of conflict that needs to be resolved.

"Creating and resolving conflicts is key."

Conflict makes stories engaging and suspenseful.

Mystery

From the beginnings of humankind, from birth to death, we are surrounded by mysteries. Some of them are potentially threatening, others are not. In all cases, a mystery is an invitation for the mind to explore.

"Suspense!"

The mind feels driven to gather information, which may become relevant either for our survival or for our interactions with others. Mystery is compelling; it draws us in and captures our attention.

"We don't want things to be too obvious."

Films that present all the information clear and open from the beginning may succeed in some contexts, but most of the successful stories create mysteries in the narrative, gaps that are often filled and revealed towards the end of the story.

"Keep audiences wanting and craving to know more till the very end."

Mysteries are for the mind like food for the body. We crave them. Create gaps in your story and take your time to fill them in.

Parallel universes

We live only one life. And there is only so much we can do in our existence. Stories create characters through which we can experience a different existence.

"Becoming an explorer, a thief, a president, a writer…"

Stories exercise our creative muscles by transporting us for a few minutes or hours to a completely different context. During those moments our minds and the new context blend and combine. This adds new ingredients to our subconscious, which can eventually help us incubate and produce novel insights.

"Good stories are food for the mind and training for our creative muscles!"

Be bold, use stories to experience different lives and expand the context and horizons of your audience and yourself.

A great output channel

Recall great speeches by historical figures, the great monologues of your favorite movies or that unique lecture of your favorite teacher. Every great story needs a great vehicle, a channel to reach the audience in powerful ways. That channel may be an actress, a politician, a teacher, or it may be the pages of a book.

In all of these cases we find that similar tricks to the previous ones are being used to sustain the attention of our easily distracted minds.

A great orator creates suspense in the way he/she talks, making use of dramatic pauses and changes of intonation and rhythm. This also happens in the case of great musical works, full of contrast and variation.

"Contrast, suspense, twists, surprises."

Imagine a book that had a single chapter whose 300 pages had no variation in formatting, structure and pagination. The odds of that book being successful can't be very high.

"Definitely!"

Successful books create suspense in their table of contents, in the way they structure their chapters, in how they introduce them and in how they close them, anticipating the mystery that is about to arrive in the coming pages.

Hold in mind the importance of the context, format, structure and delivery channel of your story. They are a key part of its success.

Contrast

Let's focus a bit more on contrast.

In storytelling, contrast is key in relation to the characters and their experiences.

Some of the stories that have touched us the most are those where the circumstances and events surrounding the characters change in dramatic ways throughout the narrative. The changes can be external or internal. They may happen in the inner life of our characters and not necessarily in their external circumstances.

When you create a new story, enrich its context with additional characters that can provide tension and contrast.

As you draft the timeline of an event, think of other events before and/or after that can provide contrast so that both get reinforced.

Stories without contrast can also engage audiences. There are films where changes and variation are very subtle and yet are enormously profound.

In any case, stories have to engage and nothing engages as strongly as contrast.

"Find your contrast and emphasize it."

And remember, we are not talking here only about films or books. Stories are key everywhere, from the marketing of a business to politics, education, etc.

A common thread

All the previous points work in different ways with that key element: information.

"The raw stuff behind it all."

The brain craves information because throughout history having the right information could mean surviving, finding the right mate, winning a contest or discovering that crucial formula.

"Good information is gold for our minds."

But finding the information requires a lot of energy and time, and staying engaged with that process is difficult for a mind that has to constantly monitor multiple inputs and events.

"Stories make that engagement easier."

Stories structure and package information in easy to digest units. They create variation in the way the information is revealed, making use of anticipation, mysteries, conflicts, etc.

"They keep the mind engaged."

They help us sustain our attention long enough to complete the delivery of their message. And they provide original, colorful and unusual markers that stand out within the oceans of your memory and make their information easier to recall.

Creating characters

Great stories have texture, richness, variation and detail. Great characters need to have specific details to grow and develop.

"The more details you provide, the more the character grows and the easier is to engage with it."

Imagine we want to write a film script about a young man. We know the script should have tension, mystery, suspense, twists and a memorable ending. We pace around the room reflecting, thinking, remembering other films, and yet we cannot come up with anything.

"Good stories are born from…"

The fact is, it is hard to come up with anything if we start with nothing.

So far all we know is that we want to write a movie script about… a young man?

"A young man is too generic."

With such an abstract objective no wonder we cannot find a way to develop this beginning into an actual story.

Creating compelling and detailed characters is the base of great stories and in general the base of many creative projects.

"A great character establishes a direction and a context."

You may be making a film, a music work, a sculpture, a painting or any other form of art. Characters are where it all begins.

Or you may be instead designing an online business or a company around a product/service and now the characters become your users, your audience. You have to get to know them as if they were your own blood.

Creating a detailed and well-developed character or getting to know in depth your users/audience, will empower the rest of your creative path.

What is the background of this young man? What has happened in his life, from its beginnings till the moment in which the story takes place? Who are the people that matter the most to him? What are the challenges he has faced in the past and the ones that he is facing now? These and many other questions have to be answered before you can begin to develop fully your story.

"I imagine actors have to follow a similar process."

Yes, an actor would never consider performing a role without having studied every single detail about the character.

The scriptwriter or story writer has exactly the same challenge. Writing about a character that is fully unknown to us is like trying to make a painting about a topic we haven't yet decided.

So let's give it a try with this young man. Let's enrich his background story. The writing can be fragmented and doesn't have to make complete sense. You are brainstorming. Just begin to get to know him in your own words.

Ricardo is a young man in his early thirties, 33 to be precise.

"I try to be specific with the details."

Yes, the more the better. Use specific numbers and names. They help you create markers and hooks in your mind.

Ricardo was born in Palermo, in the Italian island of Sicily, where his parents still live. He has two other brothers.

During his childhood, Ricardo dreamed about travelling, but his family, being very poor, couldn't afford to send him abroad. Besides, he was the youngest of 3 brothers and often the last in line when it was time to receive the few things the family could afford.

"This is a beginning, we are starting to see the face of this young Ricardo!"

Let's continue, we want to know more about his emotions and feelings.

Ricardo loved wide open spaces, like the coastal ones around his native Sicily. Being from an island, he longed for discovering other places. He was also very artistic and loved creating sand sculptures at the beaches near his home.

At 20 he met Marina, a beautiful Sicilian girl who became his girlfriend.

"We are getting to know more and more Ricardo. But what about his challenges?"

Ricardo's father, Antonio, often vented his frustrations on Ricardo. Being the youngest and the most sensitive, Ricardo was always the target when things were not going well financially.

The older brothers were already working small jobs around Palermo and Ricardo was the only one still struggling with his studies and not bringing any money home.

Because of this, the relationship between Ricardo and Antonio grew more and more tense over the years.

"So far so good. Now we need to start thickening the base."

Antonio wants Ricardo to marry Marina. Marina's family has a decent financial position and Antonio doesn't have faith in the financial future of his artistic son.

"I sense more conflict around the corner…"

With the years, Ricardo has grown tired of Marina. He senses that marrying her will chain him forever to the little world of Sicily. What he desires is something completely different.

"It's time to take action."

One night, Ricardo takes his art tools, a rucksack and a bit of food and quietly leaves for the port where his friend Emmanuel is waiting for him in a small boat.

Ricardo leaves Sicily with his friend. They set sail towards the mainland.

"Wait a minute. We were writing about the background of Ricardo, but suddenly it feels as if we have moved on to write the actual wider story we were looking for from the beginning. What is going on?"

That's the great thing about writing the background of a character. As soon as it becomes rich and deep enough, the backbone of a story may appear anytime.

"Great characters become great stories!"

The past, personality and context of a great character are the base of infinite stories, and it is only a matter of time that whenever you start to develop that character's background, a story will start suggesting itself.

"I feel that the more specific I am, the better the chances of that happening."

Yes, be as specific as you can with the details. Write real names, numbers and locations. Explain how things look, feel and behave. The more specific you are, the more chances that a story will start arising from this process.

"Stories are great training for my creative muscles."

They exercise your creative muscles and help you deliver in powerful ways messages that can empower your products, services and relationships.

"Now that's a story!"

Let it flow

Every word is a universe. From single words stories have been born. A word. A thought. A beginning. A seed.

Life is a page, blank at the beginning, rich with anecdotes and stories at the end. And like in a fractal, pages within pages overlap as different stories are born from each other and return to the main path of our lives.

Let your words flow and create amazing stories to empower your professional and personal life.

CHAPTER 9:

The Evolution of Ideas

"The best way to have a good idea is to have a lot of ideas."

— Dr. Linus Pauling

Ideation processes have surprising parallels with Darwinian evolution. In this section we play with some analogies that help us understand even better the fascinating world of insights. Let's contemplate the nurturing process of creativity from an evolutionary perspective.

As we mentioned earlier, in his book "The Selfish Gene", Richard Dawkins introduced the concept of memes, cultural units representing ideas or behaviors that spread from person to person.

In the next paragraphs I will sometimes establish parallels between biology and the world of insights. We don't intend to establish direct comparisons between evolutionary processes in biology and in the world of ideas. They are different in so many ways. We simply use biology as a useful aid to inspire interesting reflections about the way ideas behave.

Productivity, the sex of ideas

Mutations are part of our theories about the origin and evolution of life. These mutations produce changes in life forms. And changes that contribute in positive ways to the survival of that life form, spread and remain in the generations to come.

Sexual reproduction in nature helps combine and spread mutations that may benefit specific genes. In culture, ideas can mix and blend with other ideas, giving birth to new insights that may take firm hold in a mind and spread fast through many others.

Let's connect the process we have just described to how productive innovators often are. Innovators produce massive amounts of experiments, combinations, prototypes and variations. The best of them survive. Iterations happen and the process restarts again and again. That's why productivity is so important. It accelerates the evolution of ideas by naturally selecting the best variations and discarding the ones that are not so useful.

"It's as if an unconscious competition is taking place within our neural circuits."

Think of an idea as a series of electrical intensities present at various connection points, such as the synapses. Various patterns of activation become stronger and more reinforced or fade away depending on the context we live in.

When our context resonates with a mental pattern, an idea, that pattern becomes stronger in our brains and it may begin to displace others that become weaker.

Remember the phrase "1% inspiration, 99% perspiration". Think of creative processes as evolutionary processes. They take time and require work. Creativity is a gradual process of nurturing, refining, pruning and shaping insights. A process that at times happens in isolation and at others takes place in collaboration with teammates, friends, relatives and strangers.

From the perspective of an innovator, insights that are worth keeping are those that keep you on the right path towards an innovative solution.

And just like evolution needs a diverse context surrounding the unit of selection, so our mind needs to gather a diversity of quality ingredients in order to incubate great insights.

A changing environment feeds constant evolution

Making another useful parallel with biology, evolution in nature doesn't stop working once a good combination is passed onto the next generation. The environment keeps changing and therefore evolution keeps happening. Our ideas keep evolving as well, together with the dynamic context that surrounds them. There is no such thing as a final insight, only solutions that should continue changing over time as the context around them evolves.

Survival means staying relevant

We can draw another parallel in terms of survival: when the environment changes, some genes may evolve to adapt to those changes. The organisms that hold those new genes have more chances to survive.

In the same way, insights need to keep evolving and adapting to the changing markets, business environments or personal contexts. Insights that stop evolving while the context changes soon become irrelevant.

"Our context never stops changing."

Evolution needs variation

Another useful analogy is related to mutations and variations. Just as natural evolution wouldn't happen without those "mistakes" we call mutations, so we need to encourage our ideas to evolve by introducing variation through different strategies.

"Divergence of course."

Some of these strategies can include:

- **Adapt:** Adapt insights to different contexts.

- **Rearrange, modify:** Modify insights, rearrange their configurations.
- **Combine:** Bring together unrelated ingredients or insights.
- **Substitute:** Replace parts of an insight with other elements.
- **Add/Remove:** Add or remove elements of an insight.
- **Invert:** Turn ideas upside down, invert them, challenge perspectives.

Random ingredients, like mutations, help us diverge before we converge, and can make it easier to open new avenues, to grow new activation patterns in our minds.

New insights are very fragile at the beginning. It is hard to keep them alive as they are competing against more established ideas. Their activation strength is still too weak.

"I often can't remember what I was thinking an hour ago…"

If we haven't invested enough effort in strengthening a new pattern, the habitual winds of the mind will soon erase those soft and fresh marks.

But a weak idea that contributes in positive ways to our current context will soon grow stronger and start to displace other ideas and thoughts.

And in the same way that new adaptations in nature don't start from zero, but extend instead existing configurations, ideas don't begin from zero either. Some are expansions of your existing patterns of activation. Others are adaptations of ideas started by different sources. Relying on a mixture of your own ideation processes and those of others accelerates the natural evolution of your insights.

Getting stuck

Yet another interesting analogy relates to habits, patterns that become deeply ingrained in our neural networks. Insights and ideas that take strong roots in our mind, carving deep channels and activation routes, can be hard to get rid of. It is hard to remove them even if these patterns don't resonate anymore with the changing environment.

"Just as it happens in some evolutionary processes. And what can we do about it?"

We can challenge and fight those habits using different strategies. Most of them are based on diverging and you can find them in the previous exercises outlined in the book.

To conclude, let's emphasize again the importance of random mutations. Our incubation processes generate combinations, mutations and variations born out of our accumulated ingredients. New insights are then verified and evaluated by our analytical processes.

The great thing about our mind is that the mutations that are produced are not blind guesses. They are based on the guided interaction between ingredients that have been purposefully chosen during a good nurturing process. This increases the speed and potential for unique new insights to develop.

CHAPTER 10:

Resonant Education

*"An inventor is simply a person who doesn't take his
education too seriously. You see, from the time a person
is six years old until he graduates from college he has to
take three or four examinations a year. If he flunks once,
he is out. But an inventor is almost always failing. He tries
and fails maybe a thousand times. If he succeeds once
then he's in. These two things are diametrically opposite.
We often say that the biggest job we have is to teach a
newly hired employee how to fail intelligently. We have
to train him to experiment over and over and to keep
on trying and failing until he learns what will work."*

— Charles Kettering

The incubation of creative insights can help us reflect about that
all important topic - education. For that, let's turn to physics
and create a hypothesis of how and why incubation processes work.

In acoustics, objects have different natural frequencies of vibration depending on their physical characteristics. For an object, it is
easy to vibrate at its resonant or natural frequencies.[48]

We can use an analogy to think of information, stored or fresh,
as a vibrating wave of a specific frequency and wavelength.

As information entities interact with each other, we arrive to the
phenomenon known as constructive interference.

Constructive interference happens when waves match, producing a larger cumulative effect as a result. That cumulative result is
therefore easier to notice for our consciousness. It can more easi-

ly move above that threshold that separates the conscious and the subconscious.

Thinking of this process in terms of waves helps us understand better what still remains mysterious on so many levels.

The implications of the resonance analogy reach far into the field of education.

The child is the seed

Think of the mind of a child as a set of waves that represent information. These waves can interact with other information waves around them. Some of these interactions will produce constructive interference effects and others will produce destructive (or non-constructive) interference effects.

As the child's mind evolves, the type of external waves that will produce constructive interference will constantly change. Good education can be seen as the process of surrounding the child with enough information entities that produce constructive interference.

Constructive interference is self-sustaining. It powers itself. Motivation and enthusiasm are its companions and side effects.

Forcing the mind of children to interact with information waves that don't resonate with theirs, produces destructive interference and kills motivation and enthusiasm. However, the process of surrounding a child with the right information entities is a delicate one.

"It's not that simple."

There has to be a balance between both types of interference. A balance that over time should become more biased towards the constructive side.

At the beginning, the child needs a healthy amount of non-constructive interference for the sake of introducing him/her to new areas and exploring a variety of paths. As the mind develops, motivation and enthusiasm is to be sustained with a good amount of constructive interference, while maintaining the mind open to other types of interference patterns that can and will arise when dealing with unexpected situations and other challenges.

In fact, we could argue that exposing ourselves to a certain amount of negative interference may be as important for our minds as being exposed to germs is for our immune system.

"We need to be exposed to some polarity to be fit and ready to deal with the challenges of the real world out there."

What matters is the overall sum of the process. Which type of interference is winning, constructive or destructive?

Experts state that it is good for children to be exposed to a certain amount of germs, but we also need to make sure that the germs in question will not endanger their organism too much. We need to find a similar balance with the kinds of information waves we are exposed to during our childhood. A lot of childhood problems are related to children being overwhelmed by too many information waves that don't resonate at all with their personas.

If you want to light up a fire, do you try to randomly combine anything you find around yourself? Or do you look for specific materials that you know have the potential to spark a fire when reacting with each other? What strategy will be more successful?

The first is a lazy strategy, akin to the strategies used by many education programs of the past. The second strategy requires more planning and effort, but produces a bigger payoff in the end.

The human seed

The child can be seen as well as the initial seed in the creative process of producing a flexible and harmonic adult mind. To produce a beautiful adult mind, we have to begin from a child's mind whose motivation and enthusiasm must be organic and natural, not forced.

In summary, learning and growth is social and interactive. We thrive when surrounded by a context we resonate with.

Great seeds for new ideas are born from the harmony that arises as fresh and stored quality information ingredients blend with each other. And a harmonious adult mind is an extension of a child's mind that thrives in a harmonious environment, blending external and stored information patterns in mainly constructive ways.

Finally, let's remember the beautiful words of the Oscar-winning actor Daniel Day Lewis in connection with the concept of resonance.

"I can't account for how at any given moment I feel the need to explore a life as opposed to another, but I do know that I can only do this work if I feel almost as if there is no choice; that a subject coincides inexplicably with a very personal need and a very specific moment in time."[49]

That's what I call resonance.

CHAPTER 11

Creative Productions

*"Genius is one percent inspiration, and
ninety-nine percent perspiration."*

— Thomas Edison

L et's now explore the foundations of creative and artistic ventures through the various general principles that many of them share.

Most creative endeavors can be divided into pre-production, production and post-production phases.

All ventures begin with an idea. The idea can be implemented through a combination of different techniques and strategies. Deciding what techniques we should use in a project should be the last stretch of a deep pre-production phase. A phase that should help us refine the answer to the question of what channels will best express our message.

Let's now take a closer look at the three stages.

The three stages

The initial stage, the pre-production phase, establishes a firm base. This base should be flexible. It is built in close interaction with future users or audiences. It has to provide a good foundation, besides being able to shift and change in response to movements in markets and audiences.

Traditionally, pre-production stages were built to be quite rigid and fixed. This was fine for those times in which the dynamics and behaviors of markets and audiences changed slowly. Today, pre-production needs to be lean, agile and flexible. Communication and feedback from future customers is essential from day one.

Pre-production is essential even in the creative projects that seem the most spontaneous and random. It is not a matter of how long it takes. Pre-production can take seconds or years. It is about establishing a good initial foundation on top of which our production can have the best chances for success.

After the pre-production, the production stage implements the plan. Subsequently, the post-production stage refines the result. They both depend crucially on the base established by the pre-production phase.

Pre-production can be as simple as deciding on a theme or location, the type of subjects we are interested in, the range of resources we require, the setup of our equipment and the schedule and timeline of the project.

In the case of more complex productions, the number of people and elements involved can increase significantly.

In general what we are trying to do during the pre-production phase is to fill in any gaps we may have in relation to our challenge. This makes for a much smoother production phase.

There are a number of areas we have to consider when working on our pre-production.

Concept

The idea and the vision are the most important thing and everything should be connected to them. The equipment, the location, the crew, the timing and all other details depend on that initial seed.

Some creatives and innovators like to leave their initial idea and plans in a vague and fuzzy state on purpose. After preparing the crew, location, props and timing, they maintain enough flexibility and freedom to steer the final idea in various directions as the production develops.

Furthermore, starting a creative project without any idea is also a possibility and some creatives work in that way. What you are really doing in these cases is not so much to begin without an idea, but simply deferring the finding of your key insights until the very moment in which the production stage is happening. For this to be effective, the team and leader in charge need to have fit and healthy creative muscles. Deferring the entire idea or parts of it to the production stage has obvious risks, but potentially very unique benefits as well.

"This reminds me of the importance of context."

Yes, some unique insights are only triggered when the participants are on stage, when the final context surrounds them and the pressure of the event is present. That's why many creatives like to shape and change their ideas and scripts right during the production stage in response to the new insights that are born right there and then.

"What about rehearsals?"

Rehearsals are of course connected to the above. But they often cannot replace the unique mixture of feelings, vibrations and events that takes place during the final production. It is not easy to imitate the atmosphere and context of the real production, when actors give everything they've got, when speakers gather all their intensity, when it's an all or nothing situation.

In some unique cases, it is possible to gather a talented crew and the necessary resources, enter a stimulating context together and incubate right there and then the key insights that the team will work on.

This is not for the faint of heart and it requires well-developed CT muscles, but it is extremely stimulating, inspiring and motivating when it works. Many successful innovators engage on similar processes.

"Exciting and definitely challenging!"

Those are extreme examples. Most projects and most innovators prefer to sacrifice that ultimate freshness and instead engage on a more tranquil and predictable path.

Think of a horse. CT is a more impulsive and unpredictable horse with tremendous power and possibilities. AT is a more controllable but slower horse. Combine them in different ways to create your own strategies.

Ultimately, few things can beat preparing a production well in advance, especially if specific details are essential for the ultimate success of the project. Location, crew and similar resources are hard to improvise if the aim is to achieve top quality or very specific results. So defining our ideas with great granularity and detail, and arranging all aspects of the production as precisely as possible are very useful processes, provided we keep our mind open to considering the many unexpected opportunities that can arise during the production phase.

"Flexible foundations."

Flexibility is always essential, because often only the real time interaction with the subjects and locations may awaken us to different unexpected angles or perspectives of our idea that we may have missed during pre-production. Being ready to grab those insight bubbles when they appear is key.

Becoming the subject

Getting to know our subject, understanding it, riding its depth elevators, is a key part of any pre-production process.

If we are painting or filming a landscape, we should first visit it and study it from multiple angles. If our creative project is focused on a person, we can hold several meetings to create a connection with that individual and explore the essence of that character as much as possible.

Become the subject, own it inside out.

Equipment

Our equipment and resources are key factors in translating our vision into a final product.

As we start out as creatives, we are often highly concerned with finding equipment that can serve for multiple purposes.

"For all the imaginable purposes if possible."

Notice how we can establish an analogy here with the generic simplifications and abstractions of analytical thinking. The more purposes a tool serves, the more compromises it has to make and the further it gets from the specific behavior and features we really need.

The features of the equipment we need to shoot wild tigers in the jungle are very different from the ones we need to capture macro photography of flowers or portraits of children.

And the range of colors, surfaces and other materials an artist may use changes depending on the media, be it acrylics, oils or watercolors. Same happens in other creative areas.

For best results, your equipment should closely match the challenge you are facing.

Scope

It is very possible to carry with us equipment that can cover all the scenarios we may possibly encounter, but there will be a tradeoff between the excess of weight, time and other complications required by the extra material and the overall quality of our final results.

Being a jack-of-all-trades while maintaining a good overall quality across many areas is possible, but far more difficult in terms of energy and time required than specializing in a single area. As the saying goes, "jack-of-all-trades, master of none."

By trying to do everything you don't send a clear message to the markets and audiences about the meaning of your message. What makes you different and unique? What makes you instantly recognizable? By diversifying too much, the range and variety of your works may become a distraction in itself. The essence of your message becomes harder to grasp, label and categorize, harder to put into words. And words, in the end, are our main channel of communication with others.

Quality and quantity rarely go together. To focus on quality and deliver solutions that reach deep into people's hearts and minds, we need to identify specific challenges within specific communities, challenges that need innovative solutions. And we need to breathe, explore and become one with those specific contexts.

"We need to go deep!"

Yes, by going down on specific depth elevators your style becomes more concrete, distinct and clear, helping you stand out from the competition.

When you remain at the shallow surface, at the shoreline from which you can see multiple areas and disciplines, your competition is very large. The shallow waters are easy to walk and most people spend their time there. When you invest time and effort to plunge deep into the massive ocean of possibilities, your competition goes down significantly. Not many are willing or able to abandon the comfort and safety of the shallow waters in order to sail through the complex challenges and storms of that ocean.

Riding down the depth elevators your logistics get simplified as well. The equipment you need to use or carry will be the one that specifically fits the project at hand.

"I often worry about the equipment and logistics…"

It is natural for those who are new to innovation to emphasize equipment, because at those stages we are focused on exploring. Like children in a playground, we discover which techniques we enjoy the most and we experiment with the possibilities offered by different tools.

"We are getting to know in depth the tools of the trade."

As professionals, ideas and concepts are the top priority. Once an idea has been found, we proceed to choose the equipment that best expresses that idea.

"The equipment follows the idea, not vice versa."

Yes, that is the best path towards quality and efficiency.

In summary, a good pre-production should prepare you to achieve your objectives using the least amount of resources and equipment while maintaining quality across the board.

Location

Location is context. Context reinforces meaning and provides depth. It is key for all kinds of creative ventures, from media productions to business gatherings, brainstorming sessions and other activities.

Choosing a location in advance allows us to concentrate on what is really important, expressing our idea or concept in the best way possible.

The location can be indoors, like a meeting room or a film-making studio, a painter's atelier or an old building. Or it can be outdoors, in a green meadow or in the streets of a city.

In some projects the location may not be so relevant for the work itself but it is still crucial because of the psychological influence it has on us.

"The context around us influences how we feel."

The ideal location has to resonate with our personality.

It would be tempting to say, for example, that the ideal location for an artist should be quiet and tranquil, a context where the artist can fully focus on the work. The reality is that some creatives thrive in completely opposite circumstances. Some people need a chaotic environment to be inspired, or their project may resonate with specific environments that are far from a tranquil oasis.

"So the idea and the person come first and afterwards comes the location."

Yes, and that location will directly impact our performance and output, so a close relationship and a good resonance between the concept, the team and the location should exist at all times.

"Any location related challenges I should be aware of?"

Find out in advance if permits are required. It is wise to avoid wasting the day because of a missing permit. This is especially important if the event involves large teams, which will be more noticeable outdoors.

But even If you are working on your own and go unnoticed, if your venture is commercial, it is very important to inform yourself about any needed permits, as it is possible that you will have to show them eventually as your project expands, enters competitions or gains visibility.

Timing is everything

The right timing can make all the difference.

"Planning schedules carefully is critical."

This is essential, for example, in the case of media productions. If we are shooting a film and we intend to use only artificial lighting indoors, we will be ok working at any time of the day as long as we block any external light sources entering the area. If we intend, however, to combine natural and artificial lighting, or we want to work indoors but making use of natural light that comes through the windows or doors, the time of the day in which we shoot will be just as critical as if we decide to work outdoors.

Those are obvious considerations. But think now of a business meeting. The time of day at which an event takes place has a significant impact on our levels of energy, ability to concentrate and even mood.

So plan your timings carefully.

Crew

You may be working on your own or within a team.

If we are leading a large project, we will need the support of a number of people to carry out our venture successfully and your crew is a critical part of the success you are looking for.

Even if you work alone, it's still very important to understand the dynamics that take place when you work within a larger team, as eventually it is very likely that you will either collaborate with others or work for others.

Many innovators work both on their own and within groups. It is important to be flexible and ready to work both ways, especially today, when collaborations and large-scale productions are so commonplace.

Should I do everything myself?

At some point most innovators have to deal with the ever-present temptation of wanting to do everything by themselves. They think they have the skills to pull it off, and most often they do. But that is not the point.

Innovation cannot be separated from productivity. Being efficient and productive can enhance the quality of your results by iterating your concept through multiple scenarios and variations. By wanting to do it all by yourself, you risk spending too much energy, effort and time while sacrificing the productivity you could achieve when uniting the skills and efforts of a larger crew.

"We don't need to be heroes."

Yes, you don't need to be a hero. It's possible that you may be able to do it all by yourself and in certain small projects that may actually be the best strategy.

"Sometimes you only learn certain things when you do it all by yourself."

Working on your own you may also avoid delays caused by communication processes and other interpersonal interactions.

But as the complexity of a venture increases, the benefits of interacting and working with others soon outweigh the drawbacks. Changes and iterations happen faster. Multiple perspectives and angles enrich the creative process. Feedback loops help refine and correct challenges quickly.

So whenever you find yourself in charge of a large production, even if you could potentially do most of the work, pick the one or two areas that you are most passionate about and focus 100% in those.

"Specialize for the benefit of your productivity and the overall quality of the production."

Put the rest in the hands of skilled collaborators who can work under your supervision, thus ensuring that your vision will be properly cared for throughout all the stages of the project.

Even when your project is small, be open to welcome others into the venture as things develop.

Small details can be crucial for the success of any venture and doing it all on your own may prevent you from noticing many of them or paying them enough attention.

"Time and energy are limited."

In a media production, an assistant may help you hold a reflector or prevent light from hitting the lens of a camera.

Even if you don't work regularly with make-up artists, stylists, assistants and other similar professionals, have in mind that anybody around you can fulfill some of those roles under your direction.

"Asking politely for help can take you places."

Other times, people may see you working and come to offer their support spontaneously. Be open to the world and to the opportunities that may cross your path.

As you prepare and organize your crew/team, there are some typical roles that will appear over and over. Let's review some of them without linking them to specific types of projects. This will open your mind to how these roles may appear in fields where they may not be common. Imagine a painter working with a make-up artist, or a sculptor working with a music composer to create an art installation. Open your mind to an infinite world of combinations and possibilities. Diverge before you converge.

Assistant

In any creative venture there may be one or more assistants. Their functions can vary enormously and their main purpose is to assist the team leaders so that they can focus on making sure that the quality of the vision and concept is maintained across the production.

Assistants may help setup or move equipment and give a hand with the logistics of the production as well as any permits needed. They become essential communication links between the leaders and other parts of the team or crew.

Their functions, in summary, are of an infinite variety. Assistants will free your time to focus on the areas that matter the most.

Make-up

Any venture that works with people and involves visuals can potentially benefit from working with a make-up artist. Good make-up artists understand how light interacts with different kinds of skin as well as different fabrics and materials. With their palettes they manipulate tones, shades, contrasts, shadows and highlights according to the needs of your project.

Some of them specialize in special effects that can enhance your projects with unusual touches. This is good for making your results stand out from the crowd.

If you intend to work with make-up artists find them early in the pre-production process, because you will need plenty of time to test and decide the final materials and styles.

It is typical to think about make-up artists in the context of photography or filmmaking, but what about business? Make-up artists can dramatically impact the aesthetics of a CEO or add that crucial touch to the group company picture.

Whenever you are working with visuals and people, consider the benefits of adding a make-up artist to the mix.

Stylist

When clothing matters, a stylist can make the difference between amateurish and refined looks. Good stylists have a sixth sense when choosing fabrics and clothing that best suit your concept and vision. If they don't find a suitable solution, they will build the ideal one, combining materials in incredible ways. It is a real joy to see them at work, exercising their creative thinking and bringing to life their insights.

Early meetings are again important to give time to the stylist to prepare and gather props and materials, as well as to design and build new combinations.

So when clothing is in the game, consider raising the level with a stylist.

Set designer

Set designers are in charge of directing both the design and the construction of the sets you need for your project.

Your location is your set. But sometimes natural locations cannot provide what we need and then we build custom sets. This may be required for media productions but also for business meetings, celebrations and other kinds of gatherings.

Whenever your surroundings don't fit your requirements, consider making things happen with a set designer.

Music composer

Music is an essential part of numerous creative undertakings. It should be in sync with the general vision of the project. That's why the communication and feeling between directors and composers is critical for the overall success of the project.

Because music is often so crucial, working with a composer is a balancing act. On the one hand, we need to give the professional the space and time necessary to work comfortably. On the other hand, we need to make sure that the results blend seamlessly with the rest of the production, reinforcing the vision of the director.

Music can make the difference between success and failure in many creative ventures. If you are not a composer yourself, there are many ways to get great music for your project:

(a) If you need it fast and the music doesn't need to be completely unique, consider stock music libraries. You can get fantastic music pieces for a reasonable price.
Examples:
[Web] premiumbeat.com
[Web] stockmusic.net

(b) If you are not in a great hurry and need exclusive music that is 100% unique, hire a composer. Find one at websites such as:
[Web] upwork.com

Actors/Models

Sometimes other human beings are your main subject.

Fluid communication between the director and the actors is essential. The actor becomes the brush through which the director expresses the vision.

Get to know the people you work with, not only at work but also outside of it. Get to know them as human beings first. Build trust.

Some good ways to find the right actors or models for your project are:

(a) Make a casting. A casting is typically an open event where candidates demonstrate their skills and their suitability for a role or project. It's like a job interview but for actors and models. A good casting can make all the difference on the road to success.
"Great casting directors are very much in demand!"

(b) In some cases the best person for your project is right there in front of you. It can be one of your friends, a relative or somebody you just met for the first time yesterday. Some famous directors have found their key actors/models in this way.

Audiences

Your venture is intimately linked to your users or audiences since the very first minute.

We create and innovate to produce solutions to challenges connected with specific communities. Waiting till the end of our productions to think of those communities is like boarding a random plane today and deciding in the middle of the flight that we want to land in Paris. It may be too late!

"We should start thinking of our audience from day one."

Share your idea with selected groups that represent that community. Get feedback. Make sure that your message resonates with that audience and if that's not the case review your target community or the idea itself. Repeat this process at various stages during the production.

To keep the process as objective as possible, these test groups should have no connection whatsoever to us. Avoid testing with family and friends as much as possible. They may give you constructive feedback, both positive and negative, but their opinion is often too biased because of your strong connection to them.

Also, keep in mind that an isolated test with a single group cannot be very representative of the general opinion. Avoiding feedback can be just as bad as going against your own impulses because of specific feedback you have received from a single group.

Therefore diversify, get multiple perspectives and test with a few groups as different from each other as possible.

Above all, be honest to yourself. You don't have the obligation to change things because of any feedback you receive. The obligation you have is to reflect on that feedback and to be open to what you feel and think as a consequence.

If you receive feedback that implies doing large changes on your project, pause and reflect. Did you already have similar thoughts in the past but avoided them till now? Does your intuition tell you that the opinion of this group is likely to be replicated across many others? Or the opposite?

Don't rush. Reflect on it. And keep testing until you feel a definite impulse to either leave the product as it is or change it.

It is way better to use a few days in this process than to keep flying in the wrong direction that takes you away from your "Paris". Because once your project is well advanced and New York is in sight, it is going to be hard to get back to Paris. Not impossible, but it will require an extra investment of time and resources you may not want to deal with.

"So early feedback is a must."

Agile and lean methodologies promote quick launches and multiple iterations. For this process to work, feedback is essential at all times.

"We need to look for that great fit between our challenge and our audiences or markets."

Yes, but have in mind that a new creative venture will never please everybody. It may well be the opposite. And if the venture is really innovative and different, you should expect, in fact, a good amount of disagreement at first. Initial resistance is to be expected whenever surprising breakthroughs and really innovative ideas are first shared with the public.

"So we need to be ready to accept a certain amount of rejection when we innovate."

The most unique innovations can at first be too shocking for most people, provoking general rejection. Only some minorities may be able to adapt to radical new ideas when they are first shared. So what you are looking for, when you test your product, is not necessarily if a lot of people like it. That would be great but it is still secondary to your main objectives. The main objectives are two:

1. First, to find out if their feedback confirms that the product communicates your vision/message correctly. Do they understand what the project is all about?
2. And second, if their feedback confirms that the product solves the specific need or challenge you identified within the target community.

If a good percentage of people understand your message/vision and the product is solving the challenge you identified, you are on the right track.

And remember that those communities keep changing and your vision has to move with them. Constant gathering of feedback as well as a flexible development process are keys for achieving success.

A team of teams

Each of the professionals we have mentioned may in turn direct a team of their own. Once you trust a professional, it is important to let him/her manage their own people and teams without interfering. Getting in the middle will waste resources and may create tensions and confusion.

Remember that productivity is key in creative projects. The inevitable uncertainty that is often the companion of innovators requires a counterbalance, a clear division of roles and tasks for the sake of efficiency.

And now, go and create!

CHAPTER 12:

Climbing Marketing Peak

"Don't worry about people stealing your ideas. If your ideas are any good, you'll have to ram them down people's throats."

— Howard Aiken

Our creative and innovation processes have produced great results. Now it's time to explain to our audiences how our solution fits with their challenge. Welcome to marketing.

The right story

Perception is powerful.

Would you like to be able to hear sound originating from anywhere around the world? What about having communication capabilities that can project messages anywhere on earth?

"Spectacular. I'm interested!"

Now, would you like to learn how to develop and program a technology application that interacts with users to send and receive audiovisual messages?

"Eh…"

I bet that doesn't sound so spectacular.

And yet, both paths take us to the Internet and the same tools we use on a daily basis.

"I see, perception is everything!"

Marketing is all about building exciting stories to communicate our messages. We take the facts and dress them in beautiful colors, we make them shine just as we do the same with ourselves when we want to impress our partners.

"People's perspectives depend so much on the way we present things, I see!"

Learning to sing can sound like an abstract and complex challenge. It is hard to mentally fill in the gaps and the distance between our current vocal capabilities and those of the great singing masters.

"It is hard to find the motivation…"

But what if we put it this way: would you like to change the way you breathe in order to make more efficient use of the oxygen that is being inhaled by your lungs?

"Mm, that's related to my health… interesting."

Would you like to have more energy and feel more rested?

"Oh yes!"

Would you like to learn to support your voice in better ways in order to control the muscles in your mouth and vocal organs more efficiently? That way you will project and communicate your messages, including songs and speeches, with more confidence, feeling more powerful and being more convincing.

"Definitely!"

We may now understand better what singing is all about. It is not that abstract anymore. The essence of singing is not the songs, but us, our body, our health and confidence, and we can easily relate to those things.

"What made the difference?"

The details, the story we built around the message. The story provided information and increased our understanding of what learning to sing really means for us and why it is something important.

With the right story, the internet also takes on a new meaning. Suddenly we see it as a wonderful gift that allows us to extend our senses and capabilities in incredible ways. We are able to hear, speak, and sense reality all around the world instantaneously. Isn't that amazing?

The facts are still the same, but how we explain those facts, the story we build around them, is what makes the difference.

"That's marketing!"

And now, let's begin with a title.

To title or not to title?

A title is a symbol, an abstraction we choose to represent a project. It may facilitate the communication of a message to an audience. But it can just as well simplify the message in the wrong way or confuse the audience.

"Why would it confuse the audience?"

We may have created something whose complexity goes well beyond what can be expressed using words. If that is the case, trying to come up with a title may backfire, creating an interpretation that has little to do with the essence behind the message.

Let's say that we begin a project by choosing a title. For example: "The silence of war."

"Interesting title."

Yes, but as we work and explore the idea, our original impulse may change and branch into so many different perspectives, directions and angles that we may end up deciding to remove the title because we feel that no name, word or symbol can do justice to the richness and ambiguity contained within the work.

"I get it, but some products always require a title."

Yes, sometimes we have no choice but to use a title. It is often seen and accepted that people display paintings and photographs with no titles. But we hardly ever find a film or a music piece without one. Filmmaking is very tied to marketing and marketing is all about creating quick and easy to remember connections between a product and an audience. Language is the easiest way to create those links. So for a film and many other creative works, a title is a must.

"A good title always helps."

Yes, great titles help audiences interpret our creations faster. Giving them a name is like giving them a starting point, an anchor from which they can begin to explore our work.

"Without a title the audience needs to put on more effort."

The audience would have to figure out by themselves where to begin when interpreting the work.

"But that also encourages people to diverge while interpreting the work."

Yes. This can be very interesting and liberating, which is why many contemporary modern art pieces have no titles.

"I sense this is connected with closure…"

Once we are given a name, the process of converging accelerates. We lose the freedom to interpret what is in front of us in any way we like. The title immediately introduces a bias and begins to push our interpretations along a predefined path.

"But it also makes our job easier as an audience."

Indeed. As creativity and business keep converging, marketing brings them together, linking them to audiences through titles and other easy to interpret abstractions.

Why do we need marketing?

Imagine a small dot among hundreds of millions of other dots. Now imagine trying to locate your dot among all the others. There are even more websites on the internet and somewhere there is your web, the voice and face of your service, product, work or yourself.

Today, in a society as saturated as ours, investing our energy on producing quality work is only the beginning. And that may be hard to accept, especially for innovators who see the implementation of their insights and the insights themselves as the core of their efforts and the key for success.

It is tempting to think that if we produce something good, they (the audiences) will come.

"But what is something good? What is quality?"

We are part of a society made of billions of human beings. Whatever we do cannot be separated from that society and from the markets whose preferences and motivations constantly shift and mutate. We need to ask ourselves, what is our objective as innovators? There are several answers to this question:

(a) To produce something that resonates mainly with ourselves, not necessarily with a wider audience. Such product will obviously not have much potential as a business offering. Marketing is a non-issue because the objective is only us. This scenario is typical of many artists who don't fit with the entrepreneurial mindset.

(b) To produce something that resonates with us and with those closest to us (our family, friends and friends of friends). In this case, a modest amount of marketing, through social networks and similar channels, should be enough to gain a small following. Investment is negligible or none.

(c) Finally, the case that is most common is when you want to reach and influence large numbers of people who are completely unknown and unrelated to you. Here, the marketing you need becomes a huge mountain that you must climb, a peak that you want to reach as soon as possible in a complex race against multiple competitors. Your final objective is not just to arrive but to remain up there for as long as possible.

The marketing mountain

This is no conventional mountain. The marketing mountain is constantly changing. One day you look and the peak can be seen in a certain direction, but next week it has shifted to a different position. In order to reach the peak of the marketing mountain, you need to have flexibility, resilience and a good deal of real time information about your market.

[Web] torchprinciple.com/marketingmountain

"I can imagine that in order to reach such a shifting and mutating peak the best will be to travel light, carry little luggage and be ready to change course at any time…"

Yes, imagine that you spend many months isolated from the rest of the world, working intensely on the planning of a long expedition to be the first to reach a certain peak. As part of your preparations, you accumulate some very heavy baggage. And right after you end that phase, you are put on a plane that drops you off at the base of this huge mountain. You are told that you need to reach the peak as quickly as possible.

"You have to be one of the first to get there."

Anxiety builds up and you begin to wonder: do I have the right equipment to get up there quickly? Will I be dragged down by the weight of my heavy baggage? What dangers will I encounter on the way? Who are those competing with me and what's their situation?

Because you have been locked away, separated from the rest of the world for a long time, your knowledge of the current context, the mountain and the competitors, is minimal.

"Our chances are not looking good."

The same happens if you try to reach the marketing peak with a product or service that you have kept isolated from the rest of the world for a long time. You may soon have to deal with a range of issues: your baggage (your product) does not adapt to the context (the mountain), and your progress is slow or nonexistent. You have been working thinking of a mountain that does not exist anymore.

"The current mountain has changed so much!"

Your competitors outpace you. Their equipment and products adapt better to the market. Some carry baggage and products similar to yours but they are more refined and better suited to the context. You realize it is too late to catch up with them.

"They have been tracking the mountain closely."

Marketing is a tough mountain. Ask yourself: What is the best way to reach the summit?

(a) Get the information and resources that you need to start the expedition as quickly as possible. Begin your ascent early and carefully as you continue updating your strategy in real time in response to what you find during the ascent.

(b) Plan and accumulate information for months, and once you are at the mountain, try to force your equipment and baggage to adapt to the challenge as best they can.

The second option runs the risk of endangering both your business and your health. The first option will help your business and the markets converge gradually towards the peak.

Just as the success of the production of a film depends largely on its pre-production stage, the success of any venture begins with a strong base. Those crucial first stages have an enormous influence on your chances of successfully climbing the marketing mountain.

"And from that point on, real time tracking is essential."

You cannot separate your challenge from the competitors, neither from the obstacles along the way, nor from the peak itself that keeps shifting its position as you progress.

Each one of them, the peak (the users that resonate with your solution), the competitors (the alternatives to your product) and the obstacles (challenges along the way), will shift, mutate and change often.

"We need to track closely!"

The route that you pick through the marketing mountain depends largely on those shifts and changes that you need to follow closely.

Nowadays, the recipients (users, readers and audiences) of our creations are extremely dynamic and changeable. Be it about a film or a business startup, it is crucial that we monitor their needs, preferences and features continuously. Those peaks will keep shifting, sometimes dramatically in a matter of days or hours. This deep tracking, this need to understand your context on a daily basis, applies to everything, professional ventures and personal life.

Regular monitoring of our target audiences should be compatible with a degree of stability in our expedition. Routes, once the investment to open them has been made, need to be explored for some time before their potential and convenience is properly evaluated. Monitoring our audiences will allow us to gradually reflect on the tradeoffs involved in continuing on the current route or considering alternatives.

For some innovators, this process may feel like a distraction that moves us away from what really matters, crafting, developing and creating a message/service/product. Yet again, times have changed and we don't live in the renaissance when contexts were so much less dynamic.

If you want to reach a global audience, be it for business or for getting more followers, exposure and visibility, you must keep track of your dynamic audience. You cannot pretend to navigate a river full of rocks in a straight line. Being well informed of the context around you is the best insurance you can have.

"We need to be flexible and open."

Which can sometimes collide with people's egos. We want to stick to a plan because it is our plan.

"Ego alert!"

We started it, it was our idea, and to change it because of a shifting context, to let that context modify our route, can feel like losing control and ownership of that plan. So how flexible and adaptable we are is sometimes related to our sense of ownership and control.

"And what can we do about that?"

Entrepreneurs and artists can see themselves as the facilitators, the guides and the channels that bring some value, a solution, to a community.

"So the star is the value we provide."

Yes, the star is the value that transforms the community. We are the facilitators and vessels that transport that value, making the community aware of its existence.

Notice the connection between what we just said and the field of education:

- The most inspiring teachers are those that behave as guides, facilitators and mentors. They provide value in the form of deep knowledge and they generate a dynamic community of students.
- At the opposite end, we have teachers that have a high sense of ownership over the knowledge they are communicating and their position as leaders of a group. Part of their motivation is linked to maintaining their status above others.

Separation and closeness. Isolation and distance to the context. We return to the same issues that make all the difference when we climb the marketing mountain.

Being separated and isolated from your audience (as a teacher, business entrepreneur or creative artist) generates a false sense of security, encourages unrealistic expectations, distorts perception and keeps you away from reality.

Being close to the community and your audiences generates valuable feedback, encourages empathy, improves communication, keeps expectations realistic and tames our ego.

"This ego often fights back."

Many times we want to maintain that isolation and separation because we are scared to find out what our position in life really is. When we open ourselves to a community, the cards are on the table and the truth shines.

"We need the courage to face it all…"

Yes, it requires courage to face feedback and facts, but the process gives us key information and the opportunity to tweak our position and influence our present and future in positive ways.

"So in general, isolation can really become an issue."

A degree of isolation is useful and essential at some stages of the innovation cycle. But any excess is harmful and may gradually move you away from the shifting reality and the routes that best resonate with your challenge.

In summary, be agile, track your potential customers and context in real time, and create amazing stories to inspire your audiences.

Finally, although this is not a book about marketing, to end this chapter we will quickly introduce a few terms related to internet marketing that you can then explore in more detail on your own.

SEO, SMM and SMO: It's about the content

The internet extends your senses and your reach. Mobile apps and websites are the billions of vessels that navigate the cyberspace competing for the attention of billions of destinations we call users. In order to bring your content vehicle to the attention of the right audience, different strategies can be followed:

- **SEO:** Search engine optimization. Search engines help organize the internet by connecting specific users with specific content related to their needs. SEO encompasses a series of strategies that increase your visibility in search engines, making it easier for users to find you.

- **SMM:** Social Media Marketing. The paid advertisements which are placed under social media sites like Facebook, Twitter, YouTube, etc.

- **SMO:** Social Media Optimization. Consists of promoting your services, work or products on social media websites like Facebook.

- **SEM:** Search Engine Marketing. Consists of paid adverts placed on different platforms.

You may implement any of those solutions on your own or you can hire a consultant/expert at websites such as:

[Web] **upwork.com**

Start implementing these strategies to climb higher and get closer to the peak of your marketing mountain.

"Time to climb!"

CHAPTER 13

Creative Business

"The organizations of the future will increasingly depend on the creativity of their members to survive. Great Groups offer a new model in which the leader is an equal among Titans. In a truly creative collaboration, work is pleasure, and the only rules and procedures are those that advance the common cause."

— Warren Bennis

Today, business is more complex than ever. The pace of technological change and the globalization of markets have created a dynamic environment that is in constant flux. Changes are hard to predict and uncertainty is often our companion.

Complexity and competition are the challenges. Innovation is a must if we want to stay ahead of competitors. Businesses are realizing that the tools they have traditionally used, the step-by-step slow tactics of logic and analysis, are unable to cope with these challenges.

"We need reinforcements!"

That reinforcement was there all along. We only need to give it space and combine it properly with the always essential analytical side in order to obtain a balanced mind, ready to innovate and to work with the complexity of our world.

In this fast changing context, basing business decisions mainly on AT processes can often lead to costly mistakes. We need a new approach, an approach that balances the rigors of analysis with the flexibility of creative thinking. We need strategies that help us diverge more at the beginning in order to bring to light the subtle insights which often fail to make it into our conscious realms. To get there we have to begin with the environment in which our business takes place.

An ideal business environment

"What is an ideal business environment?"

In such an environment:

- The nature of both analytical and creative thinking is understood and valued.
- Managers encourage a free flow of ideas and value them for their overall merit.
- Employees must be autonomous enough to be able to exercise their CT. That way they can fulfill their potential both at a personal and a professional level for the good of the company and of themselves.
- Happiness is a respected and promoted value.

"Happiness you say?"

The importance of happiness

Yes, happiness. More and more businesses are realizing that the satisfaction of their employees translates into better work and more benefits for the company.

"But how do we describe that happiness, or what is it linked to?"

That satisfaction is often linked to autonomy, flexibility and safety, as opposed to environments where employees may feel pressured, threatened, restricted or enslaved.

"You are talking about motivation."

Yes. Innovation combines analytical and creative thinking, conscious and subconscious processes. Employees are more likely to engage spontaneously with these processes if they enjoy their work environment and the tasks they have to perform, and if they feel they have enough control over what they do.

"That's clear. But isn't that spirit hard to maintain in organizations that grow very large?"

Maintaining the spirit

Let's understand why. The best businesses in the world were created by freelancers. People who took risks, combining analysis and creativity to understand the complexity of their environments. They found ways to produce value that resonated with their customers.

But as businesses grow large, a shift happens. Something that often mirrors the transition from childhood to adulthood. Something that can happen in successful ventures of any kind.

With success often arrives the fear of losing what you gained. Do we agree with this?

"Yes."

And with fear comes in turn an increased emphasis in control and analysis. Fear pushes you to try to control the events around you.

"Fear makes me crave security and control."

This, in turn, implies an increased emphasis on AT. An emphasis on converging, not diverging.

"We move away from other more unconventional, spontaneous and unpredictable ways of thinking."

Over time, these businesses are eventually overcome by new startups which make use of the entire range of thinking strategies.

"So those large companies are self-limiting themselves."

They behave as if they had a hand tied to their backs or were standing on only one leg. Literally!

We know that succeeding is not necessarily very hard. What is hard is staying at the top. But you cannot expect that to happen if you get to the top making use of your full potential, and once you are there you cut off one half of it for fear of losing your position.

"They weaken their potential by dedicating part of it to try to secure their position."

They want to make it stable and permanent.

"But nothing can be truly permanent, everything is in constant flow, whether we like it or not."

Such a strategy soon becomes a trap. Just as in football the best defense consists in having a great attack, the best guarantee for staying at the top of your market is to keep innovating, maintaining your creative muscles fit and ready to perform.

"So as the business grows, we must keep our creative muscles fit and fresh."

Structured entrepreneurial spirit

Yes, and let's understand why:

No matter how large a business grows, the context around it doesn't slow down. It keeps changing and evolving.

"As the business grows, resources increase, but old and new challenges remain and constantly evolve and mutate."

That's why flexibility and the use of our full mental potential continues to be a must. Businesses need to maintain their entrepreneurial spirit while taking advantage of the many benefits that a structured and well organized business enterprise can provide.

We could call it: structured entrepreneurial spirit.

"I love it, but for many organizations it may be too late if they want to change the way they function. Something tells me that these principles and strategies should be applied from day one."

It begins with education

This takes us to one of my favorite areas, education.

Think of your life as a story. A story whose narrative is for the most part very much in your hands.

Imagine that at the beginning of your story you were exposed to a variety of disciplines and encouraged to explore and grow in the ones that you resonated the most with. This would organically generate in you a self-sustaining enthusiasm and the natural discipline to engage with the world in creative and productive ways.

Changing the way things work in any organization, no matter how large and no matter how old, is always possible. There is always a degree of flexibility in every human being and in every organization. But of course, changing stubborn, unhealthy habits is always harder than creating healthy ones from the start.

"That's why our early education is key."

For a long time, education has been focused on accumulating knowledge and information.

"This obsession with accumulating, with quantity…"

After the studies are completed, the hope is that all that knowledge and the associated practice will help the student perform in the real world. But the real world is as stubborn as a pattern of symptoms that doesn't fit any of the specific diseases the books talk about.

Adapting all of this accumulated information to the real world works in cases where complexity is not too high. But when complexity is high, it can feel like we are trying to squeeze a preset key through the wrong hole. At worst it's a waste of energy, at best it's an imperfect solution. Wouldn't it be better to fully understand the new hole first, and only then build a custom key to fit it?

"Working at the roots of how we think."

Yes, more than anything, for students to perform in the real world, we need to train them to utilize their full thinking potential, from the analytical to the creative. They will then be ready to understand and adapt to the uncertainty that is a norm in today's environments.

"And that means exposing them to a variety of possibilities and fields early on in their paths."

Even further, education should be an interactive experience: you don't impose knowledge on the student. Feedback flows in both directions. Students are exposed to a variety of experiences so that they can discover which ones resonate best with their personalities and capabilities. Those are then further emphasized and pushed forward.

"Doing what resonates with you and doing it with passion and enthusiasm."

That creates productive and happy human beings. Productive and happy go hand in hand when we are using our full potential to do what resonates the most with ourselves.

Finally, let's talk about another way in which business is adapting to this fast changing complexity.

The agile philosophy

In recent years, we have witnessed the emergence of agile and lean methodologies that apply to areas as diverse as software development, entrepreneurship and design.

Think of the lean startup model, agile software development, lean UX, etc. They are a consequence of the increasing complexity and the fast evolving speed of today's markets.

Innovation needs reinforcements. By the time we think of innovating, the context has rapidly evolved and we are left too far behind.

"We need to catch up!"

Innovation needs to be built-in right into the fabric of the business itself. The context must be considered at each step of the process. Feedback and interaction with the audience and users must be continuous. And to keep pace with the shifting environment, wasteful processes must be minimized.

"That's such a contrast with how business used to be done in the past."

Working in isolation or semi-isolation, teams used to produce highly refined and detailed results that often had to be discarded or completely redone because of shifting client requirements or changes in the markets. This extremely inefficient way of working has pushed more and more professionals into considering the need to do things in lighter and more flexible ways, adapting to what the world really is, a dynamic and changing creature whose next step is hard to predict.

Agile and lean practices help us adapt to the nature of the beast. The benefits are many:

- Increasing harmony and resonance between products and audiences by closely and regularly tracking the convergence between needs and solutions.
- Saving time and money by minimizing waste.
- Quick response times that improve efficiency.

These agile philosophies and methods share a range of key processes:

(a) Concepts and ideas are triggered.

(b) A quick prototype is created, functional enough to demonstrate the concept and allow for its demonstration and testing.

(c) Validation of the prototype is made internally within the team. External tests are then performed with people unconnected to the project. All feedback is collected and analyzed.

(d) Lessons are learnt and changes applied to the project in response to the feedback.

(e) We return to b) and continue iterating through this process.

Agile CT

Agile methodologies move fast. CT, however, likes to take its time to achieve the best results.

"How do we combine both?"

To be agile in a creative way, your creative muscles need to be well trained. When your creative muscles are strong, you are able to use CT in faster ways, adapting to the agile philosophies.

Therefore, agile methodologies require faster innovation cycles. This implies the need for participants to exercise their creative muscles on a regular basis.

"Time to exercise!"

CHAPTER 14:

Extra Tips for Maintenance

"You see things; and you say, 'Why?' But I dream things that never were; and I say, 'Why not?'"

– George Bernard Shaw

The following are a series of reminders and extra tips to help you maintain your creative muscles in good shape. They complement the exercises we covered previously.

- Begin by identifying topics that interest you. Find ways to interact with others interested in similar areas.

- Balance tasks that make heavy use of AT with others that are more relaxed, free flowing and unpredictable. Do excursions, practice a sport. Get involved in music or any other artistic activity. Exercise your CT muscles by getting away from routine and the deep cliffs of your mind. Open new avenues, welcome the unexpected.

- Give yourself permission to let your mind wander with no specific purpose. Remind yourself that it is at those times when the most unpredictable subconscious insights can find the space to reach your consciousness. Engage on walking meditation in inspiring surroundings. Allow your subconscious to gradually open up to the new space you are creating in your mind.
  "Lots of ideas come to me during my relaxing walks."
  Others prefer different activities. There are infinite ways to create the space that encourages the successful incubation of new ideas. Find yours!

- Remember the importance of diverging before converging and of exercising your creative muscles. Perform random activities (activities that don't go against your principles and that are safe for you and others) with a defined direction or with no specific goal. Imagine life as a path that is being walked in exactly the same way by a billion other humans. Wouldn't you like to venture out of that path and explore what is out there along alternative routes?
  "I'm not a robot, I want to diverge!"

- Apply the same concept (diverging strongly) to writing. Sit down and start writing. Don't judge or evaluate. Just write.
  "About what?"
  You are exercising your creative muscles. What you write is not the important thing. Simply sit and write. Challenge your AT filters by letting anything that comes to your mind stream onto the paper (or digital file).
  "What if nothing…"
  Your mind is a mirror of your life and your experiences. You have a life, right? So something will come up. Maybe what you write won't make any sense, that's totally fine. The process itself is stretching your creative muscles and may lead you somewhere unexpected.
  Remember that all great things, including life itself, begin from a blank canvas, from that nothingness that seems so scary at first.
  "Doubts…"

- When doubts creep in, remember again that you are flexing your creative muscles. Exercising your body muscles in a gym can sometimes feel like a waste of time, even painfully so, but it is the base over which you can later build great achievements. The same thing happens with your CT muscles.

- Take it further. Exercise your creative courage. Build flexibility into your mind. Start singing at places where you wouldn't normally sing.
  "I don't sing."
  What about when you hum your favorite tunes in the shower or as you celebrate some good news? Singing is nothing unusual. The context in which it takes place is what you can change.

- Got a pencil or pen nearby? Draw something.
"I'm not good at drawing."
Think of your signature as a very complex drawing, because
it is! If you can draw your signature then drawing is not
the problem. Gathering the courage to move those creative
muscles is a good first step. Let those muscles work by
drawing random lines. Enjoy the lack of a goal, the feeling of creating something organic and complex that is an
extension of yourself. Think of what you are drawing as an
expression of your subconscious.
"That's exciting!"
It is, and it may reveal unexpected insights about you.

- Apply divergence to anything that blocks you.
"I am having trouble writing this job report."
Do you feel like you need some fresh air? Open a separate page and write something unrelated to your report,
as apparently unconnected as possible. Because of the way
the subconscious works, unrelated inputs can expand your
focus, bring more light to the challenge and sometimes
trigger new insights that can help with whatever is blocking
you, the job report in this case.
"I see once again the potential of diverging before
converging!"
Yes, keep exercising your CT muscles by bringing the unexpected into all sorts of activities. For example, if you are
taking a photo of your husband, friend or girlfriend, take
another moment to take an extra picture of something
apparently unrelated that you find nearby. It could be an
original doorknob or the texture of the ground below you.
Contemplate what you captured. Reflect on how it makes
you feel. Refresh your mind with the power of variation
and diversity.
"Surprise your neurons!"

- When you invite friends for dinner, transform the event
into another opportunity to exercise your CT muscles. Be
creative with the preparations. If you make a cake, add a
unique twist, surprise your audience.
"Make the experience unforgettable."

- If you are going to play a game with your friends, invent a
new game instead of playing the usual ones. Begin simple.

After repeating the experience a few times, your proposals will become more complex and engaging.

- In general, transform every occasion into something unique and memorable. It benefits everybody's minds. What will your guests talk among themselves when they leave your house? Share your creative mind with the world and in return you will receive amazing benefits!

In summary, make your days unique. Take controllable risks, celebrate interaction, feed your subconscious, balance AT tasks with others that are more unpredictable and free flowing, cultivate space in your mind and celebrate randomness.

"Live with capital L!"

Multidisciplinary diversity

Athletes know the importance of exercising all the muscles in the body, not just a few. So from time to time, put in motion a range of creative channels.

- Pick a challenge, a seed or a theme.
- Starting from your seed, write a short story or the treatment of a screenplay.
- Make a spontaneous drawing while you reflect on the seed.
- Imagine a business designed around your challenge. Who are the customers? What is the business model? What are the benefits and the risks?
- Improvise a simple sculpture or shape using any materials you find around.
- Improvise a song that explores your challenge.
- Imagine that you are dancing with your seed. Improvise a choreography. How will your seed look and act?
- Choose a set of colors for a palette that will represent your seed.

- Imagine that you are your seed. For a few minutes act and behave as your seed would. How will your challenge move and talk? Be your seed.

- Take notes of any insight or interesting thoughts that come to your mind as you go through the process.

This is a great exercise for your CT muscles. The more you do it the better you will be at connecting different areas and disciplines.

In life you constantly face a variety of challenges, and the more avenues and channels you explore, the stronger your creative muscles will become and the better they will perform when looking for innovative solutions to those challenges.

We finish this chapter with the magic of stories.

Enrich your life with stories

At the root of some of the most creative works we find stories. Stories create a rich context, a solid foundation that favors innovation through the cultivation of a rich subconscious.

Coming up with new stories can seem a daunting task but there are many strategies to speed up the process.

- As you go through your day, pay attention to the world around you.
  "What is happening right there across the street?"
  Yes, what is going on behind you with those two people laughing? Or are they having a heated discussion? Pick an event that calls your attention and imagine what happened before and what will happen in the future with the people involved. In summary, pick a seed from your surroundings and build a story from it.

- As you are sitting at a cafe or a library, notice the person beside you. Pay attention to the looks, movements and gestures of that person. Imagine what his/her life is like based on your observations.

- And now, wherever you are, at a park, a street, a shopping mall or a mountain, imagine yourself being part of a film. This film needs to attract the attention of a wide audience and communicate a deep message.

- Observe the context around you. Imagine the events that could be taking place. Who are you in the film? A robber escaping from the police, a lawyer waiting for a secret meeting to begin, a desperate father looking for his child? And why are you there? Answer these and other questions as you start to create a story right there wherever you are.

- Gather stories that people are attracted to in films and magazines. Those that are popular and any others that resonate with yourself. Give them your own twist, write your own version of your favorite ones.
  "Branch away."

- Grow new trunks from those quality seeds. If you are part of a group, improvise acting performances with others. Take on different roles.

- Note down any new insights.

Celebrate contrast

Exercising your body muscles often requires you to bring them into extreme positions before relaxing them again.

"Contrast builds strength. The same happens in your mind."

Contrast is essential in all creative endeavors. It is only because of it that we can appreciate the distinctive features of any subject.

Whatever project you are working on, think of contrasting elements you can bring into it. By including elements that oppose each other or contrast strongly, you will be reinforcing them both.

"Without contrast, life becomes flat and dull."

Apply some of the above in your daily routines and you will be strengthening your creative muscles, enriching both your professional and personal life.

"Way to go!"

CHAPTER 15

Innovation in Numbers

"Innovation – any new idea – by definition will not be accepted at first. It takes repeated attempts, endless demonstrations, monotonous rehearsals before innovation can be accepted and internalized by an organization. This requires courageous patience."

— Warren Bennis

Many people have never considered how much benefit CT can bring to their lives. The question we want to answer is: What kind of benefit and how much of it can CT bring in relation to AT?

Let's build a simulation with numbers. Using very simple math and plain language, we will build a very simplified model to quickly reflect on this issue.

Anything we do in life requires an investment. There are many kinds of investments. In this model, we will focus on just a few of the most important ones: time, energy and money.

Energy and time, though interrelated, move at different speeds. You can spend a great deal of energy in very little time. Or spend a lot of time without hardly any investment of energy. Resources required by innovation processes will be included within the financial area.

Ideally, everybody wants to obtain as much value as possible in return for as little investment as possible.

"Sounds like a good plan!"

Sure, but remember that this value expresses itself in different ways through time. It can last for a short time or stretch through weeks, months or years. Let's suppose then that the final number we are looking for is the total value, which we shall call TV. This number is born from the relationship between obtained value (OV) and applied investment (AI). That is, the more we had to invest to obtain the value, the less total value we get. And vice versa.

"I get it. I want to get as much of that TV as possible."

We shall scale all numbers in relative percentages between 1% and 100%.[50] We will consider that 100% represents in each case the maximum value we can attach to that parameter.

"Let's begin!"

The value that we obtain, if it lasts an instant, is not worth as much as when it lasts 100% of our lifetime.

"Generally, most of the time that's true."

Therefore, obtained value (OV) equals value (V) times the duration of that value in terms of the percentage of what remains of our lifetime (DV).

$$OV = V \times DV$$

In regards to our applied investment (AI), we shall simplify the model by stating that energy, time and money combined make for our total investment (TI).

"I see, the energy, time and resources I put in the process make for my total investment in this simplified model".

Yes, a lot of investment over a short time can equal a small investment sustained over a long time. Therefore, the applied investment (AI) will be equal to our total investment (TI) times its duration in terms of the percentage of the rest of our lifetime over which it is sustained (DI).

$$AI = TI \times DI$$

"Great, so both obtained value and applied investment are dependent on how long they last."

Let's continue. The obtained value is worth less if our investment is larger than if it is smaller. Therefore, total value (TV) equals obtained value (OV) divided by applied investment (AI).

$$TV = OV / AI$$

"The larger the applied investment, the less total value we receive in proportion. And vice versa."

Therefore, to obtain the total value that either AT or CT generates:

$$TV = (V \times DV) / (TI \times DI)$$

"The value we get multiplied by how long it lasts gets divided by our total investment multiplied by how long we sustain it."

This is a very simple model of an extremely complex issue. It greatly simplifies the involved parameters. Still, it is a useful abstraction that can help us reflect on this delicate balance between AT and CT.

"Let's put it in motion!"

Let's suppose that we attempt to solve a challenge by using first and mainly analytical and logical strategies (AT) and afterwards we put more emphasis on the creative strategies (CT).

When using AT we work sequentially within an environment full of abstractions and simplifications, obtaining insights that are more typical, closer to our initial departure points. When using creative thinking we make unpredictable leaps, reaching insights that lie further away from our initial position. They are more unique and original.

Because we want to innovate, we value unique and original insights much more than those that are too predictable.

"We want to innovate and stay ahead of competitors!"

So value, V, shall be larger in CT than in AT. How much larger? A lot more. A unique and novel insight can make all the difference between leaping ahead of the market and going out of business.

Let's assign a V of 100 to CT and of 10 to AT.

Next is the duration of that value, DV. Unique and novel insights are likely to bring value that lasts longer than the one brought by predictable insights. Predictable insights are soon found to provide insufficient advantage in the market and their value quickly decreases. As before, the benefit brought by unique insights lasts way longer. Let's assign a DV of 100 to CT and of 10 to AT.

"Unique insights bring more value and help us stay ahead of the competition for a longer time."

Now let's move on to the investment side of things.

Let's consider that financial investment is similar in CT and AT. In either case you require a set of tools whose cost can be considered, most of the time, to be similar.

"What about energy and time?"

For creative thinking to be effective we need to be free from strict time constraints. CT processes that intend to find innovative solutions have to go beyond our mental abstractions to work with the raw complexity of our challenge. This could potentially require more energy and time.

So how much larger is that time investment? Not that much more, and in fact it can be less. AT works sequentially. CT involves simultaneous processing. It is the uncertainty of CT that can make it last longer than AT. But because of its powerful processing capabilities, CT sometimes achieves results in a shorter period.

In terms of energy, we can state that CT processes require more energy than one would need while working with simplified abstractions. Not a lot more, but somewhat more. Being generous, let's give a TI of 100 to CT and of 50 to AT.

"CT processes in adults require more effort in general than AT processes."

Finally, regarding DI, the amount of time over which we need to sustain our investment, CT typically needs more of it. It is more specific and works closer to the raw complexity that keeps evolving, and, therefore, it needs to sustain its interactions with that complexity for longer periods of time.

AT works with simplified abstractions. In comparison with the raw materials of CT, these abstractions are more detached from reality and are likely to change at a slower pace. AT still needs to update its abstractions so the difference is not very large but it certainly exists.

"Makes sense, being more specific and working with the fine details of something that keeps changing, keeps us engaged with it intensely and more regularly."

Let's therefore give a DI of 100 to CT and 50 to AT.

So what do we get as a result?

$$\text{TV (CT)} = (100 \times 100) / (100 \times 100) = 1$$

$$\text{TV (AT)} = (10 \times 10) / (50 \times 50) = 0.04$$

"CT is the champion!"

As simplified as this model is, it is helpful to verify some of our intuitions when we work with AT and CT. What these numbers show is that AT requires an investment of energy and time that is often less than what CT requires. In addition, AT, because of the abstraction level at which it operates, also requires a less intense sustaining of that investment.

"So in the short term, AT seems like the easier choice."

Yes, but when both AT and CT are considered all the way to the end, CT delivers insights that provide much larger value and for much longer in comparison to what AT can provide by itself.

"So CT wins in the long term."

Yes, CT requires a larger initial investment but delivers a much larger total value and long-term benefit.

AT requires a somewhat smaller and shorter initial investment but delivers a much more modest value that decreases faster over time.

"So remind me again of why AT is so often in charge within our minds."

From a biological perspective, AT makes a lot of sense: it makes more efficient use of our energy and achieves good enough results. It is also capable to help us adapt to our evolving environments as long as changes are controlled and competition is modest.

"So as long as things are not too demanding, AT is efficient and capable."

Yes, the problem is that nowadays complexity and competition are high and keep getting higher in both our professional and personal lives. Contexts change at lightning speed, often in directions hard to predict. The competition around can make our product, service or ourselves irrelevant in a short span of time.

"CT becomes essential."

Yes, CT becomes essential for thriving. A relatively small extra investment of resources can bring a much larger benefit, one that helps you leap ahead of the pack and helps you stay there for longer.

"Still both AT and CT are always present and need each other, right?"

Yes. The comparison we just made is of course completely unreal because CT and AT can never work without each other. The model serves to remind ourselves why CT is so important today and why a society traditionally biased towards AT is starting to move towards a better balance between both strategies.

CT and AT need to constantly work together. Innovation cannot rely on only one of them. Both are important in creative processes, but our CT is especially relevant when we want to provide long-term value within a competitive, complex and fast evolving environment.

CHAPTER 16:

Creative Essence

"Creativity, as has been said, consists largely of rearranging what we know in order to find out what we do not know. Hence, to think creatively, we must be able to look afresh at what we normally take for granted."

— George Kneller

L et's explore in more detail what creativity means. Creativity has an enormous range of possible definitions. For our purposes we will define it as the process of making use of what is known in order to produce something new, such that it has some practical use or serves a community or individual in some way.

"From the known to the unknown!"

Yes, we move from the known to the unknown, rearranging the old in order to come up with new solutions that, most importantly, provide some value.

A matter of time

This definition immediately suggests something crucial. Creativity is all about the here and now, the current context, the present, as opposed to the past. That past becomes a base over which you stand on the way to new insights and discoveries.

"So creativity deals mainly with the state of things today, not in the past."

Yes.

"Paying more attention to what surrounds us now…"

Don't look at creativity as a separate process, but as a way of living. At its very essence, creativity simply means reorganizing what we know in order to find out and produce something new.

Being creative benefits our health, career, relationships and well-being. It is problem-solving that goes deeper and wider, beyond the possibilities that logic and analysis alone can offer.

In summary, regardless of what you are, an artist, engineer, business professional, writer, entrepreneur or journalist, creativity is a tool that can improve your life in many ways.

"A way of being… I really wish I could apply these creative behaviors in all I do, but it's not easy."

Standing up takes effort and energy

That's right, standing on the shoulders of past knowledge to reach what is new requires some effort. It also requires new thinking strategies which can be harder to access as adults.

"I recognize that effort. For example, drawing is very hard for me."

Maybe you should consider that creativity is what happens before.

"Before? Before what?"

The tip of an iceberg

When we hear the word creative or creativity many think of the skills of drawing, sculpting, designing, programming, etc.

"Sure."

But those are methods, techniques and channels. They are ways to express, communicate and implement the insights that are generated before. Those skills are the tip of an iceberg whose much larger base encompasses the roots of creativity, the understanding of the principles that are common and shared by most creative activities and disciplines.

"A common base."

Yes, think about rhythm, structure, color, movement, highlights and shadows.

Those are just some of the many parameters that are part of the common foundations of so many creative activities. They appear in music, but also in the stock market, in dance, in drawing and in public speaking, in design as well as in physics and chemistry."

Movement exists in the brush that dances over the canvas, in the delicate and invisible strokes created by the human dancer, in how light and shadow chase each other through a composition. Movement and rhythm are also key elements to understand in the fluctuations of the stock market, in the behaviors of living cells and viruses or in the changing intonation of the human voice as it delivers an important message to an audience.

"I see, we need to first understand the deeper layers..."

On the one hand, at the very top of this iceberg is the implementation of creative insights. Mastering one of these skills, for example, drawing, is easier if a natural predisposition exists. But it is a road that anybody can traverse as long as they are ready to put in the number of hours, days, months and years necessary to become an expert at it.

"It's a matter of time."

Experts say that in order to become highly proficient at playing an instrument you need to put a minimum of a few thousand hours of practice under your belt.[51] This may still not make you a virtuoso, but should be good enough for you to express yourself creatively in a comfortable way.

"But what about the rest of this iceberg? What about what lies beneath?"

Here we go: more key than the implementation skills is the process of deeply understanding the essence of the universal principles mentioned before. It is the deep understanding of those principles that will make you a master.

"So it's that base down below that makes the difference…"

Yes, the skills that lie at the tip of the iceberg are important yet limited without the deep understanding, without the strong and firm base."

"An example, please."

You may consider yourself an expert in photography, but if your understanding of lighting, composition, human emotions and other key principles is limited, your progress over time and the originality of your work will be limited as well.

"And what about the opposite scenario?"

At the opposite end, you may have a great understanding of the deep principles and then decide to invest more time in advancing your expertise of different skills. Those skills become channels, ways to express your insights and messages. By combining a strong base with enough time developing and practicing those skills you will be on your road towards mastery.

"The understanding and the skills. Which comes first?"

Start with both but make sure to continuously support and feed that base. Help it become stronger and deeper over time. That way, the tip of that iceberg will continue being rich, secure, stable and flexible for decades to come.

"Whereas a weak base could make that tip crumble easily."

That's right!

"That's all great, but not everybody has the capacity to go that deep, some people are naturally more creative than others, isn't that the case?"

Is your creative potential set on stone?

Your creative potential is not set on stone. It is not an amount of something that determines what you may or may not be able to achieve. If you think that way, you are branding yourself a non-creative being, because creative people, by definition, constantly push and overcome their limits, perceived or real.

"But when I look at successful innovators…"

You are already on the road

When we contemplate successful innovators and creators in action, we can feel the same as when watching the best athletes. They seem to be made of a different material. It is as if they came from a different galaxy. There is no chance, we think, that we may ever get so far.

"That's how I feel."

And yet, there was a time in their lives in which they thought the exact same thing. Some of them may have been given a better starting position than you (and genetics may be part of that), but the main reason why they are where they are is because of how much and how well they exercised their muscles, the physical ones in the case of athletes and the creative ones in the case of successful innovators and the most creative individuals.

When we start comparing ourselves to others, it is easy to exaggerate the distance that separates us from them.

"It's a matter of perception, I see…"

Can you write your signature? Can you kick and catch a ball? Do you sing sometimes in the shower? Did you ever have to run to catch a bus that was leaving? Do you often organize and execute plans? Are you sometimes lost in the contemplation of a beautiful sunset?"

"Sure I do…"

All of us have powerful brains whose creative muscles are ready for action. What may separate you from the best innovators is a mixture of deeper understanding and enough time practicing a variety of techniques, but most of us already have the potential and generic skills that are at the base of what later becomes a professional master.

So don't wonder if you can join that road. You are already on it!

"I'm already on it!"

Yes, and in order to grow further you need to exercise your creative muscles in the right way and for long enough to generate the progress that will take you far and deep.

"So everybody is on the same road, just on different parts of it."

People begin their paths at different places, but the road ahead is fully open for everybody.

"It's up to me to keep exercising my creative muscles."

See creativity as a series of problem-solving and thinking strategies that you can continually expand and strengthen.

"Just like when I strengthen a muscle."

That's right, think of it as a muscle that you can expand, grow and strengthen. It is in your hands what you do with it on a daily basis.

"So just like in fitness, it is about seeing obstacles as challenges, not problems."

Yes, from such a perspective all perceived obstacles are a relative nuisance. As long as you stay focused on keeping your creative muscles fit and healthy, you know you will be ok.

"And these principles, these roots, what are these, where do they come from?"

Artists of life

The source is life itself in its different manifestations. These principles are the roots and raw building blocks of creativity.

"An example, please."

Think about light and shadow. These are two poles that express a key duality in our world. The night and the day. Darkness and brightness. In turn, they also express a key principle, contrast, which is essential in all forms of creativity. Bringing together contrasting elements, juxtaposing them, we can better appreciate the unique qualities and features each of them has. We perceive light because of darkness, rhythm because of stillness and color in relation to the world of greys.

"Contrast is a powerful principle that we can apply to any topic."

Now, what happens if we disregard contrast and we focus on just one of the poles?

Imagine a creative work that is made of just rhythmic figures without pauses in between, or another made of total brightness without any darkness or shadows. This is possible, it is. It expresses something for sure.

"It sounds kind of odd."

Yes, it is constrained and limited in its potential to communicate the subtle nuances of a complex message when we compare it with the alternative of juxtaposing more than one pole together. It may also fail to engage the mind as well as other works that employ the full range between the poles.

"I feel as if contrast has been important for a long time…"

Indeed. For biological and evolutionary reasons, humans are attracted to contrast. Contrast can mean survival (for example, the contrast between the environment and a predator or a dangerous plant).

"So understanding the importance of contrast we begin to grasp its potential in relation to creativity and innovation."

Right, once you understand the importance of contrast, you can go deeper into it and begin to unravel how it works, how it interacts with our minds.

"For example?"

Let's talk about the law of simultaneous contrast in relation to perception: It tells us that when we position two complementary colors (colors that are opposite to each other in a color wheel, for example blue and yellow) next to each other, they will each be perceived as more intense, their features and traits are automatically reinforced. So position any two poles next to each other and their features appear more marked and intense when each is surrounded by their opposite.

"Fascinating, bringing opposites together reinforces both. And this applies only to colors?"

It applies to anything: light and shadow, harmony and dissonance, rhythm and stillness. As opposite as they are, they need each other and depend on each other to shine stronger and deeper, to reach audiences in powerful ways.

"Opposites attract, reinforce each other and engage audiences."

So keep this in mind: working with extremes (or poles) reinforces them and the overall message you are trying to convey. Working with only one pole is sometimes necessary, effective and interesting but runs the risk of weakening the pole itself and the message.

"There are exceptions of course."

Yes. These are not mandatory laws, just guidelines, reminders. However, they work so well in the vast majority of cases that they often help us find the best solutions.

"I can feel the importance of this principle, the contrast, in how we live our lives."

When life is a monologue without enough contrast we feel more insecure, shallow, weakened and scared of the complexity around us. But when life is a diverse mixture of poles and experiences, a multidimensional journey full of contrast, we come out stronger and deeper.

Just think of yourselves, the readers of this book. You are a very diverse audience full of contrast. Compare that with an audience made of people with similar background, age and occupation. Sounds way less exciting, right?

"Totally!"

Let's summarize:

As you go deeper and deeper into creativity's universal principles you are expanding the base that will feed all your creative endeavors. One of those principles is contrast. Understanding contrast benefits all your innovation and creative activities. Ignoring it may weaken you and your creative processes.

Reflecting on these poles that feed on each other, and on the delicate balance that keeps them alive, is a great way to keep your creative muscles sharp and fit.

"It's a deal, let's go deep!"

CHAPTER 17

Creative Personality

"If you hear a voice within you say, 'You cannot paint',
then by all means paint, and that voice will be silenced."

– Vincent Van Gogh

Being creative is a way of living and also a way of being. "So do you need to have a specific kind of personality in order to be creative?"

Not at all. But there are certain personality traits that facilitate creative thinking, and others that strongly resist it.

As we look back at the greatest creative geniuses the world has known, we can identify key behaviors they share. One of them is perseverance despite obstacles and rejections.

"They keep going."

These geniuses interpreted what others would define as "failure" as opportunities to advance and progress.

Innovating implies taking risks, jumping into the unknown and embracing uncertainty. We cannot expect to reach our goals on the first try. The creative process takes time and often multiple iterations. This is what discourages many people who give up their creative challenges after a couple of attempts, attempts that they label as "failures".

"Typical impatient AT behavior."

Yes. AT wants closure and wants it quickly. But innovation and creativity require a different mental strategy, flexible, iterative and evolutionary.

"One that stretches our thinking skills in every direction."

By taking us out of our comfort zones, this strategy forces our minds to work harder to make sense of the world, combining and merging our experiences in unexpected directions.

"The creative process makes us deeper and richer beings."

Think of the opposite scenario: when we stay most of our time in our comfort zones we are opening the doors to atrophy, physical and mental. Atrophy of the body, which triggers pain, and atrophy of a mind that imprisoned in its abstract analytical fortress, will start to accumulate fears and anxiety.

Looking at the world through the analytical lens means living in the past, in the memories and in what is already known, as opposed to living in the present, where anything can happen, where novelty is the norm and challenges open doors to new opportunities.

AT wants to make our life easier but too much of that love and support can weaken your mind.

Creative people are also conscious of their capacity to continuously reshape their mind. As human beings we have this wonderful ability to reflect on ourselves and on our own mental processes. This gives us the incredible opportunity to reshape at every moment the way our mind works, to gently steer its way into any direction we choose. Even the strongly ingrained habits of the mind can be changed or eliminated, sometimes by creating better habits that compensate the previous ones. This requires perseverance. Whatever the outcome, exercising your creative muscles will produce benefits in all areas of your life.

More about creative personalities

Creative personalities are highly sensitive and generate enough mental space to be receptive to the movements of their subconscious. Being sensitive means being receptive to the vast amounts of inputs that are constantly bombarding us. It is easy to engage our

AT autopilot, minimizing the energy we use to deal with the world. This efficiency deprives our subconscious pot of quality ingredients.

"Without those, creative thinking processes lose their magic!"

To innovate, we need to bypass the filtering process of our minds and access the raw information we are constantly swimming through. Wherever you are, picture yourself in an ocean of information. Get used to engage that present with your creative muscles, and your future will be richer and deeper in every way.

On the other hand, creative personalities are able to create enough space in their minds. This implies taming the incessant analytical chatter generated by AT processes.

In our busy lives it is easy to enter a vicious cycle of overanalysis regarding the pros and cons of our present, past and future. This generates a noisy environment in which it becomes hard to notice the subtle and fragile insights arising from our subconscious.

Creativity requires an open, flexible and broad focus, and that means relaxation and space. Think of the subtle subconscious insights as the thin and beautiful sound of a violin in the middle of a constant hurricane. It is hard to hear anything if we don't manage to calm the storm within us.

A sensitive and open mind is ready for anything that may come its way. This is also the attitude of those that face life as if they are experiencing it for the first time. The opposite is a know-it-all attitude. An attitude that closes you mind to anything new and different.

Imagine the infinite stream of information in which you constantly swim. Imagine how it combines and recombines with your existing knowledge at subconscious levels until fleeting and delicate new insights arise. These insights can easily go unnoticed unless your mind's attention and focus are broad and sensitive enough to detect them.

Therefore, when the context calls for it, a heightened sensitivity and a broader focus are key traits of a creative personality.

Perennial student

Creatives are natural students. For them, knowledge is always relative and incomplete, open to question and reinterpretation.

"Everything is in flow!"

Yes, our bodies are, but also our interpretation of any event and the events themselves. Learning is a process of gathering perspectives that are always open to revision. These students are like supple branches, adaptable and flexible.

The paradox of persistence

We are often reminded about the importance of perseverance and sticking to our plans. On the other hand, CT enjoys the uncertainty and encourages flexibility and spontaneity.

How can we bring together those two perspectives? In a world where complexity is reaching new heights and everything is in constant change, perseverance with a flexible attitude is the point at which those two perspectives meet.

On the one hand, you need to stick to your route for long enough in order for novel insights to emerge. On the other hand, you need to have enough flexibility to be open to other promising avenues that may come your way.

"There is such a thing as dying of perseverance! "

Persevering for too long, when it becomes clear that you are driving through a road with no exits, is clearly counterproductive. Realizing when that is happening is tricky. Having the courage to acknowledge it is even harder.

It is hard to reach the right equilibrium as you walk on the tightrope. Remember, creativity requires courage, patience and confidence.

As fresh as a good friend

Creative personalities understand the importance of sharing and interacting with others. One of the best ways to prevent falling off the cliffs of closure during the nurturing stage of creativity is to interact often with colleagues and friends, exchanging thoughts and perspectives. This keeps the ingredients moving and combining in your subconscious pot. Remember, you don't want things to settle too soon.

Sometimes, we settle too soon and narrow down our perspectives as a consequence of too much isolation. As innovators, sometimes we feel the temptation to do everything in secret, hiding from the world.

"Somebody may steal my idea!"

NDAs, patents and similar processes are sometimes key for protecting our unique intellectual property. But there are still many other things we can share. That process of sharing can bring us many benefits.

Some of the key geniuses in history spent a big part of their time interacting and exchanging knowledge with their friends and colleagues.

"Were they not scared of having their ideas stolen?"

These geniuses understood the very key and important distinction between having an idea and implementing it.

Experienced creatives realize that in a world brimming with talent there are many chances that our idea is not as unique as we think.

"But I assure you that…"

And even if it is unique today, are we ready to trade the immense benefits of interacting with others and receiving their feedback for the hypothetical advantage of being the very first ones to implement that insight?

"Well, but if nobody else knows…"

Experienced creatives know that there is a massive distance in terms of effort, time and motivation between having an idea and implementing it successfully. And that the importance of an idea goes well beyond the initial visionary stage. So when choosing between obscurity and the benefits of sharing, experienced creatives choose the second option.

"So you mean that when you are overprotective of your seeds…"

You suffocate them. Being overprotective, you can suffocate seeds, ideas, people, your partner or anything else. You become an obstacle. An obstacle between them and their much needed nourishment. In the case of challenges and ideas, their nourishment are quality ingredients that come from your interaction with the world and other people.

Yes, we live in a world full of patents and complex legal issues related to intellectual property. This is one of the biggest concerns for many creatives. But as the experience of many famous startup founders demonstrates, before worrying too much about complex legal issues you first need to demonstrate that you can build a sustainable and viable business. That is a long and hard nut to crack, and to crack it you need all the support, all the feedback and all the quality ingredients you can gather.

"That reminds me of YouTube…"

If the YouTube founders had worried too much about IP issues, they would have never become what they are today. IP issues are important, but not the most important thing at the beginning of your path. Obsessing over the uniqueness of your idea is like dreaming with the fantasy of cooking the most unique dish in the world. It distracts you from what really matters: gathering the ingredients you need to implement your solution.

"Hard work rules."

Yes, it is all about hard work built on top of a great idea. But hard work is 99% of it all. It is not a race to protect the idea. Without going into details, protecting ideas fully is at best very complex and expensive and at worst it can be impossible. What really matters is to implement that idea as well and as fast as you can.

"So being first is not the most important thing."

Think of some of the top technology companies in the world. Google was not the first in its field, it came after Netscape. Facebook came after MySpace. And we could continue listing more examples.

"But what if I really need to protect some parts of my venture?"

There is no doubt that at some stage there will be proprietary designs, algorithms and other parts of your implementation that you will need to protect during the production phase of any venture. And the patent and trademark registration processes are designed to deal with that. But there will always be large parts of your idea that you will be able to share and exchange with others. Sharing helps you gather new perspectives and detailed feedback that otherwise would be hard to access.

"I guess it's hard to tame our ego…"

This is a good moment to remind ourselves of the struggle that creatives often have to maintain with their egos: being an innovator, a creative or an entrepreneur, requires a high level of self-confidence. Uncertainty surrounds you and you feel exposed and vulnerable. You need a good amount of confidence to stand your ground and some would say a healthy dose of ego as well. But ego, like stress, is another wild horse. And it is quite easy for it to get out of control.

"It can grow and grow like…"

You may view this ego as a balloon that you can inflate more or less. The more inflated it gets, the bigger it becomes and the bigger you want it. And you forget that the bigger you make it, the closer you get to…

"An explosion!"

Yes. An ego out of control will take you eventually back to square one or lower, alienating your relationships and paralyzing your actions. Self-confidence requires balance, as most things in life do.

"And the solution for that is…"

Feel free to interact with others in relation to your challenges. Try to involve people from all backgrounds and not only experts. Every person holds a trove of experience and unique ingredients, fresh perspectives that you can add to your project. Each of them can be a potential audience, user or customer for your product, service or creation. Treasure them because somewhere in one of those interactions may lie the magical ingredient, that pinch of salt that provides the ultimate touch needed for success.

"So experts are not necessarily the best sources."

You would be surprised. Sometimes it is the amateurs and beginners who come up with the most original insights. Excess of knowledge can prevent divergence and push you towards typical and predictable solutions.

"When the existing mental patterns are deep, it can be hard to open new ones."

Knowing less, but not too little, can make it easier to diverge and divergence encourages unpredictable interactions.

In general, the balance between knowing too much and too little is a delicate one. Having insufficient knowledge about your challenge restricts enormously the possibilities of your incubation processes. Having too much knowledge, on the other hand, increases the difficulty of avoiding the paths of least resistance in your mind that lead you to predictable solutions. The solution lies in cultivating a mind that absorbs the information you need and yet is able to keep exercising an open and broad awareness, avoiding premature closure and giving time for that information to blend and combine with other areas of your experience. So as you listen and interact with others, don't try to impose your perspective on them. Respect their views. They will often be different to yours. Celebrate that. Celebrate diversity. What would your subconscious pot look like without diversity?

"Other people's perspectives could influence me in many ways…"

The fact that their views are different does not mean that you have to change your project or recipe in any way. Their perspectives are fresh ingredients to consider for your mix. And what happens when you combine their views with your existing ones is something you should not rush to judge. Give time and space to your incubation processes. Let things blend and mix as they wish. Trying to accelerate that process will drive you towards premature closure, which can keep you away from the most unique and valuable insights.

Remember to carry with you a way of recording any interesting angles and perspectives. Fresh ingredients, like fresh food, deteriorate quickly.

Motivation

Finally, let's return to the cooking metaphor. The best cooks are those that are passionate about their craft and the best innovators are those with a passion for learning. If you share that passion, if that fire is fresh and alive inside of you, all your dishes will be original from the start. Motivation is indeed at the base of all the magic to come.

Stay fresh!

CHAPTER 18:

Creative Quotes

Get inspired with these quotes from historical personalities. These quotes remind us of the importance of creative divergence and of exercising our creative muscles.

"Every child is an artist, the problem is staying an artist when you grow up."

– Pablo Picasso

"If you hear a voice within you say, 'You cannot paint', then by all means paint, and that voice will be silenced."

– Vincent Van Gogh

"Great is the human who has not lost his childlike heart."

– Mencius (Meng-Tse), 4th century BCE

"Have no fear of perfection, you'll never reach it."

– Salvador Dali

"Curiosity about life in all of its aspects, I think, is still the secret of great creative people."

– Leo Burnett

"You can't wait for inspiration, you have to go after it with a club."

– Jack London

M. A. Rosanoff: *"Mr. Edison, please tell me what laboratory rules you want me to observe."* Edison: *"There ain't no rules around here. We're trying to accomplish something!"*

– Thomas Edison

"Imagination is the beginning of creation. You imagine what you desire, you will what you imagine, and at last, you create what you will."

– George Bernard Shaw

"It isn't the incompetent who destroys an organization. The incompetent never gets in a position to destroy it. It is those who achieved something and want to rest upon their achievements who are forever clogging things up."

– F. M. Young

"It's easy to come up with new ideas; the hard part is letting go of what worked for you two years ago, but will soon be out of date."

– Roger von Oech

"Creativity, as has been said, consists largely of rearranging what we know in order to find out what we do not know. Hence, to think creatively, we must be able to look afresh at what we normally take for granted."

– George Kneller

"Think left and think right and think low and think high. Oh, the things you can think up if only you try."

– Dr. Seuss

"Creativity comes from a conflict of ideas."

– Donatella Versace

"Don't think. Thinking is the enemy of creativity. It's self-conscious, and anything self-conscious is lousy. You can't try to do things. You simply must do things."

– Ray Bradbury

"Creativity is just connecting things. When you ask creative people how they did something, they feel a little guilty because they didn't really do it, they just saw something. It seemed obvious to them after a while."

– Steve Jobs

"You see things; and you say, 'Why?' But I dream things that never were; and I say, 'Why not?'"

– George Bernard Shaw

"We all operate in two contrasting modes, which might be called open and closed. The open mode is more relaxed, more receptive, more exploratory, more democratic, more playful and more humorous. The closed mode is the tighter, more rigid, more hierarchical, more tunnel-visioned. Most people, unfortunately spend most of their time in the closed mode. Not that the closed mode cannot be helpful. If you are leaping a ravine, the moment of takeoff is a bad time for considering alternative strategies. When you charge the enemy machine-gun post, don't waste energy trying to see the funny side of it. Do it in the "closed" mode. But the moment the action is over, try to return to the "open" mode— to open your mind again to all the feedback from our action that enables us to tell whether the action has been successful, or whether further action is needed to improve on what we have done. In other words, we must return to the open mode, because in that

mode we are the most aware, most receptive, most creative, and therefore at our most intelligent."

– John Cleese

"Without the playing with fantasy no creative work has ever yet come to birth. The debt we owe to the play of imagination is incalculable."

– Carl Jung

"To raise new questions, new possibilities, to regard old problems from a new angle, requires creative imagination and marks real advance in science."

– Albert Einstein

"To be creative you have to contribute something different from what you've done before. Your results need not be original to the world; few results truly meet that criterion. In fact, most results are built on the work of others."

– Lynne C. Levesque

"Once we rid ourselves of traditional thinking we can get on with creating the future."

– James Bertrand

"The essential part of creativity is not being afraid to fail."

– Edwin H. Land

"The things we fear most in organizations – fluctuations, disturbances, imbalances – are the primary sources of creativity."

– Margaret J. Wheatley

"There is no doubt that creativity is the most important human resource of all. Without creativity, there would be no progress, and we would be forever repeating the same patterns."

– Edward de Bono

"The creative person wants to be a know-it-all. He wants to know about all kinds of things: ancient history, nineteenth-century mathematics, current manufacturing techniques, flower arranging, and hog futures. Because he never knows when these ideas might come together to form a new idea. It may happen six minutes later or six months, or six years down the road. But he has faith that it will happen."

– Carl Ally

"The achievement of excellence can only occur if the organization promotes a culture of creative dissatisfaction."

– Lawrence Miller

"When the 'weaker' of the two brains (right and left) is stimulated and encouraged to work in cooperation with the stronger side, the end result is a great increase in overall ability and... often five to ten times more effectiveness."

– Professor Robert Ornstein, University of California

"Innovation – any new idea – by definition will not be accepted at first. It takes repeated attempts, endless demonstrations, monotonous rehearsals before innovation can be accepted and internalized by an organization. This requires courageous patience."

– Warren Bennis

The way to get good ideas is to get lots of ideas and throw the bad ones away."

– Linus Pauling

"To have a great idea, have a lot of them."

– Thomas Edison

"That so few now dare to be eccentric marks the chief danger of our time."

– John Stuart Mill

"Creative thinking is not a talent, it is a skill that can be learnt. It empowers people by adding strength to their natural abilities which improves teamwork, productivity and where appropriate profits."

– Edward de Bono

"An inventor is simply a person who doesn't take his education too seriously. You see, from the time a person is six years old until he graduates from college he has to take three or four examinations a year. If he flunks once, he is out. But an inventor is almost always failing. He tries and fails maybe a thousand times. If he succeeds once then he's in. These two things are diametrically opposite. We often say that the biggest job we have is to teach a newly hired employee how to fail intelligently. We have to train him to experiment over and over and to keep on trying and failing until he learns what will work."

– Charles Kettering

"Every act of creation is first of all an act of destruction."

– Picasso

"All human development, no matter what form it takes, must be outside the rules; otherwise we would never have anything new."

– Charles Kettering

"Anyone can look for fashion in a boutique or history in a museum. The creative explorer looks for history in a hardware store and fashion in an airport."

– Robert Wieder

"If you do not expect the unexpected you will not find it, for it is not to be reached by search or trail."

– Heraclitus

"Genius is one percent inspiration, and ninety-nine percent perspiration."

– Thomas Edison

"The organizations of the future will increasingly depend on the creativity of their members to survive. Great groups offer a new model in which the leader is an equal among Titans. In a truly creative collaboration, work is pleasure, and the only rules and procedures are those that advance the common cause."

– Warren Bennis

"Don't worry about people stealing your ideas. If your ideas are any good, you'll have to ram them down people's throats."

– Howard Aiken

"Some men look at things the way they are and ask why? I dream of things that are not and ask why not?"

– Robert Kennedy

"In every work of genius, we recognize our once rejected thoughts."

– Ralph Waldo Emerson

"The innovation point is the pivotal moment when talented and motivated people seek the opportunity to act on their ideas and dreams."

– W. Arthur Porter

And we conclude with some anti-creative quotes that illustrate the need to keep our creative muscles fit to avoid narrowing our horizons in the way that we can read below:

"Everything that can be invented has been invented."

– Charles H. Duell, Director of US Patent Office 1899

"Sensible and responsible women do not want to vote."

– Grover Cleveland, 1905

"Who the hell wants to hear actors talk?"

– Harry M. Warner, Warner Bros Pictures, 1927

"There is no likelihood man can ever tap the power of the atom."

– Robert Miliham, Nobel Prize in Physics, 1923

"Heavier than air flying machines are impossible."

– Lord Kelvin, President, Royal Society, 1895

"What use could the company make of an electric toy?"

– Western Union, when it turned down rights to the telephone in 1878

"The horse is here today, but the automobile is only a novelty - a fad."

– President of Michigan Savings Bank advising against investing in the Ford Motor Company

"Video won't be able to hold on to any market it captures after the first six months. People will soon get tired of staring at a plywood box every night."

– Daryl F. Zanuck, 20th Century Fox, commenting on television in 1946

Did You Like the Book?

If you learnt something useful from the book, I would really appreciate it if you left a review wherever you purchased it. You may also send me a testimonial by email to ideami@ideami.com.

[Web] **torchprinciple.com/review**

Thank you very much.

Glossary

Agile Methodology

A methodology for the development of a product/service or other output, focused on developing small iterations with strong emphasis on autonomy, testing and feedback gathering.

Anonymous texture

Visual texture that cannot be interpreted or labeled quickly by our mind.

Depth elevator

Metaphor that represents the relationship between universal principles and specific areas, fields and disciplines. For example, rhythm in connection with dance, the variations of the stock market or earthquakes.

Insight bubbles

Metaphor that represents new insights as fragile bubbles that emerge from our subconscious processes.

Lean Methodology

In essence, lean means generating more value for the customer with less resources, eliminating all waste.

Lean UX

Applying lean principles to improve user experience.

Lightstorming

Brainstorming technique that uses anonymous textures.

Marketing mountain

Metaphor that connects marketing processes with the challenge of climbing a mountain whose peak mutates continuously in form and position, while you compete against other teams pursuing the same objective.

Negative spaces

The space which surrounds the main subject. The space occupied by the subject is the positive space. The negative space is the one that surrounds the subject. Think of an apple. The space within the boundaries of the apple is the positive space. The negative space is the space around the apple.

Paths of least resistance

Neural pathways that are often activated, thereby strengthened, generating paths of least resistance, routes along which our thinking processes tend to flow more easily.

SK-Engine

Brainstorming tool that combines guided randomness with verbal stimuli.

Soundmap

Audio track that reproduces a specific acoustic context. Examples: sounds of a jungle, of a pub, of rain, of birds singing, etc.

Soundstorming

Brainstorming technique that combines guided randomness with acoustic stimuli.

Subconscious pot

Metaphor that represents our subconscious as a cooking pot where information ingredients combine. These combinations can eventually generate insight bubbles.

Texture

It is a continuous and non-uniform variation present on a surface of any kind.

Texture elevator

Metaphor that represents the range of possibilities that exists between visual textures that are easily identified by our analytical processes and others that are harder for our mind to interpret.

The Torch Principle

Metaphor that represents the process of innovating unique solutions through the challenge of illuminating innovative ideas. Initially, these ideas are located far away from our position within a vast ocean of mental darkness. At the start of our search, our mind holds in its hands a small torch, our initial knowledge related to the challenge.

Bibliography

EDWARDS, B. (1987). *Drawing on the Artist Within.* Touchstone.

CLAXTON, G. (1999). *Wise Up.* Bloomsbury USA.

GELB, M. (2000). *How to think like Leonardo Da Vinci: Seven steps to genius every day.* Dell.

KOPPETT, K. (2001). *Training to Imagine.* Stylus Publishing.

GAWAIN, S. (2002). *Creative Visualization.* New World Library.

MICHALKO, M. (2006). *Thinkertoys: A Handbook of Creative-Thinking Techniques.* Ten Speed Press.

Endnotes

1. http://theleanstartup.com/principles ("The Lean Start-up") / https://en.wikipedia.org/wiki/Lean_manufacturing ("Lean Manufacturing") / https://en.wikipedia.org/wiki/Lean (accessed January 5, 2016).

2. http://www.humankinetics.com/excerpts/excerpts/the-bodyrsquos-fuel-sources: "As potential fuel sources, the carbohydrate, fat, and protein in the foods that you eat follow different metabolic paths in the body, but they all ultimately yield water, carbon dioxide, and a chemical energy called adenosine triphosphate (ATP)." (accessed January 3, 2016).

3. https://en.wikipedia.org/wiki/Nervous_system ("The Nervous System") (accessed January 1, 2016).

4. https://en.wikipedia.org/wiki/Long-term_potentiation ("Long-Term Potentiation") (accessed January 5, 2016).

5. http://healthcare.utah.edu/publicaffairs/news/current/08-14-2013_brain_personality_traits.php ("Myth of left and right brain debunked") (accessed January 11, 2016).

6. http://americanrtl.org/Einstein (accessed January 15, 2016).

7. http://www.virtuesforlife.com/10-great-life-lessons-from-albert-einstein/ "It's not that I'm so smart; it's just that I stay with problems longer." (accessed January 12, 2016).

8. http://www-935.ibm.com/services/us/ceo/ceos-tudy2010 / http://public.dhe.ibm.com/common/ssi/ecm/gb/en/gbe03297usen/GBE03297USEN.PDF (accessed January 17, 2016).

9. http://en.wikipedia.org/wiki/Montessori_education (accessed January 2, 2016).

10. http://www.ncbi.nlm.nih.gov/pubmed/21126528 (accessed January 21, 2016).

11. https://en.wikipedia.org/wiki/Neural_oscillation (accessed January 15, 2016).

12. http://www.choosemuse.com / https://www.crunchbase.com/organization/interaxon (accessed January 7, 2016).

13. https://en.wikiquote.org/wiki/Henri_Poincaré (accessed January 25, 2016).

14. http://www.sciencemag.org/content/328/5976/360.abstract (accessed January 2, 2016).

15. *Anger Management For The Twenty-First Century* by Century Anger Management Publishing / https://books.google.es/books?id=_yl3WalNdLgC&pg=PA61&lpg=PA61&dq=%22creative+thinking+can+trans-form%22&source=bl&ots=SfIcJMKvz4&sig=UZU2W-GNPBP_B51OvtYxrNcFBPkw&hl=es&sa=X&ved=0CD-kQ6AEwBGoVChMIzamG7_bayAIVCX4aCh175Qcz#v=o-nepage&q=%22creative%20thinking%20can%20transform%22&f=false / "Creative thinking can transform the conflict into an opportunity." (accessed January 17, 2016).

16. *Einstein's Universe: Gravity at Work and Play* by A. Zee "by Einstein's own admission, he was daydreaming when what he called the happiest thought of his life occurred to him. Perhaps he was having the dream of falling. The subconscious can work in strange ways." **https://books.google.es/books?id=tI6hr5boxg0C&pg=PA17&dq=einstein+subconscious&hl=es&sa=X-&redir_esc=y#v=onepage&q=einstein%20subconscious&f=false** (accessed January 3, 2016).

17. https://en.wikipedia.org/wiki/The_Selfish_Gene (*The Selfish Gene*) / **http://www.amazon.com/The-Selfish-Gene-Popular-Science/dp/0192860925** (accessed January 21, 2016).

18. *Creative Problem Solving: A Guide for Trainers and Management*, by Arthur B. VanGundy Page 32: "As Einstein noted: The formulation of a problem is often more essential than its solution which may be merely a matter of mathematical or experimental skill. [Einstein and Infeld, 1938, p. 29]." **https://books.google.es/books?id=Ya9G2ozV9IYC&pg=PA32&lpg=PA32&dq=%22The+formulation+of+a+problem+is%22+einstein&source=bl&ots=l9yuCB5ARy&sig=GDYZ6mklvCJNydt5QfG5o92smXY&hl=es&sa=X&ved=0CDAQ6AEwAmoVChMIjr_xiaPZyAIVTOsmCh-oD7AL5#v=onepage&q=%22The%20formulation%20of%20a%20problem%20is%22%20einstein&f=false** / Other Sources: *Encyclopedia of Creativity, Two-Volume Set, Volume 2. The Routledge International Handbook of Innovation Education* (accessed January 4, 2016).

19. **https://en.wikipedia.org/wiki/Quantum_fluctuation** ("Quantum Fluctuation") (accessed January 17, 2016).

20. *Thinkertoys: A handbook of creative-thinking tech-niques*, by Michael Michalko, Page 227 of 379 (59%) "Einstein imagined he was a beam of light hurtling through space, which led him to the theory of relativity."

21. *Surviving Transformation: Lessons from GM's Surpris-ing Turnaround* by Vincent P. Barabba. "The Albert Einstein quote "Imagination is more important than knowledge," comes from an in-depth interview by George Sylvester Viereck in the *Saturday Evening Post*." **https://books.google.es/books?id=JwviBwAAQBAJ&p-g=PT212&dq=imagination+is+more+important+than+-knowledge+einstein&hl=es&sa=X&ved=0CCYQ6A-EwAWoVChMIubGkiLvZyAIVRbIUCh18tQFl#v=onep-age&q=imagination%20is%20more%20important%20than%20knowledge%20einstein&f=false** (accessed January 21, 2016).

22. *Thinkertoys: A handbook of creative-thinking tech-niques*, by Michael Michalko, Page 261 of 379 (69%): "Albert Einstein observed that: the words of language, as they are written or spoken, do not seem to play any role in my mechanism of thought. The physical enti-ties which seem to serve as elements in thought are certain signs and more or less clear images which can be voluntarily reproduced and combined." *Drawing on the artist within* by Betty Edwards, Page 46: "Faraday, Galton, Einstein, and certain other noted scientists have reported that they solved scientific problems in visual images and only afterwards translated their thoughts into words."

23. *Dilemmas in the Study of Information: Exploring the Boundaries of Information Science* by Samuel

D. Neill / **https://books.google.es/books?id=76H-Q8UMpRFAC&pg=PA25&dq=einstein+imagi-nary+trips&hl=es&sa=X&redir_esc=y#v=onep-age&q=einstein%20imaginary%20trips&f=false** (accessed January 1, 2016).

24. *How to Think Like Leonardo da Vinci: Seven Steps to Genius Every Day* by Michael J Gelb: "In his quest for truth, and his search to understand the essence of natural systems, Leonardo went to extremes. His anatomical studies of the act of coitus, his dinner party for deformed and grotesque characters, his remarkably composed sketch of the hanging of Bandinelli, the phantasmagorical war machines, all demonstrate his intuitive knowledge that to understand a system, one must explore it, or imagine it, under extreme conditions."

25. "Genius is one percent inspiration, ninety-nine percent perspiration." Spoken statement (c. 1903); published in *Harper's Monthly* (September 1932). **https://en.wiki-quote.org/wiki/Thomas_Edison** (accessed January 23, 2016).

26. SK-Engine is an online brainstorming tool that uses guided randomness in combination with verbal stimuli to stimulate the subconscious mind.

27. Soundstorming refers to brainstorming processes that use mainly sound to stimulate the subconscious mind. Lightstorming refers to brainstorming processes that use mainly visual textures to stimulate the subconscious mind.

28. *Thinkertoys: A handbook of creative-thinking techniques*, by Michael Michalko, Page 222 of 379 (58%):

"When Einstein was troubled by a problem, he would like down and take a long nap."

29. *Drawing on the artist within* by Betty Edwards, Page 47: "In 1907, Albert Einstein recorded the creative moment when he grasped that the effect of gravity was equivalent to a nonuniform motion as "the happiest moment of my life." Quoted in Hans Pagels, *The Cosmic Code*, 1982."

30. **https://en.wikipedia.org/wiki/Theory_of_multiple_intelligences** ("Theory of multiple intelligences") (accessed January 5, 2016).

31. **https://en.wikipedia.org/wiki/Theory_of_multiple_intelligences** ("Theory of multiple intelligences") (accessed January 3, 2016).

32. **https://en.wikipedia.org/wiki/Business_Model_Canvas** ("Business Model Canvas") (accessed January 7, 2016).

33. **https://en.wikipedia.org/wiki/Harry_Potter** ("Harry Potter Books") (accessed January 19, 2016).

34. *Thinkertoys: A handbook of creative-thinking techniques*, by Michael Michalko, Page 261 of 379 (69%): "Albert Einstein observed that: the words of language, as they are written or spoken, do not seem to play any role in my mechanism of thought. The physical entities which seem to serve as elements in thought are certain signs and more or less clear images which can be voluntarily reproduced and combined."

35. *Drawing on the artist within* by Betty Edwards, Page 186: **http://www.goodreads.com/book/**

show/680042.Drawing_on_the_Artist_Within / https://books.google.es/books?id=ROh9ZGJPfv8C&p-g=PA186&dq=drawing+artist+within+sighting+dur-ero&hl=es&sa=X&ved=0CCAQ6AEwAGoVChMIpOr-bhMPZyAIViVsaCh31wQx5#v=onepage&q=drawing%20 artist%20within%20sighting%20durero&f=false (accessed January 22, 2016).

36. *Drawing on the artist within* by Betty Edwards http://www.goodreads.com/book/show/680042.Drawing_on_the_Artist_Within (accessed January 3, 2016).

37. http://www.biography.com/news/alexander-flem-ing-5-other-accidental-medical-discoveries ("Penicil-lin") (accessed January 5, 2016).

38. *Thinkertoys: A handbook of creative-thinking tech-niques*, by Michael Michalko, Page 227 of 379 (59%): Einstein imagined he was a beam of light hurtling through space, which led him to the theory of relativity.

39. *Excursions to the Far Side of the Mind* by Howard Rhein-gold: "The role of visual thinking in artistic and scien-tific creativity through the ages can be discerned in a distinct pattern of historical testimony. Autobiographical accounts of creative geniuses from Mozart to Einstein attest to the role of mental images in the creation of masterpieces."

40. http://www.goodreads.com/quotes/978797-look-at-walls-splashed-with-a-number-of-stains-or / http://www.tate.org.uk/context-comment/articles/delibera-te-accident-art (accessed January 9, 2016).

41. "Whenever he felt that he had come to the end of the road or into a difficult situation in his work, he would

take refuge in music, and that would usually resolve all his difficulties" (Ronald W. Clark, 1971. *"Einstein. The Life and Times"*. p106).

42. https://en.wikipedia.org/wiki/Stress_(biology) ("Stress") (accessed January 9, 2016).

43. http://wanderluxe.theluxenomad.com/10-reasons-why-couples-break-up-after-vacation / http://www.bustle.com/articles/98465-why-the-most-common-time-of-year-for-long-term-relationship-breakups-is-during-the-holidays-because: "Holidays are often the ultimate test for relationships — it's actually the most common time of year that couples break up." (accessed January 5, 2016).

44. "I have not failed. I've just found 10,000 ways that won't work." http://www.goodreads.com/author/quotes/3091287. Thomas_A_Edison (accessed January 17, 2016).

45. https://en.wikipedia.org/wiki/Psychological_resilience ("Resilience") (accessed January 5, 2016).

46. https://en.wikipedia.org/wiki/Drug ("Drug") (accessed January 25, 2016).

47. http://ctb.ku.edu/en/table-of-contents/structure/strategic-planning/develop-strategies/main: "Also, just one strategy, affecting just one part of the community such as schools or youth organizations, often isn't enough to improve the situation. Make sure that your strategies affect the problem or issue as a whole." (accessed January 21, 2016).

48. http://www.physicsclassroom.com/class/sound/
    Lesson-4/Natural-Frequency / https://en.wikipedia.
    org/wiki/Mechanical_resonance: "Many resonant
    objects have more than one resonance frequency. It will
    vibrate easily at those frequencies, and less so at other
    frequencies." (accessed January 5, 2016).

49. http://www.hollywoodreporter.com/news/steven-
    spielberg-reveals-daniel-day-409709 (accessed January
    26, 2016).

50. https://en.wikipedia.org/wiki/Feature_scaling
    (accessed January 24, 2016).

51. http://www.businessinsider.com/new-study-destroys-
    malcolm-gladwells-10000-rule-2014-7 / http://pss.
    sagepub.com/content/early/2014/06/30/0956797614
    535810.abstract (accessed January 5, 2016).

torchprinciple.com

www.ingramcontent.com/pod-product-compliance
Lightning Source LLC
Chambersburg PA
CBHW072059040426
42334CB00041B/1373